Our Only Comfort

Our Only Comfort

Daily Devotions through the Heidelberg Catechism

STEPHEN C. SHAFFER

foreword by J. Todd Billings

WIPF & STOCK · Eugene, Oregon

OUR ONLY COMFORT
Daily Devotions through the Heidelberg Catechism

Wipf & Stock
An Imprint of Wipf and Stock Publishers
199 W. 8th Ave., Suite 3
Eugene, OR 97401

www.wipfandstock.com

PAPERBACK ISBN: 978-1-7252-9873-6
HARDCOVER ISBN: 978-1-7252-9874-3
EBOOK ISBN: 978-1-7252-9875-0

04/13/21

To Elijah, Moriah, and Joanna

You inspired me to write this book, and you inspire me still to be a father who daily shares the love of Jesus with you.

Lord's Day (Weekly) Sections

Foreword

PARENTING IS INCREDIBLY HARD work. We often tell sleepless new parents that it gets easier after the first year, but I suspect that's just reassuring fiction. Young children and teenagers continue to push us to our emotional limits. Journalist Jennifer Senior expresses it well in her book title about modern parenthood: *All Joy and No Fun*. Parenting is meaningful, and a source of joy. But it is also really, really hard.

As if this were not enough, Christian parents are told to add one more gigantic imperative to their "to do" list: Train up your children in the Christian faith. Children are growing up with their hearts and minds immersed in a cultural context that uses technology and consumerism to shape them in a particular way. This culture trains our children to ache for more material possessions and to imagine a world in which beauty and strength always seem to win. In this kingdom, the individual self is king. In contrast, Christian parents are called to help cultivate something far more countercultural in our children: to ache for God's kingdom, give themselves over to the all-encompassing path of Jesus, and to look beyond selfish interest, seeking to "'love the Lord your God with all your heart, and with all your soul, and with all your mind'" and "'love your neighbor as yourself'" (Mt. 22:37–40).

While this may sound like a beautiful vision, on an experiential level, it can feel overwhelming. How can I possibly add something else to the crazy schedule of soccer and dinner and band and medical treatments, amidst temper tantrums, homework, and short attention spans? Is Christian parenting an impossible task? Is it a set up for burn-out?

The way forward is not one more "action plan" to accomplish a set of goals through our own hard efforts. Rather, the starting point for training our children in the faith is embracing this biblical truth that the Heidelberg Catechism (HC) bears witness to again and again: by ourselves, we can't do it. We can't pull it off. It's far beyond our capacity and wisdom to achieve.

Yet, in recognizing our empty-handedness with HC, there is good news. Our life of faith, and sharing it with our children, begins with a gracious displacement: that we do *not* hope in our own brilliance or grit or moral perfection. There is a source of hope that is much more basic and steady and reliable. The opening of the Heidelberg Catechism's first question and answer points to this alternate hope. This question and answer, which in some ways summarizes the whole of the catechism, begins this way:

What is your only comfort in life and in death?

A. That I am not my own, but belong—body and soul, in life and in death—to my faithful Savior, Jesus Christ.

The biblical truth is not that we belong to ourselves, but to God. Our bodies are temples of the Holy Spirit. We belong to Jesus Christ, in life and in death. Thus, in the apostle Paul's words, "you are not your own" (1 Cor. 6:19).

Parents, remember that you are not your own, especially when parenting feels like a burden that you cannot handle. When we're tempted to think that the training of children in the faith is a task to do by ourselves, remember that we can't do it on our own, in our own strength. Instead, embrace the good news that we belong to Jesus Christ through the Holy Spirit. We've been claimed by the Triune God in baptism, adopted into fellowship with God and the family of God, the church.

Through the Spirit's power, we can invite our children to live deeper and deeper into this mundane, yet wondrous, reality of communion with God and others. Yes, we are called to raise our children "in the training and instruction of the Lord" (see Eph. 6:1–4). But rather than an anxious effort, this can emerge from a place of rest and gratitude when it flows from the deep knowledge that we are not our own, but belong to Jesus Christ.

The Heidelberg Catechism (HC) is an extraordinary tool for this very purpose, and Rev. Stephen Shaffer is an excellent guide for helping families feed upon its refreshing and biblical teaching in bite-sized pieces. The HC was written in the sixteenth century for a region in Germany that included a range of Protestant perspectives. It included the elements of what were widely considered to be basic for training Christians in the faith, both among Protestants and Roman Catholics: expositions of the Lord's Prayer, the Ten Commandments, and the Apostles' Creed. These are the ABCs of the Christian faith that adults never move "beyond" — they are fundamental biblical truths to be integrated into our lives until our last mortal breath.

The HC sets all of these components within a Protestant context that will strike many readers today as deeply countercultural: the HC's theological framework does not begin with our own capacities or heroism, but with the goodness of creation, the wide-ranging consequences of our sin, and thus the astonishing grace that the Triune God brings us, as our sole hope and deliverer.

Since it was first written in 1563, the Heidelberg Catechism has moved far beyond the hills of southern Germany. It has been translated into three dozen languages and utilized by parents and congregations around the world, inhabiting a wide range of cultural locations. While historically Reformed and Presbyterian traditions are particularly likely to use the catechism, it is also being used today in nondenominational, congregational, and other church contexts.

Does all of this mean that the Heidelberg Catechism is a "golden key," the one-step solution to training children in the faith? No. It does not claim to be that, nor does it claim to be infallible. However, its time-tested character does indicate that it can be very *useful* for communicating deep biblical truths, both to children and to parents.

For those who are interested in scholarly examinations of the Catechism, there are a wide range of resources in numerous languages. As a seminary professor, my favorite scholarly treatments of the catechism are two books by Lyle Bierma, *An Introduction to the Heidelberg Catechism* and *The Theology of the Heidelberg Catechism*. I would recommend them to adults who would like a deeper look at the history, theology, and character of the catechism.

However, just as a song is meant to be sung, a catechism is meant to be engaged, taught, and used in the relational context of discipleship. For the purpose of this formation, *Our Only Comfort* provides a beautiful, cogent, and accessible entry point for families to draw upon the riches of catechism. Stephen writes as a pastor who has served congregations in both the

United States and Canada, and he has a heart for teaching and a heart for the gospel of grace that the catechism presents. Several years after he graduated from the seminary, I remember talking with Stephen about his congregation in the rural midwest. He was leading a "confirmation" class engaging materials like the Heidelberg Catechism. The youth were not familiar with it, and it captured their attention. And through Stephen's teaching, friends of youth at the church started to attend to listen as well. Stephen was able to communicate to the youth in a way that implicated their daily living.

While Stephen speaks and writes in a way that connects with others, he does so as a pastor and theologian who has a deep well of biblical and theological understanding. His reflections are simple without being simplistic, written with elegance and verve. In doing this, *Our Only Comfort* is a gift to the church today. While there are helpful resources to *study* the characteristics of the Heidelberg Catechism, a scholarly resource is not necessarily best for *using* the catechism toward its intended end.

The catechism is to be experienced as a biblical song, helping both children and adults know and love the tune of the good news. In singing this song, we can deepen our knowledge — in our heads and our hearts — of the extravagant love of God, who delivers us from the pit of alienation to sing in Spirit-enabled gratitude. As we sing, we can discover our Christian identity anew. Rather than acting as if we are heroes who will save the universe, or the saviors of our children, we are freed to hope in the One who alone provides the deepest comfort and consolation. Because of this, we can embrace our calling as children of the Father, empowered by the Spirit to serve the Lord in gratitude, knowing that in life and in death, we belong to Jesus Christ.

J. Todd Billings

Preface

How do we transmit the Christian faith?

As I held my son in my arms for the first time, I thought about how God has entrusted my wife and I with the spiritual nurture of this precious boy. In order to leave the hospital, all the nurses needed to see was that I knew how to change a diaper and put him in the car seat. I knew nothing about being a father, and I felt the weight, responsibility, and privilege of the task of raising this boy to love and serve the Lord. But how do I do it? Do I simply live by example and hope he picks it up by osmosis? I certainly hope he sees Christian faith and character in me, but I knew example wouldn't be enough. Do I give over that responsibility to his Sunday School teachers? No matter how excellent the teachers are, I feel the personal weight and responsibility for raising my child in the Christian faith. As important as it is to have the support and teaching of fellow believers, I need him to learn from me what it means to know Jesus, have faith in him, and follow him.

But how do I do it?

I wrote this book to learn how to teach my children the Christian faith. I grew up in a non-confessional church and never experienced 'family devotions.' I come to this practice as an adult searching (together with my wife) for the best way to raise my children to know the LORD. I knew the value of regularly worshipping on the Lord's Day, Sunday School, and even mid-week programs in the church. I had grown up with a lot of good programs in the church that helped me to learn about God, the Bible, and the Christian Faith. However, I did not know what that meant for our time together as a family.

It turns out I was not alone.

Why the Heidelberg Catechism?

Upon entering the Reformed Church, I discovered that there already existed a resource for teaching children and new Christians the basics of the faith: the Heidelberg Catechism. Throughout church history parents, pastors, and Christians of all stripes had been wrestling with how best to teach children the faith. They developed what were known as catechisms, from the Greek *katacheo*, "to teach orally." Some catechisms contained short paragraphs while others were formatted as a series of questions and answers that could be taught and memorized. In 1563, young professors and theologians, Zacharius Ursinus and Casper Olevianus, were asked to write a catechism for the region of the Palatinate (which contained the city of

Heidelberg) in modern-day Germany, explaining the core teachings of the Christian faith, with a particular emphasis on the core teachings of the Protestant Reformation. The resulting Heidelberg Catechism contained 129 questions and answers.

The Heidelberg Catechism was written as a summary of the Christian faith that could be used to teach young children and converts. It was drawn from Holy Scripture and intended as a tool to help Christians read scripture more faithfully. It contains three main sections. First, it details the fateful situation of humanity separated from God by sin (Misery). Second, it speaks of the salvation found in Jesus Christ (Deliverance). Lastly, it talks about how we are to live in light of God's gracious redemption (Gratitude). As it moves through these sections, the Heidelberg Catechism gives extended treatments on the Apostles' Creed, the Sacraments, the Ten Commandments, and the Lord's Prayer. All of this was part of its overall project of teaching the basics of the Christian faith.

The catechism was not only used as part of individual instruction, but as part of the regular worship and formation of the people of God. It was also used in the ongoing teaching ministry of Reformed Churches to help deepen congregants into the broad teachings and practices of Scripture. To that end, the 129 questions were divided into fifty-two sections, one for each Sunday (Lord's Day). That way a church (or family) could go through the catechism in the space of a year.

The more I read the Heidelberg Catechism, the more I grew to love its theology and its pastoral heart. I wanted to use this as the basis for teaching my children how to love and follow Jesus. However, I soon discovered that use of the catechism was on the decline, and I knew no one who was actually using it to teach children the faith. It was still occasionally used in church classes for those preparing to make profession of faith, but I knew no one using it in their home with their children. As I grew to love how simply and clearly it taught what was contained in the Scriptures, I wanted to find a way to help my children to learn Jesus through the Heidelberg Catechism (to borrow a phrase from Barth). The result is this book of daily devotions for families.

How To Use This Book

This devotional is divided into fifty-two weeks, following the divisions of the catechism into fifty-two Lord's Day sections. The Sunday reading and devotion will be directly drawn from the catechism. The rest of the week will be spent dwelling on Scripture passages relating to that week's teaching. Each devotion will have a similar pattern. It will begin with a passage of Scripture (or, in the case of Sunday, from the catechism). It will be followed by a short meditation on that passage to foster reflection and discussion. The devotion ends with a time of prayer prompted by a verse from the Psalms, the prayer book of the Bible.

The Psalm verses are meant to aid you as you seek to respond to God in prayer. Use them as you need them. For centuries, the people of God have let the Psalms lead them in prayer. The Psalms stretch us to pray in ways we might not do naturally. For instance, "You will tread on the lion and the cobra; you will trample the great lion and the serpent" (Psalm 91:13) might invite us to pray for God's justice upon the wicked (lion and cobras) and call our minds to his great promise to crush the head of the serpent (found in Genesis 3:15, fulfilled in Jesus). "For you, LORD, have delivered me from death, my eyes from tears, my feet from stumbling" (Psalm 116:8) might lead us to pray with gratitude for our salvation in Jesus Christ, while

"Create in me a pure heart, O God, and renew a steadfast spirit within me" (Psalm 51:10) might lead us to confess our sins before God and ask him to make us holy. "Open my eyes that I may see wonderful things in your law" (Psalm 119:18) could lead us to pray for God to help us understand his Word more clearly. The Psalms also invite us to bring the whole of our hearts before God. For instance, "Enter his gates with thanksgiving and his courts with praise; give thanks to him and praise his name" (Psalm 100:4) is an invitation to a prayer of joy, while "I am worn out from my groaning. All night long I flood my bed with weeping and drench my couch with tears" (Psalm 6:6) would lead to a prayer of sorrow and lament. As you reach the end of each devotion and come upon a verse from the Psalms, let the psalm set the tone, then pray as the Spirit leads in light of the scripture, conversations, or needs of the day. If your prayers head in a different direction, that is okay. Know that it is more important that you are praying with your family than that you pray "in just the right way."

Our Only Comfort is designed to be used together around the table. The content may be challenging for some younger children, but it should be a good fit for middle school and high school age children. However, if your children don't understand everything the first time you read it through, give them the space to let it sink in and ask questions. You can always come back to these sections the next time you read through these devotions.

Can't get together around the table? Put the book in your car and have your child read it on the way to school or hockey practice. Set it in their room and make reading together before bed a nightly routine. Again, it is more important to be having the conversations about faith than where you are having them.

While it can be good for one person to lead the devotion, it is also good to have participation. When reading the catechism, have one person ask the questions and another answer. During the week, have a different person read the Bible passage than the person who reads the devotion. Continue to switch it up to give each participant new chances to engage with the texts. Then proceed to read the devotion and discuss what you learned as time allows.

Our Only Comfort seeks to answer the question, "How do I transmit the Christian faith?" by providing a daily practice of scripture, prayer, reflection, and conversation so that, by God's grace, you and your family may grow in the Christian faith.

It is an incredible joy and responsibility to raise children in the Christian faith. There is no magic bullet when it comes to children and faith. However, as you gather around your table, my prayer is that God uses this set of devotions so that you and your children are "wholeheartedly willing and ready from now on to live for him" (Heidelberg Catechism Q&A1).

Acknowledgments

WHILE MY NAME GOES on the cover, this book would not exist without the many people who supported and encouraged me along the way.

To my family: Terry & Terri Wing, Tim Shaffer, Laura Ackley, and Rien and Anja Noordam. By raising me and those who matter most to me, you have demonstrated what it looks like to shepherd a child in the faith. Your relentless encouragement and love through the years have borne fruit well beyond these pages.

To North Holland Reformed Church, who hired a long-haired teenager and loved him until he joined you (and even cut his hair). For seven years together, you demonstrated the gracious and loving heart of the Reformed tradition and the beauty of the gospel. My ministry in the Reformed Church and certainly this book would not have happened without you. A special thank you to the RIOT group for receiving my first attempts at discipling and to Rev. Josh Van Leeuwen for showing me what it means to be a pastor.

To the Reformed Church of Stout in Stout, Iowa. You were the best first church Olga and I could ever imagine. You loved us through our early days of ministry and through the birth of our three children. It was while regularly gathering with you to pray for all our children that this book began to take shape. A special thank you to the catechism class (Angela, Kerigan, Jack, Jill, Jayne, Missy, and Kim) for listening so well, asking such good questions, and even memorizing Question and Answer 1 with me. My time with you stoked my desire to write this book.

To Bethel Reformed Church in Brantford, Ontario, where most of this book was written. Your passion for families and for the spread of the gospel forced me to think deeper and wider as I wrote this book. A special thank you to the Vellenga family for testing out early versions of these devotions and providing feedback. Outside of my own family, it is with you, Bethel, that I am most eager to share this book.

To Michael Thomson, my editor at Wipf and Stock. Thank you for believing in this book and having a vision for how this could impact the church.

To Todd Billings, who has been a constant source of support and encouragement in my journey as a pastor-theologian. Through time in your home, in the classroom, and even out to lunch in various spots around Holland, you have shown me what it means to love the Lord and to do theology for the sake of the church. It is not an understatement to say this book would never have gotten off the ground without your help. To Madelyn Vonk, who spent a long Christmas break reading and providing feedback on the book, the final version is significantly better for your contributions.

To Elijah, Moriah, and Joanna. Every page of this book was written with you on my heart. Every night your Mom and I pray that the Lord would give you sharp minds to know him, soft hearts to love him and your neighbor, and strong hands to serve God and the world around you. I am daily impressed with how God has already answered that prayer. If this book does nothing more than lead you to know you belong to Jesus Christ and stir you to love the Lord more deeply, I will count it a success.

To my beloved wife, Olga. You gave me the time and space to write, even when it meant more work for you. You prayed for me when I struggled and never thought I would finish. You listened as I talked my way through difficult sections and offered advice when I was finally willing to listen. In every way, your love and support made the journey of this book not only possible, but wonderful.

Finally, I give thanks to the Lord, Father, Son, and Holy Spirit, for saving me from my sins, calling me into pastoral ministry and parenthood, and also strengthening and sustaining me through every step of this book. May this work be faithful to your Word, fruitful for your kingdom, and bring glory to your name alone. Sola Gloria Dei.

Belonging to Jesus—Lord's Day 1—Sunday

Q1. What is your only comfort in life and in death?

That I am not my own,

> but belong—body and soul, in life and in death—
> to my faithful Savior, Jesus Christ.
> He has fully paid for all my sins with his precious blood,
> and has set me free from the tyranny of the devil.
> He also watches over me in such a way
> that not a hair can fall from my head
> without the will of my Father in heaven;
> in fact, all things must work together for my salvation.
> Because I belong to him, Christ, by his Holy Spirit,
> assures me of eternal life
> and makes me wholeheartedly willing
> and ready from now on to live for him.

Q2. What must you know to live and die in the joy of this comfort?

A. Three things:

> first, how great my sin and misery are;
> second, how I am set free from all my sins and misery;
> third, how I am to thank God for such deliverance.

In May 2008, a tornado ripped through Parkersburg, Iowa. When the first paramedics came over the hill, they could no longer find the street. What had been houses, cars, and trees was now a broken pile of rubble. People slowly came out of the wreckage, staring at devastation. When the bottom drops out of our lives, we understand the question, "What is your only comfort, in life and in death?"

Belonging to Christ is the *only* comfort we have, in life and in death. Life is fragile and each of us will die. Christ alone never fails, so we have comfort in the trials of life and in the pain of death. We are not alone in the world; we belong to our faithful Savior, Jesus Christ. Christ's hold is not broken even by death.

When the unexpected occurs, whether a literal storm or in the form of great loss, as it will for all of us, we must know three things to experience this comfort of God. First, we must know our misery. We are sinners separated from God. We need forgiveness only God can give. Second, we must know our deliverance. Specifically, we must know where to look for hope, peace, and comfort: Jesus Christ. Third, we must know how to be thankful. After hearing and receiving the gospel, our hearts might leap to thank God, but we do not know how. We need God's instruction in order to properly give him thanks and bring honor to his name.

Prayer: *Come, let us bow down in worship, let us kneel before the Lord our Maker; for he is our God and we are the people of his pasture, the flock under his care.* (Psalm 95:6–7 NIV)

Belonging to Jesus—Lord's Day 1—Monday

Read: Romans 8:14–17
"I am not my own"

AFTER YEARS OF WAITING, my parents had flown to China to adopt a little girl. I remained home, and while they were away to meet her for the first time, I picked out a teddy bear. It was important that I had this gift for my little sister when she arrived. I needed her to know she belonged. She was a part of our family, not because of blood, but because we loved and wanted her.

By the Spirit, Christians receive adoption into the family of God. By belonging to our faithful savior, Christians are brought into God's family and adopted as sons and daughters of God. Before our adoption, we were estranged from God because of our sin—enemies of God (Romans 5:10). We have been reconciled with God through Christ and are full members of his household. Like the adoption of a little girl from China, our adoption into the family of God is not based on merit or ability, but love. It is the work of the Spirit by uniting us to Jesus Christ—the one, true Son of God. Adoption is found in belonging to Christ.

Belonging to Christ is at the heart of the gospel. While my family chose to adopt my sister apart from anything she had done or would do, God knows us completely, and he still chose to adopt us as his own. What amazing grace! Belonging to Jesus is at the beginning of the catechism because the comfort promised by the gospel is found in Jesus Christ.

Prayer: *A father to the fatherless, a defender of widows, is God in his holy dwelling.* (Psalm 68:5 NIV)

Belonging to Jesus—Lord's Day 1—Tuesday

Read: 1 Peter 1:13–19
"He has fully paid for all my sins with his precious blood"

IN THE ROMAN WORLD, someone unable to pay their debts might ultimately end up in slavery. They would work for their new master until they could pay off their debt. However, a slave was not allowed to pay off his debt himself, so he would give his money to someone else who would buy his freedom for him.

We are born into a form of slavery. Our sins are debts that led us into slavery to sin, death, and the devil. Our debt was so great (and our works so worthless) that we could never pay it off. Yet Jesus Christ paid off our debt. He paid it off by giving himself in our place. We gave him nothing, but he gave his life for us. Jesus Christ, not through gold or silver, but through the shedding of his blood on the cross, has purchased our freedom.

Jesus paid our debt completely. There is no remaining balance. Being set free, we can now live holy lives as we await Christ's return. As Peter says, "live in reverent fear during the time of your exile. You know that you were ransomed . . . with the precious blood of Christ" (vv. 17–19).

Prayer: *No one can redeem the life of another or give to God a ransom for them—the ransom for a life is costly, no payment is ever enough.* (Psalm 49:7–8 NIV)

Belonging to Jesus—Lord's Day 1—Wednesday

Read: Exodus 6:1–9
"and has set me free from the tyranny of the devil"

THE CATECHISM USES "TYRANNY" to describe life under the power of the devil. A tyrant not only has power, but uses that power in ruthless, wicked, and cruel ways.

The Lord set his people free from the tyranny of Pharaoh. In slavery, Pharaoh's cruel power ruled their lives and constrained their actions to follow his will and desires. Yet, when the Israelites cried out to the Lord, he heard their cry and promised to deliver them. God broke Pharaoh's power over them and set them free "with an outstretched arm and with mighty acts of judgment" (v. 6).

The Lord sets his people free from the tyranny of the devil. Since our first parents trusted the serpent over God, we have lived in slavery to sin. The cruel power of Satan ruled our lives and constrained our actions to follow his will and desires. In our weakness, we cried out to the Lord. God promised to deliver his people. God kept his promise.

Christ has set us free. Though we still struggle against sin and face temptation and spiritual assault, our victory is secure in Christ who rose from the grave and broke the power of Satan.

Prayer: *Set me free from my prison, that I may praise your name. Then the righteous will gather about me because of your goodness to me.* (Psalm 142:7 NIV)

Belonging to Jesus—Lord's Day 1—Thursday

Read: Psalm 121
"He also watches over me"

WHERE DOES OUR HELP come from? Life seems fragile and the future uncertain. We hope that we can work hard enough or cover enough possibilities for our life truly to be secure. All of this frantic activity hides a mistrust as old as Eden. We do not trust God will provide all that we need.

Our help comes from the Lord, the maker of heaven and earth (v. 2). God faithfully preserves us every moment. God does not take time off from watching over us (v. 3). Even when we stumble and slip in life and faith, God will not let us fall completely. He is our shade—providing relief from the harshness of our journey. He gives us enough rest and relief for the next step. God shelters us from evil, so that when we experience trials, we are protected from their full fury. He watches over every moment of our life, from our coming from the womb to our going to the grave and forevermore.

God's care for us should bring us great comfort. It is not up to us to keep watch over our life. Instead, it is in God's hands, which are stronger, gentler, and more secure than ours will ever be.

Prayer: *I lift up my eyes to the mountains—where does my help come from?* (Psalm 121:1 NIV)

Belonging to Jesus—Lord's Day 1—Friday

Read: Romans 8:25–28

"In fact, all things must work together for my salvation."

EVIL IS AN OBSERVABLE fact. No one needs to convince us that wickedness exists. We see it plastered across the news every night. We watch it played out on playgrounds and in offices. We know it in our own hearts and see it every day of our lives.

God's triumph over evil is not always as observable. The claim that all things work together for good is a confession of faith. We get glimpses now—hearts changed by the gospel, children freed from poverty, families healed. Yet, believing all things work together for good is an act of hope. We hope when we do not see God's victory with the eyes, but wait with patience. We hope when we are weak and do not know how to pray. We hope when we groan too deep for words and need the Spirit's intercession.

However, Scripture tells us we *know* that all things must work together for our salvation. We can be confident and comforted in the midst of trials because evil and suffering will not have the last word, but will be overcome by the kingdom of God and its King. We know that all things work together, because we know the one who holds history in his hands.

Prayer: *He says, "Be still, and know that I am God; I will be exalted among the nations, I will be exalted in the earth." (Psalm 46:10 NIV)*

Belonging to Jesus—Lord's Day 1—Saturday

Read: John 6:33–40

"Because I belong to him, Christ, by his Holy Spirit, assures me of eternal life"

IN THE FACE OF death, the promises of the gospel are incredibly personal and urgent. Death threatens to sweep away everything before it, which requires the most sure and profound comfort—eternal life.

Jesus is the source of eternal life. In these few verses, Jesus promises three things. First, "Everything that the Father gives me will come to me" (v. 37). Jesus will not fail to redeem any that the Father has given him. Those who belong to Christ will come to him. Second, Jesus will not lose any he has been given. His grip will not slacken. He will not grow weary of holding our life and future in his hands. Third, "all who see the Son and believe in him may have eternal life; and I will raise them up on the last day" (v. 40). Those who belong to Christ, who call on his name, are assured of eternal life.

The promise of eternal life brings comfort in the face of all life's trials. We do not need to be afraid of whatever we may face. Our only comfort, in life and in death, is that we belong to Jesus Christ, who has secured eternal life for his own.

Prayer: *For with you is the fountain of life; in your light we see light. (Psalm 36:9 NIV)*

Q3. How do you come to know your misery?
A. The law of God tells me.

Q4. What does God's law require of us?
A. Christ teaches us this in summary in Matthew 22:37–40:
 "You shall love the Lord your God
 with all your heart,
 and with all your soul,
 and with all your mind."
 This is the greatest and first commandment.
 "And a second is like it:
 "You shall love your neighbor as yourself."
 On these two commandments hang
 all the law and the prophets."

Q5. Can you live up to all this perfectly?
A. No.
 I have a natural tendency
 to hate God and my neighbor.

KASPAR OLEVIANUS, ONE OF the catechism's authors, tells of a man walking down the street with spots on his face. The man does not know he is spotted, so he is able to walk happily around town. However, when someone shows him a mirror, he sees what he truly looks like. Ashamed, he tries to hide so that no one will see him. By looking in the mirror, the man is able to see himself more clearly, even if he does not like what he sees.

We are like the spotted man. This is the "misery" the catechism talks about. We may sense that something is not right with us or the world, but by ourselves we do not truly know our situation. We walk about our daily lives with this "misery" of sin and hypocrisy that marks us, but we are oblivious to it. However, when we see the law of God (all his commandments, summed up in loving God and neighbor) we begin to see things clearly. Like the man in the mirror, hearing how God calls us to love him completely and to love our neighbor forces us to see ourselves in a new light. By clarifying what God demands of us, God's law make sin plain. It reveals how far we have fallen short and the depths of our misery apart from Jesus Christ.

Taking an honest look at ourselves is not always a pleasant experience. Yet, once we have taken stock of our situation, we can be ready and eager to run to the only one who can save us—Jesus Christ.

Prayer: *Direct my footsteps according to your word; let no sin rule over me.*
(Psalm 119:133 NIV)

The Bad News—Lord's Day 2—Monday

Read: Romans 3:9–20
"The law of God tells me"

APART FROM CHECK-UPS, WE usually visit the doctor when we are not feeling well. We may have a guess about our illness, even looked up our symptoms on the internet, but we come to the doctor for diagnosis and treatment. We want the doctor to give a name to our current condition (diagnosis) and to help us return to health (treatment).

God's commands, known as "the law," diagnose our condition as sin. We might sense we are unwell. We might have looked around to try to understand why. But we do not know for sure. God's Word names our situation. When we face the commands of God, we realize how often we do not obey them. This disobedience is called sin. Paul tells us that "through the law comes the knowledge of sin" (v. 20). We were living apart from God, but we do not know this definitively until we encounter the law of God.

However, the law cannot help us return to health. When we learn that we are living in sin, the solution is not more hard work, more commands, and more burdens. The good news is that the God who reveals our painful condition has come to save us in Jesus Christ.

Prayer: *Before I was afflicted I went astray, but now I obey your word.* (Psalm 119:67 NIV)

The Bad News—Lord's Day 2—Tuesday

Read: Deuteronomy 6:4–9
"The first and greatest commandment"

JESUS CALLED THE COMMAND to love God the first and greatest commandment. It is the most important and highest commandment, but also the beginning and the end of the obedience God requires from us. Loving God is the source and goal of every other commandment.

The greatest commandment in all of the Bible is to love God. First, we love the Lord with all our hearts. This means that we love God by desiring him, turning our hearts toward him, and finding joy in him. God should be loved above everything else. Second, we love the Lord with all our soul. This means wanting what he wants and rejecting what he rejects. Third, we love the Lord with all our strength. This means all our actions and decisions should be directed toward loving God. It means loving God with our hands and in our hearts.

The catechism places this beautiful command in its section on misery. When we consider what God asks of us, we must also consider whether we do what he demands. Our failure to love God should lead us to sorrow over our sins—"For godly grief produces a repentance that leads to salvation and brings no regret" (2 Corinthians 7:10).

Prayer: *But let all who take refuge in you be glad; let them ever sing for joy. Spread your protection over them, that those who love your name may rejoice in you.* (Psalm 5:11 NIV)

The Bad News—Lord's Day 2—Wednesday

Read: Luke 10:25–37
"You shall love your neighbor as yourself"

SOME PEOPLE ARE DIFFICULT to love. Loving our family is hard enough, but strangers, cranky coworkers, and nosy neighbors seems too much at times. Who do we really have to love?

Jesus doesn't let us escape so easily. Once, a lawyer approached Jesus asking about the greatest commandments. He wanted to know the limits of who he should love so he could feel good about himself. "Who is my neighbor?" (v. 29) Jesus does not take the bait. Instead, Jesus tells a parable which reveals the character of the one *being* the neighbor. A neighbor is someone who does not pass by the suffering, who has compassion for them, binds their wounds, and even pays the cost for their recovery. The lawyer himself describes the neighbor as "the one who showed him mercy" (v. 37).

You do not get to choose your neighbors. We are to *be* neighbors by showing compassion and mercy in sacrificial ways. Like with the command to love God, we fall woefully short of loving our neighbor. Whenever we fail to love our neighbors, we should run for forgiveness and strength into the arms of the one who did not pass us by, but drew near to us, bound our wounds, and paid the price for our healing—Jesus Christ, our Lord.

Prayer: *Blessed are those who have regard for the weak; the Lord delivers them in times of trouble.* (Psalm 41:1 NIV)

The Bad News—Lord's Day 2—Thursday

Read: Deuteronomy 27:11–26
"Can you live up to all this perfectly?"

AT SOME POINT DURING every wedding, the bride and groom exchange vows. Before the vows are spoken, they are two separate people, but after the vows the relationship is cemented into the covenant of marriage. These vows include promises of how the bride and groom will live in this relationship. In marriage, there are blessings for being faithful and drastic consequences for unfaithfulness.

The relationship God established with Israel is also a covenant. Upon entering the promised land, God's people stood on two mountains—Mount Gerizim and Mount Ebal. Those standing on Mount Gerizim proclaimed God's blessings for covenant faithfulness. Those standing on Mount Ebal proclaimed God's curses for covenant unfaithfulness, ending with "'Cursed be anyone who does not uphold the words of this law by observing them.' All the people shall say, 'Amen!'" (v. 26). Those who break the commandments of God—even the least of them—stand guilty of breaking the whole covenant (James 2:10).

None of us has kept all the commands written in the law. There is no single person who could stand before God and deserve blessings and not curses. No one except Jesus Christ, who took on the curses we deserved and gave us the blessings he deserves.

Prayer: *Streams of tears flow from my eyes, for your law is not obeyed.* (Psalm 119:136 NIV)

7

The Bad News—Lord's Day 2—Friday

Read: Ephesians 2:1–5
"I have a natural tendency to hate God and my neighbor"

THE CATECHISM'S LANGUAGE OF "hating God and neighbor" often incites a gut reaction. I am not perfect, but I am not *that* bad. I am human, but I don't "hate" God and my neighbor. However, we are not just imperfect people, but those who are actively walking away from God.

We are not good people who *happen* to make mistakes. Instead, we are naturally "dead in our trespasses and sins" (v. 1). Apart from Jesus, we were "following the course of this world" (v. 2) and "lived among them in the passions of our flesh, following the desires of flesh and senses" (v. 3). It is not only that we do not do what God calls us to do (love God and neighbor), but we naturally do the exact opposite. We run away from God and try to take his place—trusting our own will over his.

The language of the catechism is strong, but true. Where do we go from here? What can we do once we admit just how bad the situation is? We come to Christ, who saves us, redeems us, raises us from the dead, and enables us to walk along a new way with him.

Prayer: *Many times he delivered them, but they were bent on rebellion and they wasted away in their sin.* (Psalm 106:43 NIV)

The Bad News—Lord's Day 2—Saturday

Read: Psalm 130
"Who could stand?"

IN MODERN COURTROOMS, WE hear the verdict after evidence is presented and witnesses questioned. Even if we are confident of the innocence or guilt of the defendant, there is no verdict until the judgment is finally given.

In the courtroom of God, the guilt of the defendant is never in doubt. "If you, O Lord, should mark iniquities, Lord, who could stand?" (v. 3). If God dealt with us as our sins deserved and passed judgment upon us, we would all be declared guilty. None of us could stand upright before God, but would be crushed under the weight of our sins.

While our guilt is never in doubt, the verdict is surprising. "But there is forgiveness with you" (v. 4). We are forgiven and declared innocent. "For with the Lord there is steadfast love, and with him is great power to redeem" (v. 7). God's judgment on sin was delivered. The guilty judgment we deserve was laid upon someone. Innocent Jesus took the place of guilty humanity.

On our own strength, none of us could stand. But because of Jesus Christ, those who belong to him can stand before God forgiven and clean. This is the great comfort of the gospel.

Prayer: *But with you there is forgiveness, so that we can, with reverence, serve you.* (Psalm 130:4 NIV)

**Q6. Did God create people
so wicked and perverse?**
A. No.
> God created them good and in his own image,
> that is, in true righteousness and holiness,
> so that they might
> truly know God their creator,
> love him with all their heart,
> and live with God in eternal happiness,
> to praise and glorify him.

Q7. Then where does this corrupt human nature come from?
A. The fall and disobedience of our first parents,
> Adam and Eve, in Paradise.
> This fall has so poisoned our nature,
> that we are all conceived and born
> in a sinful condition.

**Q8. But are we so corrupt
that we are totally unable to do any good
and inclined toward all evil?**
A. Yes, unless we are born again
> by the Spirit of God.

MOVING TO THE COUNTRY from a life in the city, the dozens of stars I had known became hundreds in that dark, rural sky. The ever-present city lights let only a few stars shine through. Only by seeing that starry country sky did I realize what I had been missing.

The catechism speaks of creation to remind us how much we are missing. The awe-inspiring goodness of creation has been turned from glorifying God to serve our selfish desires. By knowing what we lost, the poverty of our current condition becomes clear. After the fall into sin, human nature is significantly damaged. Though still in God's image, that image has been obscured and hampered by sin. Our nature is poisoned even from conception. We are no longer able to choose and do what is good in the sight of God. Instead, our hearts are inclined toward selfish and destructive disobedience.

We were made to know God, to love God, and to live with God in eternal happiness. Our misery is that we were made for such a high and glorious existence, but we rejected it. We live longing for communion with God, but are estranged from him. Only by being born again by the Spirit of God can we be reconciled to God and live into our true calling.

Prayer: *When I consider your heavens, the work of your fingers, the moon and the stars, which you have set in place, what is mankind that you are mindful of them, human beings that you care for them?* (Psalm 8:3–4 NIV)

Created & Fallen—Lord's Day 3—Monday

Read: Genesis 1:26–31
"God created them good and in his own image"

IN THE BEGINNING, EVERYTHING was good. It is hard for us to imagine. It was not just a world without death, pain, tragedy, mourning, hatred, and sin, but it was a world filled to the brim with the good blessings of God. Light was separated from darkness, sea from sky. Water pulled back to reveal land, and everything was filled with life. The seas, the land, and the sky all teemed with life. Seven times God calls his creation "good." Seven is a number that indicates completeness. Creation was completely good.

At the center of it all was a garden. In that garden, God placed a man and a woman. After six days of creating fish and trees, birds and snakes, livestock and insects, God created humankind in his image. While all of creation points back to its creator (Psalm 19), this male and female pair have the unique place of bearing the image and likeness of God. They were to lead the chorus of creation in praising the Creator. Though we do not know all of what this "image" contains, they are given dominion over creation (1:26), set to work the garden (2:15), and called to fill creation with their offspring (1:28).

Prayer: *The heavens declare the glory of God; the skies proclaim the work of his hands.* (Psalm 19:1 NIV)

Created & Fallen—Lord's Day 3—Tuesday

Read: Psalm 8
"to praise and glorify Him"

AS MY SIX MONTH old lay on the edge of her blanket she stared in wonder at the blades of grass. She touched and tasted them. I couldn't help but marvel at God's creation along with her. There is so much detail in even the smallest blade of grass, and God created so much more: trees, mountains, rivers and lakes; birds, fish, reptiles and lizards; elephants, tigers, moose and deer.

The psalmist also marvels at God's creation. He sees the world around him, marveling at God's handiwork in creating the sun, moon and stars. With all that is around us we can feel mighty small and insignificant. Yet, the psalmist writes of humanity, "You have given them dominion over the works of your hands; you have put all things under their feet" (v. 6). Through that care, God wants us to live into who he made us to be: creatures who praise and glorify God.

My daughter marveled at even the smallest bit of creation. She was awed by God's handiwork. The psalmist concludes by proclaiming, "O Lord, our Sovereign, how majestic is your name in all the earth!" (v. 9). As you look at the world around you today, praise and glorify God for the wonders of his hands.

Prayer: *Lord, our Lord, how majestic is your name in all the earth! You have set your glory in the heavens.* (Psalm 8:1 NIV)

Created & Fallen—Lord's Day 3—Wednesday

Read: Genesis 3:1–13
"The fall and disobedience of our first parents"

I ONCE HELPED PUT siding on a house. Two of us were putting up the siding when I accidentally broke a piece off of one of the corners. Panicking, we saw no one else had noticed and quickly put up the next section to cover over our mistake. Our first instinct was to hide.

We have been hiding from God since our first parents fell into sin. Adam and Eve sewed fig leaves together and hid from God among the trees of the garden. Neither their clothing nor the trees could truly hide them and make their sin disappear. Instead, they hide, they cover up, and they blame.

We still hide today. We cover our shame with the fig leaves of success, blame, or even good deeds. But, like Adam and Eve, we must be clothed.

In the garden, God seeks out Adam and Eve. He calls them out of hiding in order to stand before him. "What is this that you have done?" God asks (v. 13). God responds with judgment, but also with grace. He clothes them at the cost of an animal's life. The clothing that truly covers our sin—the righteousness of Christ—came at the cost of the life of Jesus Christ.

Prayer: *The Lord delights in those who fear him, who put their hope in his unfailing love.* (Psalm 147:11 NIV)

Created & Fallen—Lord's Day 3—Thursday

Read: Psalm 51
"We are all conceived and born in a sinful condition"

I COULD SEE THE glimmer in his eye—that look that said, "I know I shouldn't do this, but I want to anyway." My son shook his head no, and went ahead and grabbed hold of the floor lamp, intending to pull it down.

Young children seem to get a rush out of doing what they're not supposed to do. The psalmist writes, "Indeed, I was born guilty, a sinner when my mother conceived me" (v. 5). We have all been born into sin. How can a baby be sinful? Think of it this way: We don't need to teach our children to do wrong things, but we do have to teach them to do the right thing. They sin quite well on their own, without any help from me.

When I see that glimmer of "naughtiness" in my children's eyes, I am continually reminded of my need for a savior. I see myself—and my sin—in my children. I cannot do any good on my own. I am no different than my children. I daily need to ask forgiveness and to seek God's will for my life. It is only by the work of His Spirit that I am able to do any good.

Prayer: *Surely I was sinful at birth, sinful from the time my mother conceived me.* (Psalm 51:5 NIV)

Created & Fallen—Lord's Day 3—Friday

Read: Genesis 9:18–29
"so corrupt that we are totally unable to do any good"

HERE ARE A CHAIN of events: fruit consumed, sin committed, nakedness revealed, and curse spoken. Which story in the Bible is being described? We might think of Adam and Eve, but this is also the story of Noah after the flood. Noah takes and consumes fruit in the form of wine, sins in his drunkenness, lies naked in his tent, then utters a curse. The same pattern we see in the garden, replays itself in the vineyard. The heart of the human race was not changed by the flood.

In the judgment of the flood, God hit "reset" on creation. God looked upon the earth and saw that "every inclination of the thoughts of their hearts was only evil continually" (6:5). God's response is to cleanse the earth, saving only Noah and his family in the ark.

Yet after Noah exits the ark, God repeats the same judgment about the human heart: "For the inclination of the human heart is evil from youth" (8:21). Even after God cleansed the world with the flood, the human heart remained unclean. No amount of water could cleanse the human heart. It took something far greater, far more powerful to truly cleanse us and set us free—the blood of Christ.

Prayer: *God is our refuge and strength, an ever-present help in trouble.* (Psalm 46:1 NIV)

Created & Fallen—Lord's Day 3—Saturday

Read: John 3:1–8
"unless we are born again by the Spirit of God."

"HOW DID THIS CHILD ever fit in me?" No more than a couple weeks after birth and the child is growing rapidly. By three months, the child is barely recognizable in both size and personality.

Nicodemus, the Pharisee, was confused. Jesus said, "No one can see the kingdom of God without being born from above" (v. 3). That does not make sense. Babies begin in the womb, but once they leave they don't return. People do not naturally crawl back into their mother's womb to be born again. It cannot happen.

Jesus speaks of human birth as a way of talking about salvation. The change that comes in salvation is as radical and new as the change from being in the womb to life outside it. The Spirit's work of rebirth is not "possible" in the normal way of speaking. This rebirth, or regeneration, is not "natural." The salvation of a single sinner is as miraculous and astonishing as a grown man being born a second time.

Regeneration—being born again—also highlights our own powerlessness to give ourselves life. No one gives birth to themselves. A baby doesn't create itself. It is created. It is given life. In the same way, in our fallen situation, we don't need a spiritual leg up, or some advice, or holy medicine—we need to be given life. We need rebirth—regeneration. We cannot make it happen, but it occurs by the work of the Spirit.

Prayer: *the Lord has done this, and it is marvelous in our eyes.* (Psalm 118:23 NIV)

Q9. But doesn't God do us an injustice by requiring in his law what we are unable to do?
A. No, God created human beings with the ability to keep the law.

> They, however, provoked by the devil,
> in willful disobedience,
> robbed themselves and all their descendants of these gifts.

Q10. Does God permit such disobedience and rebellion to go unpunished?
A. Certainly not.

> God is terribly angry
> with the sin we are born with as well
> as the sins we personally commit.
> As a just judge,
> God will punish them both now and in eternity,
> having declared:
> "Cursed is everyone who does not observe and obey
> all the things written in the book of the law."

Q11. But isn't God also merciful?
A. God is certainly merciful,

> but also just.
> God's justice demands
> that sin, committed against his supreme majesty,
> be punished with the supreme penalty—
> eternal punishment of body and soul.

A KING GIVES A man some land. He tells him to till, plant, and harvest from the land. Yet, the man rebels against the king. Because of one man's treason, the whole family loses the land: his wife, his children, and his grandchildren. The king is just in this.

We are like that man's children. Our first parents—Adam and Eve—were created able to keep God's commandments completely. Yet, they committed treason against God and lost that ability for themselves and for all their children. We are "so corrupt that we are totally unable to do any good and inclined toward all evil" (Q8). God is just when he punishes sin. The catechism uses language that is uncomfortable to many modern ears: "God is terribly angry" with our sin. While our anger might be petty, vindictive, and cruel, God's anger is not. His anger is completely fitting and right. God's punishment fits the crime. Eternal punishment, the supreme penalty, is the just judgment upon our sins, which are "committed against his supreme majesty" (Q11).

We have lost the farm and cannot get it back ourselves. Sin has consequences in this life and the next. Yet, God who is completely just is also merciful. God in mercy will carry out that judgment on himself in the person of the Son, Jesus Christ—our one, true mediator.

Prayer: *Help, Lord, for no one is faithful anymore; those who are loyal have vanished from the human race.* (Psalm 12:1 NIV)

Justice & Mercy—Lord's Day 4—Monday

Read: Romans 5:6–21
"They . . . robbed themselves and all their descendants of these gifts."

SCIENTISTS WHO SEEK TO prevent the rapid spread of diseases often search for the source of the infection. They trace the spread backward in order to find the first person, first location, or first event that caused the disease to spread. The initially infected person is called "Patient Zero."

Adam is Patient Zero for the human race. While Adam and Eve together disobeyed God, the Bible places responsibility firmly on the shoulders of Adam. For "sin came into the world through one man, and death through sin, and so death spread to all men because all sinned" (v. 12). Sin is an epidemic that infects every person on the planet, and the disease is fatal. Sin leads to death. The sin that initially started in Patient Zero, Adam, has now come to infect the whole human race.

This fatal disease of sin has a cure. Just as there was one man who brought sin and death into the world through his sin, there is a person, the God-man Jesus Christ, who brought life and salvation into the world. Apart from Jesus Christ, sin is always fatal. But through the righteous life and sacrificial death of Jesus, salvation and life are given in the face of death.

Prayer: *All have turned away, all have become corrupt; there is no one who does good, not even one.* (Psalm 14:1 NIV)

Justice & Mercy—Lord's Day 4—Tuesday

Read: Ephesians 4:17–32
"In willful disobedience, robbed themselves"

WHEN I FIRST STARTED playing the guitar, my fingers ached constantly. The strings pressed painfully into my soft fingers. Yet, after a few weeks of regular practice, the pain faded. The repeated action of pressing the strings had formed callouses. These callouses eliminated the pain by lessening the feeling in the tips of my fingers.

Our hearts can develop callouses as well. Giving ourselves to our sinful desires over and over again makes our hearts callous—numb and deadened to the prick of the Holy Spirit through our conscience. These callous hearts are hard and unable to respond to the calls of God. Paul names this as the common state of human life apart from Christ. When we sin, at first it can hurt. Despite the thrill of disobedience, our renewed hearts often feel uncomfortable and unsure. However, the more we do it, the more calloused and numb our hearts become to those particular sins.

Instead of hard-hearted, Christians are called to be "tenderhearted" toward one another (v. 32). With hard hearts, we miss out on what God is trying to tell us or give us. Our hearts are to be soft and directed toward "true righteousness and holiness" (v. 24). Our new hearts are designed to have new desires: to speak the truth, to share, to build up, and to forgive.

Prayer: *My sacrifice, O God, is a broken spirit; a broken and contrite heart you, God, will not despise.* (Psalm 51:17 NIV)

Justice & Mercy—Lord's Day 4—Wednesday

Read: Psalm 5

"God is terribly angry"

WHEN SCRIPTURE SPEAKS OF God's anger, it is not speaking of "anger" in the common way we do. Even when we are angry about the right things, our anger can be tainted with malice and aggression. God's anger is perfect. It is never directed toward the wrong thing. It is never out of proportion. The Lord is "not a God who delights in wickedness; evil will not sojourn with you" (v. 4), and "The boastful will not stand before your eyes" (v. 5). God's anger is a form of his justice, love, and holiness. As the holy God, evil cannot live in God's house or even stand before his eyes. As the just God, the Lord stands against wickedness and sin, even to its destruction. As the loving God, the Lord guards and disciplines us for our own good.

Yet, entry into the presence of God is not based on our goodness, but on God's abundant love (v. 7). Before the anger of God, we all deserve punishment, but in Jesus Christ, God made flesh, one with the Father and sent by the Father in love, we are covered with grace (another word for "favor") as with a shield (v. 12). In Jesus Christ, the grace of God covers us and by his steadfast love, we can enter into the very presence of the Father.

Prayer: *But I, by your great love, can come into your house; in reverence I bow down toward your holy temple.* (Psalm 5:7 NIV)

Justice & Mercy—Lord's Day 4—Thursday

Read: Micah 2

"As a just judge"

THERE IS A HUGE difference between saying "God will forgive me" and "God will forgive me anyway." By saying "God will forgive me," we recognize our sin and need for God's forgiveness. "God will forgive me anyway" is a statement of permission. I can sin without consequences. God's forgiving love becomes an excuse for selfish indulgence.

At times, Israel assumed that God would never judge them. Israel knew God's ways better than anyone. Yet, they robbed people of their land and stole their homes. God was not watching, they thought, and he would never judge his own people. Micah reveals how wrong they were. God does not show favoritism. As a just judge, God condemns all sin, whether committed by people who know him or those who do not. In the days of Micah, judgment meant Israel losing her place in God's land and going into exile. For all of us, our sins mean exile from God.

The God who judges also promises to break open a way for us—a way out of exile, a way through judgment, a way into his everlasting peace. God promises Jesus to come and break a way out of bondage to sin into the true freedom of walking as disciples of Christ.

Prayer: *Against you, you only, have I sinned and done what is evil in your sight; so you are right in your verdict and justified when you judge.* (Psalm 51:4 NIV)

Justice & Mercy—Lord's Day 4—Friday

Read: Exodus 34:1–9
"God is certainly merciful, but also just."

"It's not a big deal," our friends say, but inwardly we feel guilty. We know our parents are loving and forgiving, but what will they do? Will they forgive me? What punishment will there be? Our expectations and fear are connected to what we know about the kind of people our parents are.

God is neither a permissive buddy nor a cruel tyrant. Instead, God is both perfectly just and full of mercy. God had lead the Israelites out of Egypt, remained patient as they groaned in the desert, and had been gracious to them when they faltered in their obedience. Israel knew God's mercy and his judgment. When the people made a golden calf idol and began to worship it, the Lord sent Moses down the mountain, where he smashed the tablets of the covenant God had carved. Judgment was executed upon the people, and three thousand were killed. Israel knew God's just punishment upon sin as well as his mercy in the midst of sin.

When he hears of God's justice and mercy, Moses bows down and worships God. We should respond in the same way. We know the kind of God we serve. He is just in punishing sin, but always ready to show mercy.

Prayer: *Hear my prayer, Lord; listen to my cry for mercy.* (Psalm 86:6 NIV)

Justice & Mercy—Lord's Day 4—Saturday

Read: Matthew 25:35–46
"eternal punishment of body and soul."

Just before the year 2000, there was a lot of anxiety about the end of the world. People feared when the clock struck midnight computers would crash and civilization would collapse. January 1 came and went, but the world did not end. Christ had not returned, and Christians continued to wait.

But Christ will return. At that time, the nations will be gathered and the Son of Man (Jesus) will separate people like a shepherd separates sheep from goats as they enter the pen. The sheep on his right will be those who belong to him and whose lives bore fruit of compassion for the hungry, the thirsty, the stranger, the naked, the sick, and the imprisoned. Jesus says that those who show care for the least show care for Jesus. The goats on his left do not belong to Jesus and have not produced the fruit of compassion. Christ's return culminates in a final judgment where the unrighteous "will go away into eternal punishment, but the righteous into eternal life" (25:46).

Jesus' words should humble us and lead to compassion. Apart from Christ, the end of all things would be a time of fear. But in Christ, we will enter the kingdom of God.

Prayer: *Blessed are those who have regard for the weak; the Lord delivers them in times of trouble.* (Psalm 41:1 NIV)

Q12. According to God's righteous judgment
   we deserve punishment
   both now and in eternity:
   how then can we escape this punishment
   and return to God's favor?
A. God requires that his justice be satisfied.
   Therefore the claims of this justice
   must be paid in full,
   either by ourselves or by another.

Q13. Can we make this payment ourselves?
A. Certainly not. Actually, we increase our debt every day.

Q14. Can another creature—any at all—pay this debt for us?
A. No. To begin with,
   God will not punish any other creature
   for what a human is guilty of.
   Furthermore,
   no mere creature can bear the weight
   of God's eternal wrath against sin
   and deliver others from it.

Q15. What kind of mediator and deliverer should we look for then?
A. One who is a true and righteous human,
   yet more powerful than all creatures,
   that is, one who is also true God.

GOD OWES US NOTHING, but gives us everything. Our next breath, a long life, good health, a successful career. God does not owe us these things. Yet God is gracious and kind. He gives us all that we are, all that we have, and holds our life and the universe in his hands.

We owe God everything, but, in our sin, we give him nothing. We continually refuse to give God what he deserves. We owe God obedience. If we kept God's commands perfectly from this moment on, we would only be doing what we already owe God. Our good deeds would not pay off the debt of our sin, only stop us from adding to it. However, we do not even do this. Instead, we continually add to our debt as we sin. Our accounts are always in the red. If we received what we deserved, there would be nothing but judgment.

Our hope is found in Jesus. God owes us nothing. Yet our salvation is sure and certain, because God has promised salvation and accomplished it through the life, death, and resurrection of his Son. God owes us nothing, but gives us everything, including salvation through his Son, Jesus Christ.

Prayer: *The Lord is my strength and my defense; he has become my salvation.*
(Psalm 118:14 NIV)

Our Great Debt—Lord's Day 5—Monday

Read: 1 Thessalonians 1:4–10
"His Justice Be Satisfied"

WHEN JESUS COMES, HE will set all things right and make all things new. Christ's return will include just judgment upon those who do not know and obey God, where God's holy love will take the form of wrath upon sin. Jesus will come in victory, meaning all that opposes his rule—sin, death, and the devil—will be vanquished.

There is a wrath that is coming (v. 10). There will be a judgment, and none of us will be able to stand on our own strength. Not the best person you have ever met, nor the worst. All of us would stand condemned. Either we stand on our own righteousness and finally fall, or we must stand on the righteousness of another and be rescued. Jesus who comes in royal, just judgment also rescues us from the wrath that is coming. Jesus the judge is Jesus the rescuer.

What do we do, having heard that Christ is coming again? Turn to God from idols. We must leave behind what we have clung to for our identity, our hope, our sense of worth, and cling to Christ. God has been patient and kind to us, but this should lead us to repentance, to turn to serve the living God.

Prayer: *Rise up, O God, judge the earth, for all the nations are your inheritance.* (Psalm 82:8 NIV)

Our Great Debt—Lord's Day 5—Tuesday

Read: Isaiah 53:1–11
"the claims of this justice must be paid in full, either by ourselves or by another."

WHY DID JESUS HAVE to die? The claims of justice must be paid in full. He didn't *have* to die. He *chose* to die. We are the ones who are deserving of death. No matter how hard we try, we still sin. Even the youngest of us are not innocent. In our home we often have to remind our toddler not to push his little sister, and remind his sister not to pull her brother's hair. Genesis 6 speaks of our hearts being inclined to evil all the time. Someone needs to pay for that sin in our lives, and the payment is death.

However, God had a plan. Our Father God chose to send his son Jesus into the world to die in our place, so that we would not need to take the punishment. "He was wounded for our transgressions, crushed for our iniquities; upon him was the punishment that made us whole, and by his bruises we are healed" (v. 5). God chose to take the punishment that we deserved upon himself, so that we didn't have to pay it. Isn't our great God amazing? He loved us so much that he took our punishment.

Prayer: *Have mercy on me, O God, according to your unfailing love; according to your great compassion blot out my transgressions.* (Psalm 51:1 NIV)

Our Great Debt—Lord's Day 5—Wednesday

Read: Matthew 18:21–35
"Not by ourselves"

SOME DEBTS ARE TOO big to pay back. Jesus' parable talks of a slave who owed 10,000 talents. At the rate of an average worker, it would take over 150,000 years of labor in order to pay back the debt. When the King comes to collect on the debt, the slave begs for time. There was never going to be enough time for the slave to pay him back. However, the master is gracious and forgives him the debt. A second slave owed the first one hundred denarii (or one hundred days' wages). This is not a small amount of money. However, compared to the debt the first slave had owed to his master, it was pocket change.

For us too, some debts are too big to pay back. As sinners, our debts are greater than the slave who owed ten thousand talents. 150,000 years would not even make a dent. Nothing we do will ever be able to pay off that debt. Instead, we need our king to forgive us. We need to hear, "out of pity for him, the lord of that slave released him and forgave him the debt" (v. 27). We need God in Christ to do for us what we cannot do for ourselves.

Prayer: *Hide your face from my sins and blot out all my iniquity.* (Psalm 51:9 NIV)

Our Great Debt—Lord's Day 5—Thursday

Read: Hebrews 10:1–18
"God will not punish any other creature"

SOUNDS OF PLAY SUDDENLY turn to tears. My daughter proclaims she should not be on time out, but her toy dinosaur should be. After all, she says, the dinosaur was the one who hit her brother, not her. She wants the toy to take the punishment for her.

In the Law, animals took the punishment for human sins. Whenever someone sinned, there would need to be a sacrifice. An animal took the punishment for the human's sin. However, this system was only ever to be a pointer to Christ. No animal can truly bear the weight of human sin. "It is impossible for the blood of bulls and goats to take away sins" (v. 4). If we are not going to bear the weight and punishment for our sins, we need a better substitute than bulls, sheep, and goats. Only Jesus can bear the weight of our sins, and not ours only, but the sin of the whole world.

My daughter's dinosaur was not put in time out for her. The toy could not bear the consequences of her actions. No animal or creature can truly bear the consequences of our sins. Only Jesus Christ, fully God and fully human, can bear the weight and save our souls.

Prayer: *Cleanse me with hyssop, and I will be clean; wash me, and I will be whiter than snow.* (Psalm 51:7 NIV)

Our Great Debt—Lord's Day 5—Friday

Read: Hebrews 7:23–28
"Our mediator"

When God brought the people out of Egypt, he led them up to Mount Sinai. The people were warned not to touch it, for the mountain was holy with God's presence. In order for the people to come before the LORD, God established a priesthood through Aaron. Aaron's sons would serve as priests, offering sacrifices and ushering people into the presence of God.

Generation after generation priests served in the temple, but each eventually died and was replaced by another. It seemed a never-ending cycle. Yet it all pointed ahead to Jesus. Jesus is our great high priest. Jesus died, rose again, and dies no more. The work he does in bringing us before the Father, saving us, and interceding for us continues forever. He does not die so his work does not fail. He offered no sacrifices for his own sins (for he had none), but offered himself as a sacrifice for the sins of others.

This is our Savior, our hope, and our joy—Jesus Christ. When the catechism names our plight and asks "What kind of mediator and deliver should we look for?" it points us directly to Jesus, our great high priest, who saves completely and forever.

Prayer: *My soul thirsts for God, for the living God. When can I go and meet with God?* (Psalm 42:2 NIV)

Our Great Debt—Lord's Day 5—Saturday

Read: Jeremiah 23:1–8
"The Lord is our Righteousness"

Jesus said, "Blessed are those who hunger and thirst for righteousness, for they will be filled" (Matthew 5:6). There is a worldwide famine of righteousness, and all of us are hungry and thirsty.

The days of Jeremiah were no different. Jeremiah prophesied at a time where those entrusted with leading Israel were failing them. There was a famine of righteousness in the land. They scattered the flock, destroyed them, and drove them away, instead of protecting, nurturing, and guarding them. God promised not only judgment upon these shepherds, but that God will be the shepherd of his people. He will gather them up and bring them back to the fold. He will also raise up a righteous Branch, a son of David. The name of this king will be "The LORD is our righteousness." When we hunger and thirst for righteousness, we must come to the LORD, come to the righteous son of David.

Jesus is Lord, both the Good Shepherd and the son of David who reigns on the throne. He is both the God who gathers and the Son who rules. He is the righteous one we must come to when we hunger and thirst.

Prayer: *Righteousness and justice are the foundation of your throne; love and faithfulness go before you.* (Psalm 89:14 NIV)

Jesus, Our Mediator—Lord's Day 6—Sunday

Q16. Why must the mediator be a true and righteous human?
A. God's justice demands
 that human nature, which has sinned, must pay for sin;
 but a sinful human could never pay for others.

Q17. Why must the mediator also be true God?
A. So that the mediator,
 by the power of his divinity,
 might bear the weight of God's wrath in his humanity
 and earn for us and restore to us righteousness and life.

Q18. Then who is this mediator—true God and at the same time a true and righteous human?
A. Our Lord Jesus Christ,
 who was given to us
 to completely deliver us
 and make us right with God.

Q19. How do you come to know this?
A. The holy gospel tells me.
 God began to reveal the gospel already in Paradise;
 later God proclaimed it
 by the holy patriarchs and prophets
 and foreshadowed it
 by the sacrifices and other ceremonies of the law;
 and finally God fulfilled it
 through his own beloved Son.

In describing the work of Christ, the catechism uses the term "mediator." If a couple are fighting and cannot solve it themselves, they can call a mediator, such as a pastor, lawyer, or counselor. A mediator would work with both people to mend and heal the relationship. Drawing from Scripture, this is the picture we are given of the work of Christ: Jesus is our mediator.

This mediator must have certain qualifications to fit the role. First, our mediator must be truly human. We have offended God and we must pay for sin, but we cannot pay it ourselves. We need a mediator who is human like us, who can represent us to God and do what we cannot do. Second, we also need a mediator who is truly God. Our debt must be paid, but we cannot pay it ourselves. Only God in his infinite power could bear the punishment of sin without collapsing. In God's grace, God has become our mediator in Jesus Christ. He took on flesh as Jesus Christ, becoming both the human mediator and the true God we need, so that the human race could be reconciled to God.

Jesus is our mediator, mending what is broken, setting right what is wrong, and making peace between us and God. He is both truly human and truly God, our perfect mediator.

Prayer: *Our help is in the name of the Lord, the Maker of heaven and earth.* (Psalm 124:8 NIV)

Jesus, Our Mediator—Lord's Day 6—Monday

Read: Hebrews 2:10-18
"Why must he be very man?"

IT FEELS GOOD TO be understood. When life is stressful at work or home, it feels good to sit down, talk, and be heard. Sometimes, "understanding" is all we can do. Sometimes we cannot fix what is wrong. We can understand, but we cannot make it right.

Jesus not only understands, but makes things right. The Son took on humanity in order to save humanity. Jesus is not ashamed to call us brothers and sisters. He took on every part of us in order to rescue every part of us from sin. "Therefore he had to become like his brothers and sisters in every respect, so that he might be a merciful and faithful high priest in the service of God, to make a sacrifice of atonement for the sins of the people" (v. 17). Jesus came not just to know what it felt like to be us, but to redeem and save us in all the ways that we need to be saved.

It feels good to be understood, but it is better to be saved. Jesus not only understands all that we face in life but redeems all of our life. He took on all we are so that he might save all that we are. He took on a human mind to redeem our minds and make them holy. He took on a human heart and will to redeem our hearts and redirect our desires. He entered into real life with human relationships and interactions, including being hated, mocked, and betrayed, to heal and sanctify us. He took on a human body, in all its fragility, to rescue our bodies and make them holy.

Prayer: *Israel, put your hope in the Lord, for with the Lord is unfailing love and with him is full redemption.* (Psalm 130:7 NIV)

Jesus, Our Mediator—Lord's Day 6—Tuesday

Read: John 1:19-34
"Why must the mediator also be true God?"

I GET TROUBLED BY how Apple names its products. The iPad. iPhone. iTunes. iPhoto. All together, Apple packages them as iLife. Yet, the iLife sells. The iLife, where *I* am the star and *I* run the show. The iLife, where I am always center stage. However, the Christian life is not an iLife. It's a God-life.

Down by the Jordan, everyone wanted to know who John was, but John wants everyone to know who Jesus is. Some people thought John was the Messiah, some that he was the return of Elijah, and others that he was the prophet sent by God. John claimed only to prepare the people for the coming of the Messiah. Everyone wanted to know who John was, but John wanted everyone to know who Jesus is. Jesus is the Lamb of God. He is the lamb God provides to remove the sin of the world. Jesus is true God, in the flesh, walking on earth, baptized in the Jordan, for us and for our salvation. John lives to point others to Jesus.

The Christian life is never the iLife. Like John, we live to point others, not to ourselves, but to Christ, the true God in the flesh, the Lamb of God who takes away the sin of the world.

Prayer: *Give praise to the Lord, proclaim his name; make known among the nations what he has done.* (Psalm 105:1 NIV)

Jesus, Our Mediator—Lord's Day 6—Wednesday

Read: 1 Timothy 2:1–6
"One Mediator—Jesus Christ"

IN *PILGRIM'S PROGRESS*, THE main character, Christian, heads up a highway burdened with a heavy load. He enters this narrow path through a single gate. There are walls on either side of the highway called "Salvation" and at the top of the hill stands a cross. When Christian comes to the cross, his sins fall away from him and are swallowed in the tomb. Though the scene climaxes at the cross, Christian could only arrive there by passing through the narrow gate.

Jesus Christ is the single gate through which we enter into the narrow path of salvation. There is only one way to God, only one way to have our sins removed—through Jesus Christ. As Paul proclaims, "there is one God; there is also one mediator between God and human-kind, Christ Jesus, himself human, who gave himself a ransom for all" (vv. 5–6a). There is only one mediator, only one who can bridge the gap between us and God so that our sins are forgiven and swallowed by the grave: Jesus Christ.

Have you come to Christ and had your burden removed? Have you watched your sin roll into the grave and be seen no more? If so, praise the Lord! Worship Jesus who poured out his life for your sins. If not, come to Christ today to find hope, joy, and relief.

Prayer: *Our God is a God who saves; from the Sovereign Lord comes escape from death.* (Psalm 68:20 NIV)

Jesus, Our Mediator—Lord's Day 6—Thursday

Read: Ephesians 1:1–14
"Given up for us"

LIFE CAN SOMETIMES FEEL like anything but blessed. Jobs are lost, marriages are bruised and broken, children struggle in school, loneliness and isolation remove us from family and friends. Sickness, depression, and death flood our lives.

Yet in the midst of all of this, God's Word proclaims something stunning: Before you were born, before you even knew about God, God already chose you as his own in Jesus. He had already decided to die for you, to adopt you into his family, and to bless you in and through Jesus. This love and blessing cannot be shaken by circumstances, no matter how difficult. We find blessings not in our circumstances, but in Christ. From before the creation of the world through the blood of Christ shed on the cross to the giving of faith and the marking with the promised Holy Spirit—Salvation is God's work and rests in God's hands. It is God's blessing of us in Christ. "In him we have redemption through his blood, the forgiveness of our trespasses" (v. 7). The blessing of God comes to us through the Cross. Our life comes from Christ giving up his life for us. Our peace comes through his suffering.

In a world where life can feel anything but blessed, Christ has given himself up for us. This is blessing beyond what we can see with our eyes, but blessing that stretches out to eternity.

Prayer: *May God be gracious to us and bless us and make his face shine on us—so that your ways may be known on earth, your salvation among all nations.* (Psalm 67:1–2 NIV)

Jesus, Our Mediator—Lord's Day 6—Friday

Read: Genesis 3:13–21
"already in Paradise"

THE OPENING PART OF the story often tells us both the problem the characters are facing and points to the possible solution. *The Fellowship of the Ring*, the first book in the *Lord of the Rings* trilogy, opens with the problem of the Ring and the possibility of destroying it. *Beauty and the Beast* begins with the curse and the promise that true love would break it.

In Genesis 3, we are told both the problem of our world and the promise of God to set it right. The problem is the curse we suffer under as a result of our sin. Yet, tucked into the painful news of the first sin's fallout is a promise in the curse upon the snake. "I will put enmity between you and the woman, and between your offspring and hers; he will strike your head, and you will strike his heel" (v. 15). A child will come from Eve who will crush the serpent. The rest of the Bible can be rightly seen as the search for this child.

The child promised long ago has come: Jesus Christ. At Calvary, the great serpent, Satan, struck Christ's heel, but it was his head that was ultimately crushed. The Catechism writes, "God began to reveal the gospel already in paradise." Before the story had even gotten fully underway, God was promising restoration to come. Already, here and now, Christ has begun the work of redeeming all things. In Christ, the curse of Eden has been thrown asunder and God has fulfilled his promise.

Prayer: *You will tread on the lion and the cobra; you will trample the great lion and the serpent.* (Psalm 91:13 NIV)

Jesus, Our Mediator—Lord's Day 6—Saturday

Read: Hebrews 1:1–4
"At last through his Son"

IMAGINE THREE BLIND MEN place their hands on different parts of an elephant, but none know it is an elephant. Each claims it is a snake, tree, or rope depending on what they are touching. Some claim this is how we know God: blind men touching only a part, ignorant of the whole. An elephant itself is unable to tell the men what and who they are touching. However, God has not been silent with us.

God spoke to the patriarchs, to Israel on Mount Sinai, and through the prophets. He told us who he is, who we were to be, and promised that he would one day come and bring us to himself. In the last days, the Word became flesh as the man Jesus Christ. Jesus is the one the prophets spoke about and is the most perfect speech of God, "the reflection of God's glory and the exact imprint of God's very being, and he sustains all things by his powerful word" (v. 3). We know who God is because he has revealed himself to us.

We are not groping in the dark. No longer like blind men fumbling in the dark, we are people who have heard the voice of the LORD and trust in his word, trust in his Son, through whom he has spoken.

Prayer: *I will listen to what God the Lord says; he promises peace to his people, his faithful servants—but let them not turn to folly.* (Psalm 85:8 NIV)

Q20. Are all people then saved through Christ just as they were lost through Adam?

A. No. Only those are saved
 who through true faith
 are grafted into Christ
 and accept all his benefits.

Q21. What is true faith?

A. True faith is
 not only a sure knowledge by which I hold as true
 all that God has revealed to us in Scripture;
 it is also a wholehearted trust,
 which the Holy Spirit creates in me by the gospel,
 that God has freely granted,
 not only to others but to me also,
 forgiveness of sins,
 eternal righteousness, and salvation.
 These are gifts of sheer grace,
 granted solely by Christ's merit.

Q22. What then must a Christian believe?

A. All that is promised us in the gospel,
 a summary of which is taught us
 in the articles of our universal
 and undisputed Christian faith.

Q23. What are these articles?

A. I believe in God, the Father almighty,
 creator of heaven and earth.
 I believe in Jesus Christ, his only begotten Son, our Lord,
 who was conceived by the Holy Spirit
 and born of the virgin Mary.
 He suffered under Pontius Pilate,
 was crucified, died, and was buried;
 he descended to hell.
 The third day he rose again from the dead.
 He ascended to heaven
 and is seated at the right hand of God the Father almighty.
 From there he will come to judge the living and the dead.
 I believe in the Holy Spirit,
 the holy catholic church,
 the communion of saints,
 the forgiveness of sins,
 the resurrection of the body,
 and the life everlasting. Amen.

IF AN UNBELIEVING FRIEND came up to you and asked, "What is the Christian faith?" what would you say? How would you summarize something so large and deep in a quick way? Some spur of the moment answers might be good and true, others might be false or incomplete. If we have to summarize "all that is promised us in the gospel," what should we say?

We are not the first to wrestle with this question. One of the earliest and best summaries of Christian teaching is the Apostles' Creed. It is called "Apostles," not because it was written by the apostles, but because it contains the summary of what they taught. We call it the Apostles' Creed because its teaching is "apostolic." The Creed, just like the Heidelberg Catechism, is not as authoritative as the Bible. Instead, it seeks to summarize the teachings of Scripture in a way that can be easily remembered and publicly spoken. It contains the core teaching of our "universal and undisputed Christian faith."

The Heidelberg Catechism explains each line of the Apostles' Creed because it summarizes the core of the Christian faith. When we know this summary, we are shaped to read scripture well and confess a faith that is rich, true, and deep. The next time someone asks about the Christian faith, we can say, "I believe in God the Father almighty . . ." and be able to explain what we mean when we say those things.

Prayer: *They tell of the power of your awesome works—and I will proclaim your great deeds.* (Psalm 145:6 NIV)

True Faith—Lord's Day 7—Monday

Read: John 3:16–21
"through true faith are grafted into Christ"

SOMETIMES, KIDS DO NOT want to eat their dinner. It does not matter what you say, they do not want to eat it. All they need to do is open their mouth, and they would be fed and enjoy the wonderful food we have made for them.

Faith is like opening wide our mouth to receive the salvation God has provided for us. Like children opening their mouth for food, faith requires vulnerable trust in God's goodness. Jesus Christ was sent into the world to save it (v. 17). Salvation comes into our lives through belief in Christ. Like a wide open mouth, faith is how we receive Jesus' saving work into our lives. Yet, not every one is open to receive Jesus Christ. Those who do not believe are "condemned already" (v. 18). The salvation of Christ is right in front of them, but their mouths remain closed. They do not believe in Jesus, and their souls starve without him.

May we each be open in faith to receive Jesus Christ, our only Savior. Like a child opening its mouth wide to receive good food, we are called to open wide to receive Christ in faith so that we "may not perish, but may have eternal life" (v. 16).

Prayer: *I am the Lord your God, who brought you up out of Egypt. Open wide your mouth and I will fill it.* (Psalm 81:10 NIV)

True Faith—Lord's Day 7—Tuesday

Read: Romans 10:1–13
"True faith is . . . a sure knowledge"

IMAGINE TELLING SOMEONE YOU really enjoy their friendship, but do not want to know anything about them. You do not want to know their birthday, favorite color, or favorite hockey team. This would seem silly to you because a real relationship is about knowing and being known. No meaningful relationship lasts if you do not know each other.

We cannot have a relationship with God apart from knowing him. Our deepest relationships are more than knowing a lot about each other, but they are certainly not less than that. Trust requires knowledge. This was the problem experienced by Israel apart from Christ. They have passion and love for God, but they do not truly know him. This leads them to build their life on a false foundation (v. 3). Faith—like love—requires knowledge. We need a sure knowledge of God provided by God, otherwise we will base our life and hope on our whims, wishes, or fantasies. To be in a true, lasting relationship with God, we must know God.

Thankfully, God has not left us in the dark about himself. In the Bible, through the preaching of the gospel, and through prayer, we come to know God. Only in knowing him and being known by him, can we truly place our trust in him.

Prayer: *You, God, are my God, earnestly I seek you; I thirst for you, my whole being longs for you, in a dry and parched land where there is no water.* (Psalm 63:1 NIV)

True Faith—Lord's Day 7—Wednesday

Read: Genesis 15
"True faith is . . . a wholehearted trust"

SOME PEOPLE VIEW FAITH like stockpiling food. It is best to buy in bulk. You need to have enough to get by. However, true faith is more like shooting an arrow than stockpiling food. It matters more where faith is pointed than how much you have. It must be pointed in the right direction—toward Christ.

Abraham's faith was set firmly on God. "He believed the Lord; and the Lord reckoned it to him as righteousness" (v. 6). The Lord had come to him with a promise. And Abraham trusted God's promise. Abraham trusted with his whole heart, but, more importantly, he put his trust in the right place—in the God who keeps his promises. It was not the amount of trust he had that was crucial, but who he trusted. Abraham trusted God and trusted God's promises to him.

When we set our faith firmly on God, we become children of Abraham. It is in aiming our trust at the God who promises to save us that we become part of the family of Abraham. Faith is not a shot in the dark, but is laser-focused on the promises of God. Christian faith is trusting in Christ, the fulfillment of all God's promises.

Prayer: *I cling to you; your right hand upholds me.* (Psalm 63:8 NIV)

True Faith—Lord's Day 7—Thursday

Read: Ephesians 2:1–10
"True faith . . . which the Holy Spirit creates in me"

ON OUR WEDDING DAY, my wife and I received a lot of gifts for our new life together. It took time before we finally opened the gifts. When we lived without them, the gifts had still been given, but they remained in the wrapping paper and gave us no benefit. People gave the gifts on our wedding day, but we only really got them when we opened them.

Salvation is a gift from God. Because of our sin, we are separated from God and unable to find our way home. While we were dead, God made us alive (v. 4). While we were far from God, Christ brought us near. This gracious salvation of God is "not your own doing; it is the gift of God" (v. 8). We receive this new resurrection life through faith, but this faith itself is a gift of God. We do not buy our salvation or earn it through our works. It is a gift.

Yet, this gift must be opened. If the gift of salvation remains unopened, it does no good for us. Salvation is a gift, but the Holy Spirit must create faith in us so that we open the gift of salvation that Christ has given us.

Prayer: *It is better to take refuge in the Lord than to trust in humans.* (Psalm 118:8 NIV)

True Faith—Lord's Day 7—Friday

Read: Romans 10:1–17
"creates in me by the gospel"

SOME NEWS CALLS FOR a response. The war is over. The victory is won. A child is born. Life-changing news can bring relief and joy, but only if it is told.

Gospel means "good news." The gospel is a message—good news—that is shared with others. We come to faith through hearing and believing this news. The gospel is the announcement of what Jesus has done on the cross and in the empty tomb. God chooses to create faith through the proclamation of the gospel, through the sharing of good news. "For one believes with the heart and so is justified, and one confesses with the mouth and so is saved" (v. 10). Without hearing the gospel, we cannot believe in Christ. Without someone sharing the gospel, we cannot hear it. Without someone sent by God, there is no one to share (vv. 14–15). Without hearing the gospel, we cannot experience the joy, peace, comfort, and salvation Christ brings. Jesus Christ died and rose again, but without hearing the gospel, we cannot believe and experience joy.

"So faith comes from what is heard, and what is heard comes through the word of Christ" (v. 17). It is by hearing the good news of Christ that the Holy Spirit creates faith in our hearts. Just as we have heard the gospel, may we be those sent to share it with others.

Prayer: *Sing to the Lord, praise his name; proclaim his salvation day after day.* (Psalm 96:2 NIV)

True Faith—Lord's Day 7—Saturday

Read: Jude 1–4
"the articles of our universal and undisputed Christian faith"

WHEN PLAYING SPORTS, IT is important to be able to tell the teams apart. Separate jerseys with different colors help players to pass the ball to their teammates and not their opponents.

The Apostles' Creed functions like a team's jersey. It helps distinguish between those who hold the true faith and those who do not. It helps reveal who belongs to the church and who does not. Jude describes the Christian faith as a contest. "The faith that was once for all delivered to the saints" is being challenged. People have crept in unnoticed and claim that they are teaching the true faith when, in fact, they "pervert the grace of our God" (v. 4). How should the church distinguish between the "salvation we share," the "faith that was once for all entrusted to the saints" (v. 3) and this twisting of the faith? They need to know which team the teachers are playing for.

The ultimate test of faithful teaching is embracing the whole of scripture, particularly the gospel. However, the church has consistently employed the Apostles' Creed as a summary of that teaching. In speaking the Creed, we confess ourselves to be people contending for the faith that was once for all delivered to the saints.

Prayer: *My soul faints with longing for your salvation, but I have put my hope in your word.* (Psalm 119:81 NIV)

Q24. How are these articles divided?

A. Into three parts:

    God the Father and our creation;

    God the Son and our deliverance;

    and God the Holy Spirit and our sanctification.

Q25. Since there is only one divine being,
    why do you speak of three:
    Father, Son, and Holy Spirit?

A. Because that is how

    God has revealed himself in his Word:

    these three distinct persons

    are one, true, eternal God.

WHILE THE WORD "TRINITY" does not appear in the Bible, it was used from early on in the church to name the God revealed in the Bible. There was no word to describe the God of the Bible, who is one God—Father, Son, and Holy Spirit. Therefore, the church invented the word "trinity" to speak of the nature of God.

In the doctrine of the Trinity, we find the beating heart of the Christian faith. There is only one God. The Father is God, the Son is God, and the Spirit is God, but there are not three gods, but one God. All three are equal. All three are God. All three are one. The Trinity shapes how we worship, pray, and understand salvation. We praise the Father in the Son through the Spirit. We pray to the Father, but we pray in and through Jesus Christ, empowered and guided by the Holy Spirit. We are reconciled to the Father through the Son in the Spirit. Every aspect of the Christian faith is shaped by the Trinity, because every aspect of the Christian faith has to do with God. As the catechism reminds us, this "is how God has revealed himself in his Word" (Q25).

Prayer: *Lord, our Lord, how majestic is your name in all the earth!* (Psalm 8:9 NIV)

The Holy Trinity—Lord's Day 8—Monday

Read: Psalm 139
"God the Father and our creation"

STARING AT THE ULTRASOUND, I listened as the doctor told us our tiny son already had fingernails and eyelashes. I was amazed that God created this little boy and set him to grow in his mother's womb. God not only created all things cosmic—the sun, moon, and stars—but knitted us together in our mother's womb.

Our Father, our creator, cares for us. He knows us. "O Lord, you have searched me and know me" (v. 1). He knows the paths we have taken, our words before we speak them, and our days before we live them. Because God knows us, he hems us in, protecting us and preventing us from falling too far from his grace. This knowledge of our lives—in their beauty and brokenness—does not lead God to retreat from us, but to draw near to us. Even in the darkest places of our lives, we are not far from his presence.

The Father created everything and he cares for his creation. Not only when I look at the abundant fields and tall trees, but when I look into the face of my children or glance in the mirror, I am seeing God's creation. The Creation that God cares for and protects.

Prayer: *You have searched me, Lord, and you know me.* (Psalm 139:1 NIV)

The Holy Trinity—Lord's Day 8—Tuesday

Read: John 14:1–14
"God the Son and our deliverance"

JESUS' DISCIPLES WANT TWO things: to know where Jesus is going and for Jesus to show them the Father. Jesus' responses reveal his unique relationship to the Father as the Son of God and his unique mission.

First, Jesus brings us to the Father. Jesus says, "I am the way, and the truth, and the life. No one comes to the Father except through me" (v. 6). We can only know God the Father and be in relationship with him through his Son, Jesus Christ. Jesus wipes away our sin through his death and resurrection, overcoming our separation from God. In his life, his dying, and his rising, Jesus the Son brings us to the Father.

Second, Jesus shows us the Father. The unique relationship between the Father and the Son allows Jesus to reveal the Father to us. Jesus tells us "the Father may be glorified in the Son" (v. 13), and "I am in the Father and the Father is in me" (v. 10). The work of Jesus reveals the heart of the Father.

Jesus is the only way to get to God and the only way to know God. As the unique Son of God, Jesus has a unique mission to show us God and bring us to God.

Prayer: *Restore us, O God; make your face shine on us, that we may be saved.* (Psalm 80:3 NIV)

The Holy Trinity—Lord's Day 8—Wednesday

Read: John 16:1–15
"God the Holy Spirit and our sanctification"

SOMETIMES THE MOST LOVING word you can say is "No." No, that will hurt you. No, that will hurt someone else. Other times, the most loving word is "Yes." Yes, I love you. Yes, I will be with you. Yes, you matter to me.

The Holy Spirit says both "Yes" and "No" to us. The Holy Spirit will bring conviction (v. 8). The Spirit will speak an emphatic "No" over all in us that opposes the will and truth of God. It will help us see God's will in the Bible and prick our consciences when we stray. The Spirit will also guide us into the truth (v. 13). The Spirit will bring understanding and lead us to walk in the truth of God's Word. Lastly, the Spirit will glorify Jesus (v. 14). The work of the Spirit in our lives and in our world will make the name of Jesus "the name that is above every name."

God the Spirit says both "no" and "yes" to us. The Spirit comes into our lives to say "no" to everything that is sinful and opposes God's will. The Spirit also says "yes" to us and uses the Word of God to glorify Jesus and lead us in obedience to him.

Prayer: *Turn my eyes away from worthless things; preserve my life according to your word.* (Psalm 119:37 NIV)

The Holy Trinity—Lord's Day 8—Thursday

Read: Matthew 28:16–20
"Because that is how God has revealed himself in his Word"

WHY BELIEVE IN OR talk so much about the doctrine of the Trinity? I have Jesus. I worship God. Why is the doctrine of the Trinity important for us?

The Great Commission gives us two reasons the Trinity matters: identity and mission. We are baptized in the one name—Father, Son, and Holy Spirit. This Trinitarian formula is at the heart of Christian identity. The one God who claims us in baptism has one name—Father, Son, and Holy Spirit. The Trinity matters because we belong to the Triune God.

Christians are also called into the Trinitarian mission. Jesus sends his people on a mission to proclaim the good news, baptize, make disciples, and teach obedience to the commands of God. There is no Christian faith and no Christian mission apart from the one God—Father, Son, and Holy Spirit—who calls, sends, and empowers the church to make disciples of all nations. The Trinity matters because we are sent out in the name of the Triune God.

The Trinity is central to who we are and what we are called to do as Christians. We enter into the Christian life by being baptized and sent out in the one name—Father, Son, and Holy Spirit.

Prayer: *Let the name of the Lord be praised, both now and forevermore.* (Psalm 113:2 NIV)

The Holy Trinity—Lord's Day 8—Friday

Read: Matthew 3:13–17
"these three distinct persons"

WE HAVE BEEN LOOKING at the different works of the three persons of the Trinity. We spoke of the Father's work at creation, the Son in redemption, and the Spirit in sanctification. While we rightly say each person has distinct work, Jesus' baptism highlights that the three persons are united in the work of God.

All three persons of the Trinity are on full display in Jesus' baptism. Jesus, the Son of God, is being baptized. The Spirit of God is descending on Jesus like a dove. The voice of the Father speaks from heaven. Father, Son, and Holy Spirit are all involved at Jesus' baptism. While we can distinguish the work of the Father (creation) from the work of the Son (salvation) from the work of the Spirit (sanctification), we cannot separate them. All three are present, active, and united in every part. The Father and the Spirit are just as involved in the work of salvation as the Son, and the Son and Father are just as involved in sanctification as the Spirit.

Jesus' baptism shows that the Trinitarian persons are distinct, but not separate. The one God in three persons is united in the work of creating the world, redeeming sinners, and bringing them to glory.

Prayer: *Let them praise the name of the Lord, for his name alone is exalted; his splendor is above the earth and the heavens.* (Psalm 148:13 NIV)

The Holy Trinity—Lord's Day 8—Saturday

Read: Isaiah 44:1–8
"one, true, eternal God"

ALONGSIDE THE BIBLICAL PORTRAITS of the Father, Son, and Holy Spirit in their distinct activities is the consistent biblical belief in only one God. Christians have always and in all places proclaimed one, true, eternal God.

The Lord proclaimed through the prophet Isaiah, "I am the first and I am the last; besides me there is no god" (v. 6). Many ancient people worshipped multiple gods. They had one god to pray to for rain, one for the crops, one for war, and one for wisdom. By contrast, the whole of scripture proclaims that there is one God—the LORD—who is God over all things. God has no rivals and there is no area of creation outside his grasp. The Lord is not the highest god among a whole group of divine beings, but the one and only God. The Lord has no rivals, for he alone exists by himself, everything else he has created.

The mystery of the Christian faith is that this one, true God exists in three persons. We believe in God the Father, God the Son, and God the Holy Spirit, but there is not three gods, but one, true, eternal God, because that is how God has showed himself in his Word.

Prayer: *For all the gods of the nations are idols, but the Lord made the heavens.* (Psalm 96:5 NIV)

Q26. **What do you believe when you say,**
"I believe in God, the Father almighty, creator of heaven and earth?"
A. That the eternal Father of our Lord Jesus Christ,
who out of nothing created heaven and earth
and everything in them,
who still upholds and rules them
by his eternal counsel and providence,
is my God and Father
because of Christ the Son.
I trust God so much that I do not doubt
he will provide whatever I need
for body and soul,
and will turn to my good
whatever adversity he sends upon me
in this sad world.
God is able to do this because he is almighty God
and desires to do this because he is a faithful Father.

GOD'S FATHERLY CARE IS the standard for every father. God the Father provides for our needs, turns evil to good, and sent his Son to rescue us from our sins. This Father is compassionate and caring, strong and fair. Every earthly father falls short of our heavenly Father.

God is called Father in three different senses. First, he is the Father in relation to Christ, his only begotten Son. God is the Father because Jesus calls him "Father." Jesus stands in a unique relation to the Father. He is the one and only Son of God from eternity.

Second, God is called "Father" because he is the creator and preserver of all creation. God is the Father of all creation, because he is the reason it exists, he cares for it and "upholds and rules them by his eternal counsel and providence."

Third, God is called "Father" because we are adopted into his family through Jesus Christ. God the Father loves the Son (John 5:19), and this love passes from the Father through the Son to us. When we belong to Christ by grace, we are adopted as sons and daughters of God, and thus, with Jesus Christ, rightly call God "our Father." He is strong enough to care for our every need and he "desires to do this because he is a faithful Father" (Q26).

Prayer: *As a father has compassion on his children, so the Lord has compassion on those who fear him.* (Psalm 103:13 NIV)

Our Father and Creator—Lord's Day 9—Monday

Read: Genesis 1
"out of nothing created heaven and earth"

CHILDREN OFTEN LOVE PLAYING with blocks. With only a few different shapes, they can fashion skyscrapers, airplanes, farms, or animals. With these few building blocks, they can let their creativity flow. Yet, children cannot truly create out of nothing. We take what is there—blocks or wood or steel or soil (even ideas)—and put it together in new ways. We "make" things and "fashion" things, but we cannot create the way God does.

Only God creates. God takes nothing and turns it into something. With only a word, God creates the universe. He says, "Let there be light" and, suddenly, there is light. God tells waters to separate, tells them to gather in seas and let dry land appear, and it happens. Every time God speaks, something exists that was not there before. Before God created, there was nothing. After God created, there was the beautiful, multifaceted universe in which we live. God created the whole world from nothing.

How great is our God? All our best achievements are like children playing with blocks compared the masterpiece of God's creation. All our efforts to shape the world are like children babbling compared to the powerful, creative speech of God. Knowing God's creative power should lead us to humility and awe before God.

Prayer: *The voice of the Lord is powerful; the voice of the Lord is majestic.* (Psalm 29:4 NIV)

Our Father and Creator—Lord's Day 9—Tuesday

Read: Psalm 104
"still upholds and rules them"

IN PSALM 104, GOD is the architect laying out his creation. He set the foundations of the earth (v. 5). He controls the winding rivers and the heavy rain clouds (vv. 3, 10). He erected the mountains and carved the valleys (v. 8). The structure of the world is like a great house, built to perfection.

God is the farmer, tending the land and caring for the animals. He gives drink to the beasts of the field (v. 11). He grows grass to feed them (v. 14). "All creatures look to you to give them their food at the proper time" (v. 27). When God opens his hand, creation is filled with good things (v. 28).

God is the great host, filling his guests with joy and gladness. God provides crops so that, by the work of our hands, we have food from the earth (v. 14). More than bellies full of food, God gives us hearts full of joy. Creation is a beautiful feast that shows the extravagant love of our Creator.

God has set his table for us in the house he has built—creation itself. His loving care for us is seen in the joy we experience in this world he still upholds and rules every day.

Prayer: *May the glory of the Lord endure forever; may the Lord rejoice in his works.* (Psalm 104:31 NIV)

Our Father and Creator—Lord's Day 9—Wednesday

Read: John 1:1–14
"[He] is my God and Father because of Christ the Son"

How big is your family? Maybe you were an only child or maybe you had loads of siblings. Christians, one and all, belong to a large family.

We can call God "Father" because Jesus Christ calls us "brothers and sisters." By receiving Jesus, we are adopted into the family of God. God is our Father and Jesus is our brother. The Son came into the world so that we, who were foreigners and strangers before God, might become sons and daughters.

Adoption is a gift from God. We do not choose our families. We become children of God "who were born, not of blood or of the will of the flesh or of the will of man, but of God" (v. 13). We were chosen by God himself to be adopted into his family because of Jesus Christ.

We have a family. No Christian is an only child. Jesus Christ is the one, true Son of God, but all who belong to Jesus are children of God. We have brothers and sisters down the street, across the globe, and across the ages. This family—the church—is our one, true family, deeper than blood, longer than marriage, and firmer than friendship.

Prayer: *God sets the lonely in families, he leads out the prisoners with singing; but the rebellious live in a sun-scorched land.* (Psalm 68:6 NIV)

Our Father and Creator—Lord's Day 9—Thursday

Read: Romans 8:18–25
*"and will turn to my good whatever adversity he sends
upon me in this sad world"*

As I write this, a hurricane tears through Texas. Families are displaced. Highways have become rivers. Creation is not doing what it was intended to do. The present is often filled with pain, but there is the promise of joy in Christ.

Creation waits for that promised joy. In the present, Paul says that creation "was subjected to futility" (v. 20), frustrated in fulfilling its purpose. In the present, hurricanes cut destructive swaths, famine starves children, and disease ravages too many lives. In the present, all of creation groans for redemption.

We groan too. In Jesus Christ, something new has come into the world. Yet, we still wait and groan. What was finished in Christ has not yet come to completion in our lives and in our world. Like a woman in labor, the present is painful, but there will soon be joy.

The promise of God's fatherly care of creation is that he will set things right. We will not wait forever for the freedom and life God has promised. Even now, this world rests in the palm of God's hand, and God does turn adversity to good. Yet, one day, the waiting will cease, the futility will end, and the glory of God will be revealed.

Prayer: *I am worn out from my groaning. All night long I flood my bed with weeping and drench my couch with tears.* (Psalm 6:6 NIV)

Our Father and Creator—Lord's Day 9—Friday

Read: Revelation 21
"The End of the World"

ENGAGEMENT ENDS IN SOMETHING new and wonderful: marriage. Engagement, with all its longing and expectation, ends to give way to marriage.

At the end of all things, John sees a wedding. The holy city, the new Jerusalem, is "prepared as a bride adorned for her husband" (v. 2). The engagement is over, it is time for the wedding. The house needs to be clean and ready for the couple. All the sorrow, pain, sin, and death will be taken away. Creation will be made ready, prepared for its final purpose, to be the place where God and humanity live together. "See, the home of God is among mortals. He will dwell with them; they will be his peoples, and God himself will be with them" (v. 3). In the last days, God the Father, who created everything out of nothing, will bring creation to its fulfillment—as the house for the bride and bridegroom—Christ and his Church.

Until that day, we wait with longing and expectation. As a bride and groom dream of the future they will have together in marriage, Christians can live in hope for the day when the engagement will end and the marriage feast begins.

Prayer: *Led in with joy and gladness, they enter the palace of the king.* (Psalm 45:15 NIV)

Our Father and Creator—Lord's Day 9—Saturday

Read: Romans 8:31–39
"He is almighty God and . . . he is a faithful Father."

UNLIKE US, GOD NEVER says, "I wish I could, but I can't." As God Almighty, there is nothing outside of his power. God holds the world in the palm of his hand. He is almighty God—full of strength and power. Paul reminds us, "If God is for us, who is against us?" (v. 31). God is strong enough that nothing can stand against him. Life and death, powers and rulers, and creation itself cannot outmatch God. Those whom God loves will never be taken from his hand.

Unlike us, God also never says, "I could, but I don't want to." As a faithful Father, God is relentless in his love for his children. God exercises his power to faithfully redeem his people. "He who did not withhold his own Son, but gave him up for all of us, will he not with him also give us everything else?" (v. 32). God uses his power in love. He lifts sinners from destruction and gently, but fiercely, holds on them.

Confessing "God the Father Almighty" holds together two unbreakable attributes of God, his power and his goodness. It reminds us that God's strong hands are directed toward us in fatherly love, that nothing can separate us from his love.

Prayer: *With a mighty hand and outstretched arm; His love endures forever.* (Psalm 136:12 NIV)

Q27. What do you understand by the providence of God?
A. The almighty and ever present power of God
    by which God upholds, as with his hand,
    heaven and earth and all creatures,
    and so rules them that
    leaf and blade, rain and drought, fruitful and lean years,
    food and drink, health and sickness, prosperity and poverty—
    all things, in fact, come to us not by chance but by his fatherly hand.

Q28. How does the knowledge
    of God's creation and providence help us?
A. We can be patient when things go against us,
    thankful when things go well,
    and for the future we can have
    good confidence in our faithful God and Father
    that nothing in creation will separate us from his love.
    For all creatures are so completely in God's hand
    that without his will
    they can neither move nor be moved.

WHEN I WAS SEVEN years old, I almost died. Climbing a fifteen foot fence on a dewy morning, I reached the top when my foot slipped. I fell for a moment before my shirt caught on the fence. If it hadn't caught, I would have been badly injured or killed. Instead, my shirt "just happened" to catch on the fence.

Christians do not believe in luck or fate. I wasn't "lucky" to survive that morning. I was watched over by my heavenly Father. "All things, in fact, come to us not by chance but by his fatherly hand" (Q27).

"Providence" is God's power to provide for and to watch over all creation. God created the world and every moment since, God has cared for what he made. God provides food for the birds and makes the flowers beautiful. Even more than flowers or birds, God cares for his children. God also watches over the world. Nothing happens that is beyond his control. He is never surprised, overwhelmed, or taken off guard by what happens in the world, even if we are. Instead, God works through all these things to bring about his will for creation.

God's providence does not give us easy answers for why everything happens. Instead, it gives us someone to trust, even when we do not understand. We trust God who created the world and continues to hold it in his powerful and gracious hand.

Prayer: *Some trust in chariots and some in horses, but we trust in the name of the Lord our God.* (Psalm 20:7 NIV)

The Ever Present Power of God—Lord's Day 10—Monday

Read: Psalm 113
"The almighty and ever present power of God"

THE ROMAN EMPEROR DIOCLETIAN once wanted elevate his status in the sight of his people, as if he were a god. He distanced himself from them and shrouded himself in mystery. Most citizens went their whole lives without ever glimpsing the emperor. This is what the emperor thought it meant to be like God—distant, unapproachable, and unconcerned with the lives of the common people.

The emperor was wrong about God. God is "seated on high" (v. 5). God is a king sitting on his royal throne in heaven, holy and powerful. Yet, God does not stay distant. He "looks far down on the heavens and the earth" (v. 6). He cares about what is happening our lives. Far from being untouchable, God stoops down to lift up the poor and needy from where they sit in the dust. The high and mighty God comes near to the lowly and downtrodden and cares for them. He cares for the poor, the needy, and the barren. They are given a place to sit and a home to live in. "Who is like the Lord our God?" the psalmist asks. No one. God does not stay aloof and distant, but comes near and cares for us.

Prayer: *From the rising of the sun to the place where it sets, the name of the Lord is to be praised.* (Psalm 113:3 NIV)

The Ever Present Power of God—Lord's Day 10—Tuesday

Read: Genesis 50:15–21
"not by chance, but by his fatherly hand"

JOSEPH'S BROTHERS FEARED WHAT would happen now that their parents were gone. Years ago, Joseph's brothers sold him into slavery. Joseph was taken to Egypt, served time in prison, only to be finally exalted to second-in-command of all Egypt. Eventually, a famine drove Joseph's family to Egypt and Joseph was reconciled to his brothers. But now their father, Jacob, was dead. The brothers were afraid that with their father gone, Joseph would finally get his revenge.

Joseph saw something his brothers did not. Joseph says to them, "Even though you intended to do harm to me, God intended it for good, in order to preserve a numerous people, as he is doing today" (v. 20). Joseph saw what God had done in him and through him because of what his brothers had done. It was not chance (or even ultimately his brothers) who led him into slavery, into prison, and then into a powerful position in Egypt where he could save lives. God did that. His brothers actions were part of the larger work of God, even if they did not know it.

Nothing is outside of the guiding hand of God. Evil remains evil, but God can turn it toward his purposes. Sometimes God can even use the wicked actions of our brothers to put us in the right place to help others.

Prayer: *See if there is any offensive way in me, and lead me in the way everlasting.* (Psalm 139:24 NIV)

The Ever Present Power of God— Lord's Day 10—Wednesday

Read: Psalm 3

"Patient when things go against us"

WHAT DO YOU DO when things don't go your way? Some of us get angry. We glare, we pout, we brood. Others of us get sad. We cry, we mope, we curl up under a blanket.

God's providential care gives us patience when things go against us. When he wrote Psalm 3, David was on the run. His own son, Absalom, wanted to take David's kingdom and to end David's life. David's good life had turned sour. Yet, David is patient and unafraid. God is David's shield. David's confidence in God gives him peace and hope. He can lie down to sleep and wake in the morning trusting that God cares for him through the night. Even running for his life, David can pray, "Deliverance belongs to the Lord" (v. 8). When the world turned against him, David remained steady because God would never fail him.

God cares for us, just as he did for David. Even when we are being overwhelmed by emotions of sadness or anger, we can learn to be patient in trying times. Whether we are surrounded by thousands of enemies or struggling with just one person, God is watching over us. The God who shielded David is our shield too.

Prayer: *I lie down and sleep; I wake again, because the Lord sustains me.* (Psalm 3:5 NIV)

The Ever Present Power of God—Lord's Day 10—Thursday

Read: Psalm 16

"thankful when things go well"

WE CANNOT MAKE IT rain, nor can we pull back the clouds to reveal the sun. Farmers plant crops, but if there is no rain, the crops wither. If there is too much, they drown. The right amount of rain comes, not from all our hard work, but from God.

Every good thing comes from God's caring hand. In ancient Israel, every family had a plot of land. This land was passed down from one generation to the next. These pieces of land were separated by rows of stones known as the "boundary lines." As David sings his thanks to God, he remarks that "The boundary lines have fallen for me in pleasant places; I have a goodly heritage" (v. 6). David does not take credit for the good gifts of his life. Whenever he saw good in his life, he gave thanks to God. Every good thing he had and every blessing he has experienced comes from the hand of God.

We respond to God's good gifts by giving thanks. Rain from the sky, food on our plates, and air in our lungs all come from God. Surely the boundary lines have fallen for us in pleasant places.

Prayer: *I keep my eyes always on the Lord. With him at my right hand, I will not be shaken.* (Psalm 16:8 NIV)

The Ever Present Power of God—Lord's Day 10—Friday

Read: Psalm 23
"Good confidence in our faithful God and Father"

PEOPLE CHANGE. WE GROW up and grow older. Our hair gets longer or falls out. Our feet grow. Some changes are improvements, but others are not. We are not the same people today we were five years ago. Whether we like it or not, we are all changing.

God does not change. Unlike us, he does not need to get better. He will be as perfectly good and holy and merciful a thousand years from now as today. His love for us will not fade or change. "Surely goodness and mercy shall follow me all the days of my life, and I shall dwell in the house of the Lord my whole life long" (v. 6). God has shown David goodness and mercy continually. He provided for David day after day, like a shepherd taking care of his sheep. God walks with David in the dark and shadowy times of his life, never leaving him, but guarding him. David has known the love and mercy of God. Because God does not change, David trusts God will show him love and mercy forever.

Our unchanging God shows unfailing love toward us. We can be confident that our faithful God and Father will stay the same—tomorrow, the next day, and forever.

Prayer: *Surely your goodness and love will follow me all the days of my life, and I will dwell in the house of the Lord forever.* (Psalm 23:6 NIV)

The Ever Present Power of God—Lord's Day 10—Saturday

Read: Psalm 126
"completely in God's hand"

YOU LAUGH SO HARD you forget why. Your eyes tear up and your body shakes with laughter. You can barely speak because your mouth is so full of your laughter.

God's care for us ends in joy. Israel began in sorrow, but ended up in joy. Like the farmer who sows a few seeds into the ground to collect a good harvest, the tears we sow now will, by the working of God, turn into a bountiful harvest of joy. Our mouths will be filled with laughter and our tongues will be filled with songs of joy (v. 2). Right now, there might be tears and weeping. In the end, however, we will say, "The Lord has done great things for us, and we rejoiced" (v. 3). As Paul says, "the sufferings of this present time are not worth comparing with the glory about to be revealed to us" (Romans 8:18). What began with tears of sadness will end with tears of joy.

God's care for you ends in joy. Though you may experience sorrow now, in the end, we will have such joy in God that tears of laughter will stream down our faces. This is the promise of being in God's hand.

Prayer: *The Lord has done great things for us, and we are filled with joy.* (Psalm 126:3 NIV)

Q29. Why is the Son of God called "Jesus," meaning "savior"?
A. Because he saves us from our sins,
     and because salvation should not be sought
     and cannot be found in anyone else.

Q30. Do those who look for their salvation in saints,
     in themselves, or elsewhere really believe in the only savior Jesus?
A. No.
     Although they boast of being his,
     by their actions they deny
     the only savior, Jesus.
     Either Jesus is not a perfect savior,
     or those who in true faith accept this savior
     have in him all they need for their salvation.

YOU CANNOT *MOSTLY* SCORE a touchdown. Either you brought the ball across the goal line or you did not. If you do not do it all the way, you have not done it at all. You cannot *mostly* score a goal, *mostly* cross home plate, or *mostly* make a three point shot. You must do them completely.

Similarly, Jesus must be the perfect, complete savior or he is not a savior at all. When the catechism was written, many people looked to the saints, in particular their good deeds, for help in getting right with God. They believed that a certain amount of goodness, known as "merit," was needed to be able to be saved from their sins. Jesus, by living a perfect life, had acquired a lot of merit, but so had the church. Through participating in the church's life and sacraments, they believed Christians could access these "merits" in order to get into heaven.

There are many problems with this view, but the catechism rejects it for one primary reason: it says Jesus alone is not enough. As if Jesus brought the ball to the one yard line, but we need to bring it across into the end zone. Ultimately, this would mean we save ourselves. However, Jesus has done everything we need by living, dying, rising, and ascending to heaven. Jesus took us, in our sinful state, and brought us all the way across the goal line into the end zone. He did not go halfway or even bring us to the one yard line. He did it all.

Prayer: *Rescue me from the mire, do not let me sink; deliver me from those who hate me, from the deep waters.* (Psalm 69:14 NIV)

Jesus the Savior—Lord's Day 11—Monday

Read: Matthew 1:18–25

"'Jesus' meaning 'savior'"

HAVE YOU EVER WONDERED what your name means? For the people of the Bible, names were significant, because they often captured your identity and calling. Jacob, whose name loosely translates to "trickster," spent most of his life trying to trick his way into blessing. Moses, whose name means "drawn out," was drawn out of the waters of the Nile and drew God's people out of slavery. Jacob and Moses both lived into their names.

Jesus lived into his name, too. The angel declared, "you are to name him Jesus, for he will save his people from their sins" (v. 21). The name "Jesus" means "The Lord saves." The angel was telling Joseph what Jesus was born to do. Jesus came to save—to rescue the lost, to set free the oppressed, to cleanse the unclean, to forgive the guilty, to reconcile God and humanity, and to make the broken whole and holy. From his name itself, we get a glimpse of who Jesus is; he is the savior of his people.

Jesus' name is the Lord's salvation. Jesus lived into his name, his calling, and it is only by calling upon his name that we can know the Lord's salvation.

Prayer: *The Lord is my light and my salvation—whom shall I fear? The Lord is the stronghold of my life—of whom shall I be afraid?* (Psalm 27:1 NIV)

Jesus the Savior—Lord's Day 11—Tuesday

Read: Acts 4:1–13

"salvation . . . cannot be found in anyone else"

EXCITING NEWS IS HARD to keep quiet. You buy a gift for her birthday, you read that great new book, or find out you are having a baby and you ache to reveal it. When we experience joy and good news, we naturally want to share it.

The apostles had good news to share. Jesus is risen from the dead and in his name there is hope and salvation. After the healing of a man who could not walk, people were stunned. Immediately, the apostles told anyone who would listen that at the name of Jesus this man was set free. This same Jesus sets people free from their sins. The apostles were arrested for their teaching. Yet, they could not stop telling people about Jesus, for "There is salvation in no one else, for there is no other name under heaven given among mortals by which we must be saved" (v. 12). They could not stop sharing this good news.

The apostles knew Jesus was the only hope for every person they met, so whenever an opportunity arose, they took it. The most loving thing they could do for their neighbors was to tell them about the savior, Jesus Christ.

Prayer: *Declare his glory among the nations, his marvelous deeds among all peoples.* (Psalm 96:3 NIV)

Jesus the Savior—Lord's Day 11—Wednesday

Read: Psalm 49
"he saves us from our sins"

IN THE ANCIENT WORLD, it was the father's responsibility to rescue any family member in need. If a child got into debt, lost family land, or was trapped in any way, the father would "ransom" that child back by paying what they owed and settling the debt.

In Psalm 49, God is the Father who ransoms his children. Our situation is bleak: "Truly, no ransom avails for one's life, there is no price one can give to God for it. For the ransom of life is costly, and can never suffice" (vv. 7–8). We each have a debt that we cannot pay back. "But God will ransom my soul from the power of Sheol, for he will receive me" (v. 15). God rescues our souls from the darkest of places, even death itself. What we cannot do for ourselves and do not deserve, God in grace does for us. Not only is our debt paid, but we are welcomed back into our Father's house. The ransom is paid, and we get to come home.

The Father ransoms his lost children, bringing them back into his house. He does this by sending Jesus, God the Son in the flesh, to be lost so that we could be found. In and through Jesus, "God will ransom my soul" (v. 15).

Prayer: *But God will redeem me from the realm of the dead; he will surely take me to himself.* (Psalm 49:15 NIV)

Jesus the Savior—Lord's Day 11—Thursday

Read: 1 Timothy 2:1–7
"the only savior, Jesus"

FAMILY VACATIONS OFTEN HAVE us driving over large bridges across the Mississippi River. Without the bridges, our van would never get where we need to go. Yet, because there is a bridge, we can head to the other side.

Jesus bridges the gap between God and humanity. "There is one God; there is also one mediator between God and humankind, Christ Jesus, himself human, who gave himself a ransom for all" (vv. 5–6a). The gulf between the Creator God and us as creatures is too large for us to cross on our own. Even in a perfect world, we cannot get to God without Jesus. Not only that, but we have turned away from God, creating an immense moral gap between us and God. Everything that separates us from fellowship with God is overcome by Jesus. By humbling himself to be born in a manger and by humbling himself to stretch out his arms on the cross, Jesus has stretched himself across the gap, so that we can live with God forever.

Jesus is the only bridge, the only way to God. No other bridge will work. Only in Jesus can we enter into the loving arms of God.

Prayer: *Restore us again, God our Savior, and put away your displeasure toward us.* (Psalm 85:4 NIV)

Jesus the Savior—Lord's Day 11—Friday

Read: Psalm 16

"by their actions they deny the only savior"

I ONCE BOUGHT MY wife a pan I saw on an infomercial. It promised to last forever and food would never stick to it. Within two months, the surface had become scratched and useless. My frustration was multiplied. I was without a good pan and stuck with a bad one.

When we look for salvation apart from Christ, our sorrows are multiplied. First, we are missing out on the good that comes from life with God. In God, we have life, peace, and joy. "You are my Lord, I have no good apart from you" (v. 1). Second, whatever else we trust will only disappoint us. We are sad because we miss out on the good things of God, and we are sad because what we have is not good at all, but only pain and disappointment. We experience double sorrow. We are apart from Jesus and stuck in our sins.

However, in Jesus Christ, we experience double joy. We are set free from all those things which bound us, disappointed us, and led us to ruin. Additionally, we receive the good gifts of God. In Christ, our joys multiply.

Prayer: *You make known to me the path of life; you will fill me with joy in your presence, with eternal pleasures at your right hand.* (Psalm 16:11 NIV)

Jesus the Savior—Lord's Day 11—Saturday

Read: Hebrews 7:23–28

"All they need for their salvation"

LONG CAR RIDES ALWAYS meant worrying my batteries would run out. Whether on my phone or Gameboy, they regularly needed to be replaced or recharged so I would have enough to make it through.

Jesus never wears out and never needs to be replaced as our Savior. The priests of the Old Testament led the people of Israel in worship and sacrifice. But eventually, each of them would grow old and die. Generation after generation, new priests would be appointed to lead the people into the presence of God. None lasted. But Jesus is different. Jesus lives forever and never stops leading us into the presence of God. "Consequently he is able for all time to save those who approach God through him, since he always lives to make intercession for them" (v. 25). All we need for salvation, Jesus does for us always and forever.

We need not go anywhere but to Jesus for salvation, because Jesus never tires or fails. We may grow weary and tire, but Jesus never fails us. He saved us completely when he offered himself on the cross, and he saves us constantly as he sits at the right hand of the Father. We need no one but Jesus.

Prayer: *In your righteousness, rescue me and deliver me; turn your ear to me and save me.* (Psalm 71:2 NIV)

Christ's Anointing—Lord's Day 12—Sunday

Q31. Why is he called "Christ," meaning "anointed"?

A. Because he has been ordained by God the Father
>   and has been anointed with the Holy Spirit
>   to be our chief prophet and teacher
>   who fully reveals to us
>   the secret counsel and will of God concerning our deliverance;
>   our only high priest
>   who has delivered us by the one sacrifice of his body,
>   and who continually pleads our cause with the Father;
>   and our eternal king
>   who governs us by his Word and Spirit,
>   and who guards us and keeps us
>   in the freedom he has won for us.

Q32. But why are you called a Christian?

A. Because by faith I am a member of Christ
>   and so I share in his anointing.
>   I am anointed
>   to confess his name,
>   to present myself to him as a living sacrifice of thanks,
>   to strive with a free conscience against sin and the devil in this life,
>   and afterward to reign with Christ over all creation for eternity.

PROPHETS, PRIESTS, AND KINGS were anointed to serve God. Oil, often mixed with spices, poured on the head, hands, or feet signified God's calling. Samuel anointed David as king (1 Samuel 16:13). Elijah anointed Elisha as a prophet over Israel (1 Kings 19:16). Aaron and his sons were anointed as priests (Exodus 28:41).

Jesus is the perfect prophet, priest, and king. The prophets pointed ahead to Jesus. Jesus not only speaks God's word, but is the Word of God who speaks to us. The priests found their fulfillment in Jesus, who *offered* the perfect sacrifice and *is* the perfect sacrifice to save us from our sins. The kings were pale imitations of Jesus Christ, the true king. Jesus guards and protects us perfectly and rules us with justice, righteousness, and mercy. In his anointing, Jesus perfectly fulfills the roles of prophet, priest, and king.

Christians share in the calling of Christ. Our lives echo his because we belong to him. We are prophetic when we confess the name of Christ before the world. We are priestly when we offer our lives in service to God and others. We will be kingly when we reign with Christ in eternity. Our calling echoes the calling of Christ.

Prayer: *The Lord is the strength of his people, a fortress of salvation for his anointed one.* (Psalm 28:8 NIV)

Christ's Anointing—Lord's Day 12—Monday

Read: Matthew 5:17–20
"our chief prophet and teacher"

YOUR HOT CHOCOLATE IS gone and the mug is starting to cool in your hands. Suddenly, someone pours more into your mug, filling it all the way to the top. Warmth rushes through your hands as the mug heats and you take that next sip. It is much better to be full to the brim than empty.

Jesus came to fill God's commandments up to the brim. These commandments are good and right—the very will of God. Not one letter of them will be changed as long as heaven and earth endure. Yet, Jesus came to fulfill them (v. 17). Jesus fulfilled God's commandments by keeping them completely. He also fulfilled them by filling them up with meaning. Jesus says, "you have heard that it was said . . . but I say to you" (5:21–22). Jesus fills them up by revealing the heart of God. Not just murder, but hate is forbidden. Not just loving our neighbors, but loving our enemies is commanded.

Jesus took what was good—God's commands—and made it better by filling it up. We say that Jesus is our "chief prophet and teacher" because he reveals God's heart as he teaches us God's ways. He is the ultimate teacher showing us the heart of God.

Prayer: *The law of the Lord is perfect, refreshing the soul. The statutes of the Lord are trustworthy, making wise the simple.* (Psalm 19:7 NIV)

Christ's Anointing—Lord's Day 12—Tuesday

Read: Hebrews 9:24–28
"our only high priest"

EVERY MORNING AND EVERY evening, in ancient times, the priests would offer sacrifices on behalf of themselves and the people. Every year on the Day of Atonement, the high priest would enter into the Most Holy Place in the temple. The high priest first offered sacrifices for his own sins and then one for the sins of the people. By the blood of these sacrifices, God promised to deal with the sins of his people. Every single year, the high priest would enter the Most Holy Place and make sacrifices for the sins of the people.

We no longer need to sacrifice sheep, goats, and bulls to wipe away our sin. Once for all, Jesus has entered the presence of God the Father on our behalf. Once for all, he offered himself to "remove sin by the sacrifice of himself" (v. 26). The sacrifice of sheep, goats, and bulls pointed ahead to the one, perfect sacrifice of Jesus Christ. The priests would sacrifice again and again, but Jesus died once, and it was enough to wipe away all our sins.

As our great high priest, Jesus accomplishes what all the previous priests never could. He dealt with our sin completely and finally.

Prayer: *If you, Lord, kept a record of sins, Lord, who could stand? But with you there is forgiveness, so that we can, with reverence, serve you.* (Psalm 130:3–4 NIV)

Christ's Anointing—Lord's Day 12—Wednesday

Read: Matthew 21:1–17
"Our Eternal King"

How would you know if someone was a king? We might expect them to wear a crown or royal robes. We expect them to sit on a throne and give commands. Even if we have not seen a king in generations, we know what a king looks like.

The people of Israel knew what a king looked like. They had not had a true king in generations, only a series of wicked Herods. When Jesus came riding into Jerusalem, the people knew what they were seeing. Their king was coming, riding humbly on a donkey. It was what Zechariah had promised would happen. People spread their cloaks out before him. They began to shout in excitement, "Hosanna to the Son of David! Blessed is the one who comes in the name of the Lord!" (v. 9). They knew they were seeing a king and responded with joy.

However, Jesus did not act as they had hoped. Instead of wearing a golden crown, less than a week later, Jesus wore a crown of thorns. Instead of coming with power and sitting on a throne, Jesus came in weakness and went to the cross. He is a far better king than we could imagine.

Prayer: *Endow the king with your justice, O God, the royal son with your righteousness.* (Psalm 72:1 NIV)

Christ's Anointing—Lord's Day 12—Thursday

Read: Romans 10:9–17
"to confess his name"

Christianity is a religion of the ear. "Hear, O Israel, the Lord is our God, the Lord alone" (Deuteronomy 6:4). The prophets repeatedly declared, "Thus says the Lord Almighty." God calls through the psalmist, "O that my people would listen to me" (Psalm 81:13). More than we trust what our eyes see, we are called to trust the word spoken by the Lord.

If Christianity is a religion of the ear, it is also one of the mouth. We are people of the word heard and the word spoken. We hear Christ's word because someone speaks Christ's words. "And how are they to believe in one of whom they have never heard? And how are they to hear without someone to proclaim him?" (v. 14). Our ears may be open, but the word must be spoken. We who have heard the good news must be ready to speak it to others.

Every Christian is called to confess the name of Jesus. Christ is our great prophet and teacher, and we are anointed to be mouths that speak his words to a hurting world. The gospel can only be heard if it is spoken, in order than people can call on the name of the Lord and be saved.

Prayer: *The voice of the Lord is powerful; the voice of the Lord is majestic.* (Psalm 29:4 NIV)

Christ's Anointing—Lord's Day 12—Friday

Read: Romans 12:1–2
"living sacrifice of thanks"

IN THE OLD TESTAMENT, one of the ways Israel worshipped God was through sacrifice. One type of sacrifice, called "a thanksgiving offering" was not about sin, but gave shape to the people's gratitude to God.

The Christian life is a thanksgiving offering to God. When we do not walk according the ways of the world, but have our minds shaped by God's will and ways, we show forth our thanks to God. When we work to discern the way that God calls us to live—"what is good and acceptable and perfect"—and then walk in it, we say thanks to God. Jesus has offered the perfect sacrifice to wash away our sins and remove our guilt. We offer our lives to God in thanks for what he has done. By living for God, according to his holy and perfect ways, we give thanks to God.

Paul calls this way of life a "living sacrifice" (v. 1). We offer ourselves to God by, in turn, offering our lives to serve our neighbors. Every day of our life, we are called to pour out our lives for God and our neighbors.

Prayer: *Enter his gates with thanksgiving and his courts with praise; give thanks to him and praise his name.* (Psalm 100:4 NIV)

Christ's Anointing—Lord's Day 12—Saturday

Read: Revelation 4
"reign with Christ for all eternity"

CHRIST ALONE IS KING. Yet, the church shares in Christ's anointing (Q32). What exactly does it look like for the church to live out its kingly calling?

The church will reign with Christ in the heavenly kingdom. When God pulls back the veil on the heavenly realms, John sees a throne "with one seated on the throne" (v. 2). We also find twenty-four elders seated on twenty-four thrones surrounding *the* throne, with golden crowns on their heads. The church, represented by the elders, is present before the throne. When the chorus of praise to the Lord rings out, the elders "fall before the one who is seated on the throne and worship the one who lives forever and ever; they cast their crowns before the throne" (v. 10). The church reigns with Christ, but not for their own glory or benefit, but for the glory of God.

The church is promised to rule with Christ, but it will rule in the way of Christ and in obedience to Christ. They lay down their crowns for the sake of the kingdom, and lift their voices to the glory of the king. No longer servants, but kings, they will serve only the one true King for all eternity.

Prayer: *Let the king be enthralled by your beauty; honor him, for he is your lord.* (Psalm 45:11 NIV)

**Q33. Why is he called God's "only begotten Son"
when we also are God's children?**

A. Because Christ alone is the eternal, natural Son of God.
We, however, are adopted children of God—
adopted by grace through Christ.

Q34. Why do you call him "our Lord"?

A. Because—
not with gold or silver,
but with his precious blood—
he has set us free
from sin and from the tyranny of the devil,
and has bought us,
body and soul,
to be his very own.

JESUS CHRIST IS BOTH Son and Lord. These twin titles point to Christ's eternal relationship to the Father and to his saving work in the world. We confess both who Jesus is and what he has done.

Jesus Christ is the Father's "only begotten Son." Christ alone is the eternal, natural Son of God. "Begotten" is both biblical and technical language for the relationship between the Father and the Son. In the language of the Nicene Creed, Christ is "begotten, not made." The Son's relationship to the Father is eternal. There never was a time when the Son was not the Son, nor the Father not the Father. When we confess Jesus Christ, we say he is God the Son, the second person of the Trinity.

Jesus Christ is also "our Lord." We call him "Lord" because he has saved us. Jesus shows us what lordship means by purchasing our salvation at the cost of his own precious blood. He is Lord because he is Savior.

When the creed calls us to confess Jesus Christ as Son and Lord, we proclaim both who Jesus is and what he has done. He is the Son of God from all eternity. He is the Lord who sets us free and calls us his own.

Prayer: *The Lord is my rock, my fortress and my deliverer; my God is my rock, in whom I take refuge, my shield and the horn of my salvation, my stronghold.* (Psalm 18:2 NIV)

Jesus: Son & Lord—Lord's Day 13—Monday

Read: John 1:1–18
"eternal, natural Son of God"

THERE IS NO TYPICAL Christmas story in the Gospel of John—no angels, no manger, no shepherds, no wise men. Instead, all of that is captured in one line: "and the Word became flesh and lived among us" (v. 14). Swirling around this one Christmas line are the Spirit's words telling us who Jesus is.

In Jesus Christ, we have God with us. God comes for us. God saves us. The Son of God was there in the beginning. "In the beginning was the Word" (v. 1). He is the Word through which God spoke the world into existence. "And the Word was with God" (v. 1). He was there with the Father and the Spirit, in intimate, eternal relationship. "And the Word was God" (v. 1). John wants us to have no doubts that Jesus is God, because if Jesus is God then only he can save us.

From Jesus and through Jesus, we receive grace. Only God can give grace that saves. If Jesus is truly to be our savior, he must be God. Jesus' divinity is not an abstract teaching, but the core of our confession. In this Jesus, we have the Lord God of Israel. In this Jesus, we have the Lord who saves.

Prayer: *Our God is a God who saves; from the Sovereign Lord comes escape from death.* (Psalm 68:20 NIV)

Jesus: Son & Lord—Lord's Day 13—Tuesday

Read: Hebrews 1
"eternal, natural Son of God"

I HAVE ALWAYS BEEN a lover of books. Stories have transported me into new worlds with new people and opened me to new truths. As a lover of books, it is always a delight to meet the author.

In Jesus, we encounter the author of creation and redemption. In times past, we heard God's word from the lips of prophets, but now the Word of God has come in the flesh. Before, God sent his angels, but now God himself has come as the man Jesus Christ. "He is the reflection of God's glory and the exact imprint of God's very being, and he sustains all things by his powerful word" (v. 3). Jesus' name is greater than the angels (vv. 4–5), the angels worship him (v. 6), and he has a kingdom that will endure forever (v. 13).

Jesus is not simply an angel, or a prophet, or an amazing spiritually sensitive person, but the Son of God. He is not another chapter in the book, but is the author himself come to us. When we believe in Jesus Christ, when we place our trust in him, we are moving into the presence of the one, true God.

Prayer: *Your kingdom is an everlasting kingdom, and your dominion endures through all generations. The Lord is trustworthy in all he promises and faithful in all he does.* (Psalm 145:13 NIV)

Jesus: Son & Lord—Lord's Day 13—Wednesday

Read: Ephesians 1:1–14
"Adopted by grace through Christ"

SCRIPTURE TELLS US ELECTION is a blessing. God has "blessed us in Christ with every spiritual blessing" (v. 3). For he chose us in him (v. 4). God's choice to adopt us as his children is itself a blessing.

God's choice is a blessing because it means that salvation is not an accident. Salvation does not come through being born in the right town to the right family. Salvation through Jesus Christ was not God's Plan B after Plan A of the Garden of Eden fell through. God chose us before the creation of the world—it was intentional, purposeful, planned.

Election is also a blessing because it is *God* who does the choosing, the predestining, the adopting. From beginning to end, God has accomplished everything for salvation. From before the creation of the world, through the blood of Christ shed on the cross, to the giving of faith and the marking with the promised Holy Spirit—salvation is God's work and rests in God's hands. And God is faithful.

The good news is that the "only begotten Son" has made us sons together with him. We are adopted by grace through Christ, rescued and resting in the strong hands of Jesus Christ.

Prayer: *He brought out his people with rejoicing, his chosen ones with shouts of joy.*
(Psalm 105:43 NIV)

Jesus: Son & Lord—Lord's Day 13—Thursday

Read: John 20:24–31
"My Lord and My God"

WE UNDERSTAND THOMAS BETTER than we want to admit. Thomas doesn't want to be fooled. He wants to see. Perhaps he truly hoped Jesus was risen, but did not want to get suckered in with false hope. So, until he could see it with his eyes, he would not believe.

Sometimes we might think faith would be easier if we could just see everything with our own eyes. If we could see the wounds in his hands and feet, place our hands in his side, then it would be easy to believe.

Thomas doubts until he sees, but, by God's grace, he ends up seeing. But for the rest of us, who will never see Jesus in the flesh until he returns in glory, Jesus gives us this comfort, "Blessed are those who have not seen and yet have come to believe" (v. 29).

Jesus calls believing without seeing blessed. We might think faith is easier if we could just see Jesus standing before us. Instead, Jesus calls you blessed when you trust the testimony of Scripture and "believe that Jesus is the Messiah, the Son of God, and that through believing you may have life in his name" (v. 31).

Prayer: *Because your love is better than life, my lips will glorify you.* (Psalm 63:3 NIV)

Jesus: Son & Lord—Lord's Day 13—Friday

Read: Colossians 1:13–20
"Heights and Depths"

CALLING JESUS "LORD" CAPTURES both the heights of who Jesus is and the depths he went to in order to save us from our sins. We call him "Lord" because "with his precious blood he has set us free" (Q34). Jesus shows he is Lord by saving sinners.

Colossians 1 shows us the heights of Jesus' person and the depths of his love. Jesus Christ is the image of the invisible God. All things were created through him. He is before all things, holds all things together, rules as head over the church, and has risen from the dead. To sum up, Christ has "first place in everything" (v. 18). Yet Jesus, in whom the fullness of God is pleased to dwell, also "reconcile[s] to himself all things, whether on earth or in heaven, by making peace through the blood of his cross" (v. 20). The one who is seated on high has descended to the depths of the cross to save. This is the miracle of the gospel. This is what it means for him to be "Lord."

When we confess Jesus Christ as "Lord," we acknowledge his boundless power and complete rule over our lives. But more than that, we are trusting in his power to save.

Prayer: *Who is like the Lord our God, the One who sits enthroned on high, who stoops down to look on the heavens and the earth?* (Psalm 113:5–6 NIV)

Jesus: Son & Lord—Lord's Day 13—Saturday

Read: 1 Timothy 4:6–16
"A Good Servant"

OUR FAMILY ALWAYS ENJOYS watching the Olympic games. It is impressive and fascinating to watch people at the peak of physical performance. To reach that level requires incredible dedication and sacrifice.

Paul and Timothy also lived in a world obsessed with sports and physical prowess. Yet, "while physical training is of some value, godliness is valuable in every way, holding promise for both the present life and the life to come" (v. 8). We can train our bodies to run faster, jump higher, and be stronger, but eventually it will fade. Yet, dedicating ourselves to grow in godliness does not fade. It is an end worth toiling and striving for (v. 10). Like physical training, there will be habits we must dedicate ourselves to: words of faith, good doctrine, purity, public reading of Scripture, and teaching. Yet, like physical training, there will be things we need to leave behind, habits and teachings that don't lead us toward God.

There are no Olympic games for godliness. We struggle for godliness in the arena of our everyday lives. There is no crown in this life given for following Jesus, but if you do, "you will be a good servant of Christ Jesus" (v. 6).

Prayer: *Trust in the Lord and do good; dwell in the land and enjoy safe pasture.* (Psalm 37:3 NIV)

Q35. What does it mean that he "was conceived by the Holy Spirit and born of the virgin Mary"?

A. That the eternal Son of God,
> who is and remains
> true and eternal God,
> took to himself,
> through the working of the Holy Spirit,
> from the flesh and blood of the virgin Mary,
> a truly human nature
> so that he might also become David's true descendent,
> like his brothers and sisters in every way
> except for sin.

Q36. How does the holy conception and birth of Christ benefit you?

A. He is our mediator
> and, in God's sight,
> he covers with his innocence and perfect holiness
> my sinfulness in which I was conceived.

THE CREED HELPS US hold two truths together. On the one hand, Jesus is truly and fully human. It is not beneath God to take on human flesh. The Scriptures clearly proclaim that "Therefore he [Jesus] had to become like his brothers and sisters in every respect" (Hebrews 2:17). Jesus was fully human—mind, body, and soul—which the creed affirms in calling us to confess that he was "conceived by the Holy Spirit and born of the virgin Mary."

On the other hand, Jesus is and remains fully God. He is "the eternal Son of God, who is and remains true and eternal God" (Q35). He does not cease to be who he was in order to take on flesh and be born of Mary. In confessing Christ's birth, we are avoiding the error of denying the humanity of Christ and denying the divinity of Christ. Instead, we confess both—two natures in one person, the God-man Jesus Christ.

Additionally, this theology is practical. Because Mary bore the Son of God in her womb, Christ is our mediator, covering over all the stain of our sin with his perfect holiness. In this way, the virgin birth is not only to be confessed, but celebrated, for it points ahead to Christ's work of mediation for us.

Prayer: *Lord, you are the God who saves me; day and night I cry out to you.* (Psalm 88:1 NIV)

The Birth of Jesus—Lord's Day 14—Monday

Read: Luke 1:26–38
"Favored One"

HAVE YOU EVER NOTICED how little we really know about Mary? There is no fanfare, no pomp and circumstance. All we know is that she is a virgin and she is engaged to a man named Joseph of the house of David. That's it. This teenage girl from Nazareth was an unlikely choice for such a high calling.

The angel came to her and said, "Greetings, favored one! The Lord is with you" (v. 28). The phrase "favored one," at its root, is tied up with the word for grace. Mary is one who has received grace—that unearned and undeserved gift of God. Mary did not earn the privilege of bearing the Son of God in her womb. It came to her by grace.

Perhaps Luke does not tell us much about Mary because then we might begin to focus on her performance and not God's grace. If we heard a lot about Mary's righteousness or works of service, we might think, "That's what made her special. That's the ticket into God's good graces." Or, "I can never make it. There is no way for me."

The gospel is one of God's grace, not our performance. God in grace comes and does something impossible. Virgin Mary will have a child. How can this be? "For nothing will be impossible with God."

Prayer: *Praise the Lord. Give thanks to the Lord, for he is good; his love endures forever.* (Psalm 106:1 NIV)

The Birth of Jesus—Lord's Day 14—Tuesday

Read: Luke 1:39–45
"Amplified Joy"

HOW DO WE RESPOND when something good happens to someone else? When a classmate makes starter before you, your friend gets into the school you were waiting to hear from, or someone announces a pregnancy or engagement when you have been waiting yourself, can you feel joy for them?

Elizabeth hears Mary's voice and sings, "blessed . . . blessed . . . blessed." Among all women, Mary is to be counted as most blessed. Among all children, Mary's child is the greatest blessing of God. Of all God's words spoken to women down the ages, Mary's is the greatest to be fulfilled.

Elizabeth sees the greater blessing of someone else and praises God for her. She is not jealous or bitter that Mary has been blessed more than her. Mary's blessing does not make her blessing less. Mary's joy does not diminish her joy. Instead, it amplifies it. Elizabeth allows the joy of Mary to increase her own joy.

Elizabeth's song invites us to bless God for the blessing of others. Even if, and perhaps especially when, it feels like their blessing is greater than ours. God's gracious work in someone else does not make what he is doing in your life any less. Instead, let God's blessing of others lead us to joy as it did Elizabeth.

Prayer: *The Lord has done great things for us, and we are filled with joy.* (Psalm 126:3 NIV)

The Birth of Jesus—Lord's Day 14—Wednesday

Read: Luke 1:46–56
"Mary's Song"

IN A WOUNDED WORLD, Mary sings of the God who is turning the world right. There is nothing cute and cozy in Mary's song. She sings, for a savior is coming, one strong enough and good enough to turn the world around.

Mary praises the strength and power of God. "He has shown strength with his arm; he has scattered the proud in the thoughts of their hearts. He has brought down the powerful from their thrones, and lifted up the lowly" (vv. 51–52). God's strength reaches to the proud and powerful, to those who think themselves untouchable and rips them down, humbling them. God's arm is long and strong enough to reach to the lowly and lift them up. Mary sings of God, who uses his might to bring mercy to all who repent and believe in the good news. She sings of a God who in mercy restores the lost and gives his children a home for eternity.

When Mary sings, "My soul magnifies the Lord, and my spirit rejoices in God my Savior" (vv. 46–47), we are invited to sing along. The coming of Jesus, the child born of Mary, is the coming of the Savior. This Savior comes to set the world right.

Prayer: *The Lord sustains the humble but casts the wicked to the ground.* (Psalm 147:6 NIV)

The Birth of Jesus—Lord's Day 14—Thursday

Read: Luke 2:1–7
"Recognizing Jesus"

WRAPPED IN BANDS OF cloth and lying in a manger. Not what you would expect for a king, for a savior. The Savior, Messiah, and Lord that God promised is found in the manger.

Jesus is found swaddled just like every other baby. The King takes on the same weakness and vulnerability that every one of us endured at our birth. The Lord of the universe was wrapped in cloths and held in his mother's arm to keep warm, like us. When God came to redeem us, he took on all of us—all of who we are—that he might save all of who we are.

Jesus lying in a manger. Not on a soft bed in a palace, but in a hard stone. This is a humble place for a king. Yet, this is the way of God. Jesus will be known, not only by his humanity, but his humility. While other kings sit on thrones, he lay in a manger. While other kings exalt themselves, Jesus humbles himself, even at birth, to be a very different kind of king. Later, Jesus will wear a crown, show his power, and be exalted, but again, not in the way we would expect, but in the way of God.

Prayer: *Be exalted, O God, above the heavens; let your glory be over all the earth.* (Psalm 57:5 NIV)

The Birth of Jesus—Lord's Day 14—Friday

Read: Luke 2:8–21
"Wonderful News"

As far as the shepherds knew, there was nothing special about that night. The sun had disappeared over the horizon and the sheep needed watching. Suddenly a bright light appears and an angel stands before them. Their first response is fear and trembling, so the angel calls out, "Do not be afraid."

They receive wonderful news that transforms what seemed like an ordinary night. "For see—I am bringing you good news of great joy for all the people: to you is born this day in the city of David a Savior, who is the Messiah, the Lord" (vv. 10–11). This Savior, this Messiah, will be Emmanuel, which means God with us. God himself has come. The God before whom even the angels veil their faces has come to be our Savior. "I am bringing you good news of great joy."

The shepherds rush off to see Jesus. A group of shepherds straight in from the field is not the usual audience for a king, but maybe we shouldn't be surprised by that anymore. The God who came in a lowly manger received those on the outskirts of society. When they saw, they ran out and told everyone, for they could not keep the message in.

Prayer: *Praise the Lord, my soul; all my inmost being, praise his holy name.* (Psalm 103:1 NIV)

The Birth of Jesus—Lord's Day 14—Saturday

Read: Luke 2:22–38
"Back to Normal"

After Jesus was born, life might have settled down for Mary and Joseph. Their days and nights were filled with feeding, changing, and little sleep. All very normal for new parents. Yet, God provided two witnesses as a reminder that there is something incredibly special about Jesus.

The first witness was Simeon. He had been waiting "the consolation of Israel" (v. 25). In other words, he was waiting for God to bring comfort to his suffering people. When Mary and Joseph walk in, Simeon takes Jesus in his arms and praises God saying, "For my eyes have seen your salvation." Holding the child Jesus in his arms, Simeon proclaims that he has seen the salvation of God. To look upon the face of Jesus is to look upon the one who saves.

The prophet Anna was the second witness. She was a widow for most of her adult life, but she dedicated her life to God, "worshiped there [in the temple] with fasting and prayer night and day" (v. 37). When Anna saw Jesus, she spoke about him to all those who were looking for redemption. There are many who walk through our lives today that long desperately, even if they cannot put it into words, to hear that Jesus Christ was born to save, that in the face of Jesus there is peace, and hope, and life eternal. She did not remain silent. Will we?

Prayer: *My mouth will tell of your righteous deeds, of your saving acts all day long—though I know not how to relate them all.* (Psalm 71:15 NIV)

**Q37. What do you understand
   by the word "suffered"?**

A. That during his whole life on earth,
   but especially at the end,
   Christ sustained in body and soul
   the wrath of God against the sin of the whole human race.
   This he did in order that,
   by his suffering as the only atoning sacrifice,
   he might deliver us, body and soul,
   from eternal condemnation,
   and gain for us
   God's grace, righteousness, and eternal life.

**Q38. Why did he suffer
   "under Pontius Pilate" as judge?**

A. So that he, though innocent,
   might be condemned by an earthly judge,
   and so free us from the severe judgment of God
   that was to fall on us.

**Q39. Is it significant that he was "crucified"
   instead of dying some other way?**

A. Yes.
   By this I am convinced
   that he shouldered the curse
   which lay on me,
   since death by crucifixion was cursed by God.

JESUS IS A REAL historical person. He is as real as Abraham Lincoln, not a legendary or mythic figure. In the Apostles' Creed, only three historical figures are mentioned—Jesus, our Savior; Mary, his mother; and Pontius Pilate, the governor who gave the order for Jesus' crucifixion. The catechism tells us we confess that Jesus "suffered under Pontius Pilate" to proclaim that Jesus, though innocent, was condemned by a judge, so that we, though guilty, might be freed from the judgment of God. This is true. However, the mention of Pontius Pilate also tells us that these events took place in history. Jesus' death and resurrection is not a folktale, but a real event. We can check the records and find out about Pontius Pilate. What the gospels proclaim about Jesus really happened.

Why is it important that Jesus' suffering and death really happened and took place in history? We do not need simply a good story, but a God who acts in history. We do not need a fable to teach us something, but a Savior to rescue us. Our salvation is physical, spiritual, real, and historical. That requires a real savior, one who walked, talked, healed, prayed, and, yes, suffered under Pontius Pilate.

Prayer: *I will consider all your works and meditate on all your mighty deeds.* (Psalm 77:12 NIV)

The Cross of Christ—Lord's Day 15—Monday

Read: Isaiah 53

"by his suffering as the only atoning sacrifice, he might deliver us"

WHEN OUR FAMILY TRAVELS, we bring a lot of stuff. Toys, toiletries, and teddy bears begin to pile up. Stuffed suitcases are stacked at the door. Carrying that many bags becomes a difficult chore. The more bags, the heavier the load upon our shoulders.

Long ago, God promised he would send someone to carry the weight of our sins on his shoulders. All of us have turned away from God. Our sins fall like a weight upon his shoulders. Every betrayal, every ounce of guilt falls upon this one man until it can be said that "the Lord has laid on him the iniquity of us all" (v. 6). He would carry the weight of the sin of the whole human race and never speak a word. He could defend himself, but will not. He will carry that weight even to the point of death. By offering himself to take on the weight of our sin, he will deliver us.

Jesus is the one promised long ago. He bore that weight of sin, endured shame, rejection, suffering, and death, so that we might be free and have life in his name. In the suffering of Jesus Christ, he "shall make many righteous" (v. 11)

Prayer: *Save me, O God, for the waters have come up to my neck.* (Psalm 69:1 NIV)

The Cross of Christ—Lord's Day 15—Tuesday

Read: Galatians 3:10–14

"he shouldered the curse"

ON THE CROSS, JESUS died a cursed death. Deuteronomy 21:23 says, "anyone hung on a tree is under God's curse." By dying nailed to a wooden cross, Jesus died the death of a person who had broken God's commandments. "Cursed is everyone who does not observe and obey all the things written in the book of the law" (v. 10, quoting Deuteronomy 27:26). He died like someone who is cursed by God—cut off from God and deserving of punishment. How could one cursed by God be the Messiah? Yet, here Jesus fulfilled his calling as God's Messiah. For in his crucifixion, "Christ redeemed us from the curse of the law by becoming a curse for us" (v. 13). Each of us stands guilty before God, but Jesus Christ took on the curse for us.

Why did Jesus die by being crucified? He died this way so that we might be rescued from destruction. He died in our place, took on our guilt and punishment, so that we are counted innocent before God and walk in freedom. He was crucified for us and for our salvation.

Prayer: *the ransom for a life is costly, no payment is ever enough.* (Psalm 49:8 NIV)

The Cross of Christ—Lord's Day 15—Wednesday

Read: Hebrews 2:14–18

"he might deliver us, body and soul, from eternal condemnation"

THE ESCAPE ARTIST PLACES herself trapped underwater, a deadly situation. With the audience watching, she appears to fail, only to reappear in a moment, free and safe. The whole time there is little danger, for it is all a trick.

Jesus' death and resurrection were no trick. He entered a deadly situation: the cross. Christ suffered real agony and entered into death. Three days later he truly rose from the dead. Jesus did not come to rescue himself, but others. We were the ones trapped in the deadly situation: trapped in sin and fearful of death. Jesus voluntarily entered into our situation in order to set us free. By his suffering and death, Christ broke the power of death, defeated the devil, and set us free from the fear of death. It was not through obvious triumph, but through apparent defeat that Jesus was victorious. By death, Jesus defeated death itself. It was not a trick, but the good news.

We do not need to fear death. While death is not good, it no longer holds us captive, because Jesus took on death and the devil for us. Jesus' deliverance sets us free from sin and sets us free from fear.

Prayer: *In your righteousness, rescue me and deliver me; turn your ear to me and save me.* (Psalm 71:2 NIV)

The Cross of Christ—Lord's Day 15—Thursday

Read: Matthew 27:11–26

"he, though innocent, might be condemned by an earthly judge"

YOU KNOW YOU SHOULD not have looked at your friend's test and you begin to sweat. When you arrive, the best student in school already sits silently with the principal. Your teacher tells the story of your cheating, but blames it on the other student. The principal walks out, tells you that you are free to go, while the other student gets detention.

Two men stood before the governor, Pontius Pilate. One was "a notorious prisoner, called Jesus Barabbas" (v. 16). The other was Jesus, who did not speak even a word to defend himself. Barabbas was guilty, but Jesus was innocent. Pilate brought the two men before the crowd and asked which they wanted released. At the crowd's insistence, Pilate released Barabbas and condemned Jesus. Jesus was condemned in place of Barabbas—the innocent one in place of the guilty. Two men stood before Pilate, and because innocent Jesus was condemned, guilty Barabbas went free.

We, like Barabbas, should stand guilty before the judge. We have all sinned. But Jesus was condemned in our place. As Phillip Bliss' great hymn says, "Bearing shame and scoffing rude, in my place condemned he stood, sealed my pardon with his blood. Hallelujah! What a Savior!"

Prayer: *Blessed is the one whose sin the Lord does not count against them and in whose spirit is no deceit.* (Psalm 32:2 NIV)

The Cross of Christ—Lord's Day 15—Friday

Read: Matthew 27:27–31
"during his whole life on earth, but especially at the end"

JESUS FACED RIDICULE AND humiliation on his way to the cross. After Pilate washed his hands of Jesus, he handed him over to the soldiers. The soldiers humiliated Jesus by mocking his claim to be king. They stripped him naked and put a purple robe on him (a sign of royalty). They put a crown on his head—not a kingly crown, but a crown of sharp thorns which cut into Jesus' head. They put a reed in his hand instead of a royal scepter. They spit on him, kicked him, hit him, mocked him, and fell down and worshipped him. Jesus' whole life, but especially at the end, was a journey of humiliation.

Yet, this mocked, humiliated Jesus is, in fact, the King. While the soldiers mocked him, they also spoke the truth. When they bowed before Jesus and proclaimed him the King of the Jews, they were saying the most truthful thing they had ever said. Jesus is the King. Jesus was crowned, not in glory, but in humiliation. The soldiers mocked Jesus as they bowed before his feet. We, however, should honestly and wholeheartedly bow before King Jesus and give him all honor and praise.

Prayer: *I will exalt you, my God the King; I will praise your name for ever and ever.* (Psalm 145:1 NIV)

The Cross of Christ—Lord's Day 15—Saturday

Read: Matthew 27:32–44
"and gain for us God's grace, righteousness, and eternal life"

IN 480 BC, A small group of Spartan soldiers stood in the narrow pass of Thermopylae to defend against an invasion. In front of them was an uncountable horde of Persian soldiers. Behind them were the cities and families they loved. Running or hiding would have condemned their families to death. Instead, they stood in that gap, fought, and died.

On a Friday two thousand years ago, Jesus Christ stood in the gap and died for us. After a night of beatings and interrogations, Jesus was lead up to Golgotha to be crucified. The people passing by jeered at him, saying, "He saved others; he cannot save himself" (v. 42). They were only half-right. Jesus did not save himself in order to save others. His life was not taken from him. Instead, he laid it down. "No one takes it from me, but I lay it down of my own accord" (John 10:18). Jesus refused to save himself in order to save others.

Jesus stood in the gap for us. He bore the weight of our guilt and broke the power of sin, death, and the devil. While suffering and death lay before him, Christ endured it for the sake of the world God so loved.

Prayer: *Awake, and rise to my defense! Contend for me, my God and Lord.* (Psalm 35:23 NIV)

Q40. Why did Christ have to suffer death?

A. Because God's justice and truth require it:
>   nothing else could pay for our sins
>   except the death of the Son of God.

Q41. Why was he "buried"?

A. His burial testifies that he really died.

Q42. Since Christ has died for us, why do we still have to die?

A. Our death does not pay the debt of our sins.
>   Rather, it puts an end to our sinning
>   and is our entrance into eternal life.

Q43. What further benefit do we receive from Christ's sacrifice and death on the cross?

A. By Christ's power
>   our old selves are crucified, put to death, and buried with him,
>   so that the evil desires of the flesh
>   may no longer rule us,
>   but that instead we may offer ourselves
>   as a sacrifice of gratitude to him.

Q44. Why does the creed add, "He descended to hell"?

A. To assure me during attacks of deepest dread and temptation
>   that Christ my Lord,
>   by suffering unspeakable anguish, pain, and terror of soul,
>   on the cross but also earlier,
>   has delivered me from hellish anguish and torment.

AFTER ADAM AND EVE's first sin, God says, "'See, the man has become like one of us, knowing good and evil; and now, he might reach out his hand and take also from the tree of life, and eat, and live forever'— therefore the Lord God sent him forth from the garden of Eden, to till the ground from which he was taken" (Genesis 3:22–23). In a sinful world, it is not good for us to live forever. The combination of sinful hearts and unending life would produce only pain, suffering, and wickedness for humankind. God is merciful in keeping us from the tree of life while our hearts remain unclean.

Even though Christ has died in our place, we still die. Our death "puts an end to our sinning" (Q42). In death we can no longer commit sins, nor do we suffer from the effects of this sinful condition. However, our death is also "our entrance into eternal life" (Q42). Those who die in Christ enter the place prepared for them by Christ (John 14). In one sense, when our mortal life ends, our eternal life begins. Christians live as those forgiven and free in Christ, and we die as those who exit this life into the arms of our Savior. It is knowing this hope that allows Paul to say, "for to me living is Christ and dying is gain" (Philippians 1:21).

Prayer: *Teach us to number our days, that we may gain a heart of wisdom.* (Psalm 90:12 NIV)

The Death and Descent of Christ—Lord's Day 16—Monday

Read: Romans 5:6–11

"nothing else could pay for our sins"

TIMING MATTERS WHEN TAKING photos. Inevitably, someone had their eyes closed. Some child is pulling another's hair. We take a deep breath, count to three, and try again. We hope that with enough pictures, one of them will be just right.

God has perfect timing, for "at the right time Christ died for the ungodly" (v. 6). What made Jesus' death "at the right time"? First, Jesus died for us "while we were still weak" (v. 6). Jesus came when we were not strong enough to save ourselves. Second, Jesus died for us "while we still were sinners" (v. 8). We were like people who had slipped and fallen in the mud. While we were dirty, Christ came to cleanse us by his blood shed on the cross. Third, Jesus died for us "while we were enemies" of God (v. 10). We were cut off from God and exiled from his presence. Christ came to reconcile us to God. He made peace between us and God by his death.

We were in need—weak, sinners, enemies of God—and God demonstrated his love through the cross. Jesus Christ did not hesitate to die out of love for us. He did it all at just the right time.

Prayer: *To you they cried out and were saved; in you they trusted and were not put to shame.* (Psalm 22:5 NIV)

The Death and Descent of Christ—Lord's Day 16—Tuesday

Read: Matthew 27:45–56

"suffering unspeakable anguish, pain, and terror of soul"

"WHY" IS A QUESTION of curiosity, but also one of confusion and pain. We ask why when the cancer diagnosis comes in, when the hurricane crashes into the shore, and when a loved one walks away from the faith. Asking "why" can be a mixture of accusation against God for letting this happen and hope that it was somehow not senseless.

Jesus takes up the question "why" as he hung on the cross. "And about the ninth hour, Jesus cried out in a loud voice, saying "'Eli, Eli, lema sabachthani?' that is, 'My God, my God, why have you forsaken me?'" (v. 46). Jesus asked "why" in abandonment and forsakenness. In his darkest hour, when his friends and family abandoned him, Jesus cried out in anguish before God. As he suffered agony in his body, Jesus did not even have the comfort of the presence of his Father. He experienced abandonment and cried out, "Why?"

In Jesus, the answer to his "why" is the mystery of the gospel. Jesus experienced agony and abandonment for us. Because of that, we can know that we will never experience final abandonment by God. He cried out "Why have you forsaken me?" so that, at the end, we will never have to.

Prayer: *For he has not despised or scorned the suffering of the afflicted one; he has not hidden his face from him but has listened to his cry for help.* (Psalm 22:24 NIV)

The Death and Descent of Christ—
Lord's Day 16—Wednesday

Read: Matthew 26:36–46
"has delivered me from hellish anguish and torment"

SOME BEVERAGES COLLECT BITTER sediment in the bottom known as "dregs." In a lot of beverages these dregs are filtered out, but occasionally you will be drinking something only to find the last sip bitter and disgusting. Those are the dregs.

In the Old Testament, one of the images for God's judgment was a cup of wine. When the wicked oppressed Israel or Israel oppressed the poor and weak, God's cup of wrath was said to fill up. The judgment they would endure for their sins was said to be drinking the cup of judgment.

Jesus drank the cup of suffering down to the dregs in his death on the cross. In Gethsemane, twice Jesus prayed that there could be another way. "My Father, if it is possible, let this cup pass from me; yet not what I want but what you want" (v. 39). "My Father, if this cannot pass unless I drink it, your will be done" (v. 42). The cup of suffering and death will not pass from us unless Jesus himself drinks it. It is our cup. Out of love, Jesus drained the cup dry by dying on the cross. Jesus drank the cup of suffering so that we do not have to drink it.

Prayer: *In the hand of the LORD is a cup, full of foaming wine mixed with spices; he pours it out, and all the wicked of the earth drink it down to its very dregs.* (Psalm 75:8 NIV)

The Death and Descent of Christ—
Lord's Day 16—Thursday

Read: Romans 6:1–11
"our old selves are crucified, put to death, and buried with him"

SOME EARLY CHRISTIANS WERE baptized naked. As they came to be baptized, they stripped off their old clothes, indicating their old way of life was over. Upon coming up out of the water, they were clothed with white robes symbolizing new life in Christ.

While most people are no longer baptized naked, it was a visual reminder of the spiritual reality of baptism. Baptism is a type of death and new life. We are united to Jesus Christ by the Spirit—joined to his death and to his resurrection. In his death, all our old ways of living, our old identities, and old sinful desires have been put to death. We no longer live that way. That way died with Christ, our new life was given us in his resurrection. We died in Jesus Christ, so now we can live in him too.

Jesus' death for us changes our present and our future. It changes our future by freeing us from sin and death so that we can have eternal life. But it also changes our present, because the sinful desires of our old way of life no longer rule over us. They have been put to death. We can live free and thankful to God.

Prayer: *You, Lord, brought me up from the realm of the dead; you spared me from going down to the pit.* (Psalm 30:3 NIV)

The Death and Descent of Christ—Lord's Day 16—Friday

Read: Philippians 2:1–11
"except the death of the Son of God"

YOUR APARTMENT'S RENT IS much more than you can afford. Every month your debt gets deeper. Soon you are in over your head. Even if your debt was erased, you still could not pay the rent for the apartment. That is our condition. Every day we fall short of God's requirements. Even if our sin was removed, we would still need a way to live with God. We need someone who will not only cancel our debt, but pay our rent.

Jesus not only died the perfect death for us, he lived the perfect life for us. Jesus "being found in human form, he humbled himself and became obedient to the point of death—even death on a cross" (vv. 7–8). His life, just as much as his death, was done for us. His death erased the debt we owe because of our sin. His life provides the righteousness we need to stand before God. Jesus not only cancelled our debt with his death, but secured our future in the presence of God with his perfect life.

Jesus died the death we should have died and lived the life we should have lived. In doing so, Jesus provided everything we need for complete salvation.

Prayer: *You turned my wailing into dancing; you removed my sackcloth and clothed me with joy.* (Psalm 30:11 NIV)

The Death and Descent of Christ— Lord's Day 16—Saturday

Read: Matthew 27:57–66
"His burial testifies that he really died"

WHY DOES IT MATTER that Jesus actually died? Jesus' death for us is central to the good news. His death is not a mere metaphor, but a fact that changes our circumstances forever.

After the crucifixion, Joseph of Arimathea asked for Jesus' body and buried him in a new tomb. As soon as the stone was rolled in front of the tomb, the chief priests and Pharisees set guards to make sure the body was not stolen. The New Testament makes abundantly clear Jesus really died. If people doubted the truth of Jesus' death, they could have asked Joseph about his burial. They could have spoken to Mary Magdalene and the other Mary. These eyewitnesses confirm the truth: Jesus died and was buried. He promised to die for our sins and for our salvation. If he did not truly die, forgiveness and salvation are a hoax. Only if he truly died in our place, does our situation change.

Jesus' burial testifies that he truly died. It is of the greatest importance for Christianity that the death and resurrection of Jesus be a real event. A good story can move our hearts, but only good news can change our lives forever.

Prayer: *Sing to the Lord a new song, for he has done marvelous things; his right hand and his holy arm have worked salvation for him.* (Psalm 98:1 NIV)

Raised to New Life—Lord's Day 17—Sunday

**Q45. How does Christ's resurrection
benefit us?**

A. First, by his resurrection he has overcome death,
so that he might make us share in the righteousness
he obtained for us by his death.
Second, by his power we too
are already raised to new life.
Third, Christ's resurrection
is a sure pledge to us of our blessed resurrection.

JESUS LIVED AND DIED for us. By his death, Jesus fulfilled a life of full, righteous obedience to the Father for us, and also bore the righteous judgment of God for us. By his resurrection, we share in this righteousness. What Jesus did perfectly, in living and suffering, is not for him alone, but becomes ours because he was raised from the dead.

By rising from the dead, Jesus conquered the grave. In his resurrection, Christ is victorious over the powers of sin, death, and the devil. The promise made all the way back in the garden, that a son of Eve would crush the head of the serpent (Genesis 3:15), has been fulfilled. The resurrection of Jesus Christ is his victory.

Jesus lived and died for us, but also rose for us. Jesus is called the firstborn from the dead (Colossians 1:18) and the first fruits of the resurrection (1 Corinthians 15:23). In both cases, Jesus is the pledge and down payment of many more to come. He rose so we might share in his resurrection. By his resurrection, he shows the power by which he raises us from dead in sin to new life in Christ. His resurrection is also a promise of the future day when we will be raised bodily to dwell in the new heavens and the new earth.

Prayer: *because you will not abandon me to the realm of the dead, nor will you let your faithful one see decay.* (Psalm 16:10 NIV)

Raised to New Life—Lord's Day 17—Monday

Read: 1 Corinthians 15:12–28
"Not a waste"

"WAS MY GRANDMOTHER WASTING her life?" My neighbor stood on my porch following his grandmother's funeral, with pain in his heart and a question on his lips. Was it all a waste?

Living for Christ is only a waste if Jesus did not rise from the dead. If Christ did not rise, "our proclamation has been in vain and your faith has been in vain" (v. 14). We would even be liars, our faith would be futile, and our sins would remain. "If for this life only we have hoped in Christ, we are of all people most to be pitied" (v. 19).

Yet, Jesus rose from the grave. This changes everything. Death no longer has the last word over those who trust in the risen Jesus. Those who trust in Christ will be raised to eternal life on the last day. To pour out our life from the resurrected Lord Jesus is far from wasteful, but is the best way to live.

Did she waste her life? My neighbor wondered if his Christian grandmother's life had been spent serving God for nothing. After a brief pause, I looked him in the eye and said, "No, her life was certainly not a waste." Because Jesus is risen, it is far from a waste, but the most worthwhile life imaginable.

Prayer: *You make known to me the path of life; you will fill me with joy in your presence, with eternal pleasures at your right hand.* (Psalm 16:11 NIV)

Raised to New Life—Lord's Day 17—Tuesday

Read: 1 Corinthians 15:50–58
"The Victory of Christ"

ONE SPRAY FROM A skunk and, many baths later, the stink lingers. However, some people want to keep skunks as pets, so they have the stink gland surgically removed. The skunk remains, but the stink has been removed.

At the return of Christ, two things will happen. First, our mortal, perishable bodies will put on imperishability. We will be changed so that this world's corruption no longer touches us. We will then enter into the kingdom of God. Second, death's power over us will finally neutralized: "Death has been swallowed up in victory. Where, O death, is your victory? Where, O death, is your sting?" (vv. 54–55). Like a skunk whose spray has been eradicated, death may continue to look menacing, but its devastating power is gone. By fulfilling the law and removing our sin, Christ has crushed the power of death.

Knowing that death's destructive power has been removed by the victory of Christ, Paul calls us to do the work of the Lord with the utmost effort. We can work fearlessly, because "you know that in the Lord your labor is not in vain." Knowing that death cannot ultimately hurt us, we are free to work tirelessly for the LORD.

Prayer: *Even though I walk through the darkest valley, I will fear no evil, for you are with me; your rod and your staff, they comfort me.* (Psalm 23:4 NIV)

Raised to New Life—Lord's Day 17—Wednesday

Read: Colossians 3:1–17
"Set your eyes"

WHEN I FIRST LEARNED to hit a tennis ball, it was overwhelming. Watch your footwork. Turn your body. Keep your swing level. Mind your grip. I could not keep it all in my mind at once. I started by just keeping my eye on the ball. The rest would come, but I always needed my eye upon the ball.

Living as a disciple of Jesus Christ can be overwhelming at first. However, if we keep our eyes on Jesus, we will be okay. Our life, who we are, is hidden with Christ. So we need to keep our eyes fixed on Christ. Since he is at the right hand of the Father, our eyes should be fixed on the things of heaven. We should "seek the things that are above" (v. 1), focusing our desires and will upon Christ and his way. In other words, we need to keep our eyes on the ball.

With our eyes upon Jesus, the rest of our life will begin to fall into line. If we try to do everything at once, we will miss hitting the ball. But if we keep our eyes firmly fixed on Jesus, our swing of discipleship will begin to take shape.

Prayer: *My heart says of you, "Seek his face!" Your face, Lord, I will seek.* (Psalm 27:8 NIV)

Raised to New Life—Lord's Day 17—Thursday

Read: Romans 6:1–11
"Buried and raised with Christ"

MANY EARLY CHRISTIAN BAPTISTRIES looked like tombs. When baptized, one would descend into a grave-like pool and then, come out of the water as if rising from the tomb. "Therefore we have been buried with him by baptism into death, so that, just as Christ was raised from the dead by the glory of the Father, so we too might walk in newness of life" (v. 4).

In baptism, we die and rise again with Christ. In the gospel, we are made right with God, not because of our own deeds, but because of the finished work of Christ on the cross, which frees us from earning God's favor. However, this is not an excuse to sin. We do not sin just so God can show his grace. We must remember our baptism. Once we have tasted our new life with Christ, our desire to sin will ease and fall away. We will still face temptation, but our old self was buried in the waters of baptism, and we rise from the waters a new person—freed from sin and freed to follow God. That old person was crucified with Christ.

Live like the living, not the dead. Our lives should reflect the reality of our new life in Christ by his resurrection and not our old life that has been crucified with Christ.

Prayer: *Lead me, Lord, in your righteousness because of my enemies—make your way straight before me.* (Psalm 5:8 NIV)

Raised to New Life—Lord's Day 17—Friday

Read: Ezekiel 37:1–14
"Resurrecting a People"

BABYLON SEEMED A PLACE whence God's people would never return. Israel had no strength, no life left in them. They were cut off from God and the land he had given them. They had nothing left in their future but death, like dry bones in the desert.

Yet, the Lord will raise up his people even when they are trapped in the land of death. God brings breath and life into the place of death. Ezekiel's prophetic action foreshadows what God will do to the people of Israel. Where they were dead, God will raise them up. The people will be resurrected out of exile and restored to the land and the LORD who has compassion on them. "I am going to open your graves, and bring you up from your graves, O my people; and I will bring you back to the land of Israel" (v. 12).

However, Ezekiel's experience in the valley of dry bones points ahead to a greater, more literal resurrection. At the center of history is the resurrection of Jesus Christ from the dead, which God declares is but the first fruits of a bountiful harvest. The Lord will raise up his own even when they are trapped in the land of death.

Prayer: *My help comes from the Lord, the Maker of heaven and earth.* (Psalm 121:2 NIV)

Raised to New Life—Lord's Day 17—Saturday

Read: Philippians 3:1–11
"Knowing the Power of his Resurrection"

THERE IS A DIFFERENCE between knowing about someone and knowing someone. I know all sorts of facts about Julius Caesar, but I do not know him personally. I might know a lot about Abraham Lincoln, but I do not truly know him.

Nothing is worth comparing to the value of knowing Jesus. Not just knowing about Jesus, but knowing Jesus. Paul had every reason to think he was someone important. He was born into God's covenant people, into an observant family, trained in the best schools, going above and beyond his peers. Yet, it is all worthless compared to knowing Jesus. In fact, Paul would rather lose everything so that he would know Christ and find his life in him. He would give up everything "to know Christ and the power of his resurrection" (v. 10). The loss is worth the gain of knowing Jesus and knowing his resurrection power in his life.

Do we truly want to know Jesus the way Paul does? Not just to know about Jesus but truly to know him. Knowing Jesus personally is to find righteousness, peace, and salvation. Paul says it is worth any cost to know Christ. Do we believe this?

Prayer: *He says, "Be still, and know that I am God; I will be exalted among the nations, I will be exalted in the earth."* (Psalm 46:10 NIV)

**Q46. What do you mean by saying
"He ascended to heaven"?**

A. That Christ, while his disciples watched,
was taken up from the earth into heaven
and remains there on our behalf
until he comes again to judge the living and the dead.

**Q47. But isn't Christ with us
until the end of the world
as he promised us?**

A. Christ is true human and true God.
In his human nature Christ is not now on earth;
but in his divinity, majesty, grace, and Spirit
he is never absent from us.

**Q48. If his humanity is not present
wherever his divinity is,
then aren't the two natures of Christ
separated from each other?**

A. Certainly not.
Since divinity
is not limited
and is present everywhere,
it is evident that
Christ's divinity is surely beyond the bounds of
the humanity that has been taken on,
but at the same time his divinity is in
and remains personally united to
his humanity.

Q49. How does Christ's ascension to heaven benefit us?

A. First, he is our advocate
in heaven
in the presence of his Father.
Second, we have our own flesh in heaven
as a sure pledge that Christ our head
will also take us, his members,
up to himself.
Third, he sends his Spirit to us on earth
as a corresponding pledge.
By the Spirit's power
we seek not earthly things
but the things above, where Christ is,
sitting at God's right hand.

THE CATECHISM SPENDS CONSIDERABLE time on Christ's ascension because it was a controversial topic at the time it was written: How can Jesus be at God's right hand and present at the Lord's Supper? The Bible teaches that Jesus Christ is both God and man, fully and completely both. It also teaches that Jesus is always with us *and* that he is sitting at the right hand of the Father. Holding these teachings together, the catechism emphasizes a particularly Reformed position. Jesus Christ has a human body that is just like ours. It can only be in one place at a time. Since his ascension to heaven, Jesus' body remains at the right hand of the Father. However, that does not mean that Jesus is absent from us. While still personally united to his human nature, Jesus' divinity is present beyond the bounds of his humanity. Therefore, we can say that Jesus is truly with us and that he is truly seated at the right hand of God the Father almighty.

The ascension speaks to the heart of the Christian faith. God came down to us, in order to bring us up to God. Christ is seated at the right hand of God in heaven, and he has gone there in order to bring us to be with him. While ascended to heaven, Jesus is not far from us.

Prayer: *God reigns over the nations; God is seated on his holy throne.*
(Psalm 47:8 NIV)

Ascended to Heaven—Lord's Day 18—Monday

Read: Matthew 28:16–20
"he is never absent from us"

JUST BECAUSE SOMETHING IS simple does not make it easy. Riding a bike is incredibly complicated, but something many of us learn to do. Lifting a five-hundred-pound weight is simple, but incredibly difficult.

Jesus' last commands in the gospel of Matthew are quite simple: go, baptize, and teach. This mission, however, is not easy. Therefore, Jesus sends us with the promise of his presence and authority. We are not called to make disciples in our own name or power, but in the name and authority of Jesus. Jesus has the authority, so we can head on mission. We not only go in the authority of Jesus, but with his presence. Jesus finishes by saying, "And remember, I am with you always, to the end of the age" (v. 20). Though Jesus has ascended into heaven, he is not absent from us. He is seated at the right hand of God the Father, but as we go on mission, Christ is with us "in his divinity, power, grace, and Spirit" (Q47).

We do not head out on mission alone. We go with Jesus. His presence should give us the power and confidence to do the simple, significant task of going, baptizing, and teaching.

Prayer: *Sing to the Lord, praise his name; proclaim his salvation day after day.* (Psalm 96:2 NIV)

Ascended to Heaven—Lord's Day 18—Tuesday

Read: Acts 1:1–11
"was taken up from the earth into heaven"

"IF YOU HAVE TIME to lean, you have time to clean," my father's boss regularly told him. During the lull between customers, they would clean the fry cooker or mop the floor. Those times waiting were to be used wisely, not lazed away. There was work to do while they waited.

Christians work while we wait. Jesus went bodily into heaven. The disciples stared up toward heaven until the angels reminded them that Jesus would one day return in glory. While we wait, we have the Holy Spirit and we have a mission. The disciples were told they "will receive power when the Holy Spirit has come upon [them]" (v. 8). The Holy Spirit gives us strength and assures us of the presence of Christ. Jesus also tells us that we "will be [his] witnesses in Jerusalem and in all Judea and Samaria, and to the ends of the earth" (v. 8). The mission began right there in Jerusalem and ended at the four corners of the earth. While we wait for Jesus to return, we are called to tell the world about the mighty acts of God in Jesus Christ.

We have work to do while we wait for Christ to return. He has given us his Spirit and has given us a mission. Until Christ returns, we are called to be his witnesses to the ends of the earth.

Prayer: *Declare his glory among the nations, his marvelous deeds among all peoples.* (Psalm 96:3 NIV)

Ascended to Heaven—Lord's Day 18—Wednesday

Read: John 14:1–16
"will also take us, his members, up to himself"

SHEPHERDS WALK AHEAD OF their sheep and the sheep follow. The shepherd makes sure the way is safe, then calls back to the sheep. The sheep hear the shepherd's voice and follow, knowing the way is free from danger.

In his ascension, Jesus, the Great Shepherd, goes ahead of us. Jesus enters heaven so that we can too. Hinting at the cross, resurrection, and ascension that would soon come, Jesus told his disciples he was going on a journey to the Father's house. Jesus goes to the Father so that those who love him can go along with him. "And if I go and prepare a place for you, I will come again and will take you to myself, so that where I am, there you may be also" (v. 3). Jesus will make sure they get there by coming back and escorting them there himself. Like a shepherd, Jesus goes ahead and makes sure we will follow him where he is going.

Jesus is the only way to the Father. The only way to enter the Father's house is to trust in Jesus. We can only come into the Father's presence if we hear the Shepherd's voice and he takes us with him.

Prayer: *My soul yearns, even faints, for the courts of the Lord; my heart and my flesh cry out for the living God.* (Psalm 84:2 NIV)

Ascended to Heaven—Lord's Day 18—Thursday

Read: 1 John 2:1–6
"he is our advocate in heaven"

YOUR DEFENSE ATTORNEY IS giving the closing statement. You are guilty and the evidence is overwhelming. The judgment will be severe. Suddenly, your defense attorney stands up and says, "I know my client is guilty, but let me take the judgment. Let him go free."

Jesus ascended to heaven for us, to be our advocate with the Father. Having offered himself for our sins, he continually pleads our case before the Father. Every time we sin, we know we have one who argues our case by taking our place. The devil and our conscience continually point toward our guilt, but Jesus Christ holds forth his blood shed on our behalf. We do not have to represent ourselves before the Father. Jesus is our representative. We cannot make a case for our innocence, but Jesus Christ "is the atoning sacrifice for our sins, and not for ours only but also for the sins of the whole world" (v. 2). We are declared "not guilty" because Jesus continually is our advocate in heaven.

Jesus ascension was not for him only. He went into heaven for us. Because he went into heaven and lives to intercede for us, our hearts can rest assured that we, too, will one day enter heaven.

Prayer: *For you make me glad by your deeds, Lord; I sing for joy at what your hands have done.* (Psalm 92:4 NIV)

Ascended to Heaven—Lord's Day 18—Friday

Read: Hebrews 7:26–8:7

"in heaven in the presence of the Father"

IN THE BIBLE, PRIESTS represent God before the people and the people before God. They act on Israel's behalf offering sacrifices to God. They act of God's behalf pronouncing mercy and justice in accordance with God's word. While all prior priests did this imperfectly and temporarily, Jesus does this perfectly and permanently.

Jesus is seated at the right hand of the Father as our great high priest. He is our high priest, "holy, blameless, undefiled, separated from sinners, and exalted above the heavens" (7:26). Jesus is the perfect human representative, standing in our place before God. He is also our high priest, who perfectly represents God to us. "For in him the whole fullness of deity dwells bodily" (Colossians 2:9). Jesus is the perfect representation of God to us, since he is God himself. By ascending into heaven, Jesus Christ takes on this role of priest permanently. Other priests lived and died doing this role to the best of their abilities. Jesus does it perfectly forever.

Because we know Jesus is our high priest, we can come with confidence before our heavenly Father. We can pray with joy and expectation because Jesus is always ready to lead us into God's presence.

Prayer: *One thing I ask from the Lord, this only do I seek: that I may dwell in the house of the Lord all the days of my life, to gaze on the beauty of the Lord and to seek him in his temple.* (Psalm 27:4 NIV)

Ascended to Heaven—Lord's Day 18—Saturday

Read: Psalm 110

"remains there on our behalf until he comes again"

PSALM 110 IS FREQUENTLY quoted in the New Testament. It was consistently applied to Jesus as Lord and Messiah. The LORD almighty speaks to "my Lord," inviting him to sit at the LORD's right hand while the LORD subdues his enemies. David calls him "Lord," which means he is greater than David. In the New Testament, the Spirit reveals that David was speaking about Jesus.

Jesus Christ is the Lord seated at the right hand of the Father as king. In ascending to heaven, Jesus has been seated upon the throne, exercising his power to subdue God's enemies and set all creation right. He will "shatter kings" and "execute judgment on the nations" until he "makes your enemies your footstool." The throne is a place of power, glory, and honor. In the end, Christ's people "will offer themselves willingly on the day you lead your forces on the holy mountains" (v. 3). We will offer ourselves freely to God, clothed in righteousness.

Though every knee has not yet bowed to Jesus, he has been crowned and is seated on the throne. Until that final day, Christ rules with power, justice, mercy, and love. As he does, may we offer ourselves freely to him, trusting in our heavenly King.

Prayer: *The Lord will extend your mighty scepter from Zion, saying, "Rule in the midst of your enemies!"* (Psalm 110:2 NIV)

Q50. Why the next words: "and is seated at the right hand of God"?

A. Because Christ ascended to heaven
> to show there that he is head of his church,
> the one through whom the Father rules all things.

Q51. How does this glory of Christ our head benefit us?

A. First, through his Holy Spirit
> he pours out gifts from heaven
> upon us his members.
> Second, by his power he defends us and keeps us safe
> from all enemies.

Q52. How does Christ's return "to judge the living and the dead" comfort you?

A. In all distress and persecution,
> with uplifted head,
> I confidently await the very judge
> who has already offered himself to the judgment of God
> in my place and removed the whole curse from me.
> Christ will cast all his enemies and mine
> into everlasting condemnation,
> but will take me and all his chosen ones
> to himself
> into the joy and glory of heaven.

IN A WORLD OF injustice, the justice of God is good news. One day there will be a reckoning, a judgment. God will come in justice, set right all that is wrong, and ensure those who promote wickedness do not finally get away with it. Justice is not about petty vengeance, but about affirming the power, goodness, and faithfulness of God. It may look today like evil is triumphing, the wicked prosper, and the vipers always go free. It will not always be so.

At this judgment, our good deeds will not be weighed against our bad in hopes that our account eventually tips in our favor. Instead, in the midst of the joy of our limited faithfulness, it will be the constant reminder of the truth of Romans 3:23: "all have sinned and fall short of the glory of God." In this judgment, all of us deserve condemnation. On the basis of the works of our lives, every single person stands condemned before the judgment seat of God.

Either we fall on the strength of our works, or we stand on the strength of Christ's. If we know and trust "the very judge who has already offered himself to the judgment of God in my place and removed the whole curse from me" (Q52), then we can confess the return of Christ with confidence. We do not need to fear the final judgment, but can eagerly await the redemption of the world.

Prayer: *Do not bring your servant into judgment, for no one living is righteous before you.* (Psalm 143:2 NIV)

The Reigning & Returning King—Lord's Day 19—Monday

Read: Ephesians 1:15–23
"The King on the Throne"

WHO IS ON THE throne? The world can seem to be chaotic and out of control. The selfish get more while the selfless get less. The powerful use their strength to take from the weak. Political tensions rise, family tensions rise, racial tensions rise, and we wonder when it will ever end.

Who is on the throne of the universe? Jesus was raised from the dead and is now seated on the throne. And the Father "put all things under his feet and has made him the head over all things for the church" (v. 22). Jesus is the King of all creation. King Jesus is just and compassionate, holy and merciful, faithful and powerful. No matter how strong the powers of this world seem to be, they never sit on the throne of the world. The world is not out of control. There is a king on the throne, a king who rose from the dead, a king who is God himself.

Jesus is King. The hope we confess as the church is that one day this King's reign will be seen from shore to shore, in every nook and cranny of creation, from the highest mountains to the depths of the human heart.

Prayer: *The LORD reigns, he is robed in majesty; the LORD is robed in majesty and armed with strength; indeed, the world is established, firm and secure.* (Psalm 93:1 NIV)

The Reigning & Returning King—Lord's Day 19—Tuesday

Read: Ephesians 4:1–10
"Hail the Conquering Hero"

IN THE ANCIENT WORLD, victorious kings often made a triumphal procession through the streets. The people who gathered to celebrate the victory were given gifts as part of the spoils of war. Captives from battle were also brought and became part of the procession.

Jesus' ascension to heaven is a triumphal procession. Attributing Psalm 68:18 to Jesus, Paul says, "When he ascended on high he made captivity itself a captive; he gave gifts to his people" (v. 8). Jesus goes to the throne of heaven as a conqueror, who has defeated sin, death, and the devil. He, like a conquering king, leads captives and gives gifts. However, Jesus, instead of leading captive soldiers, has liberated those who were captive to sin and led them as freed people into the kingdom of God. Jesus conquers in order to rescue the lost. While earthly kings gave gifts plundered from their enemies, Jesus gives us the Holy Spirit. Jesus conquers in order to give us grace.

Confessing Jesus is "seated at the right hand of God the Father almighty" is proclaiming the victory of Jesus. He has conquered, returning to heaven leading his freed people into the promised land.

Prayer: *Your procession, God, has come into view, the procession of my God and King into the sanctuary.* (Psalm 68:24 NIV)

The Reigning & Returning King—
Lord's Day 19—Wednesday

Read: Philippians 3:12–21
"Run the Race"

SOME PEOPLE ENJOY AN early morning run, a competitive race, or a grueling marathon. It takes discipline and drive to run. Especially when racing, you run with the finish line in mind.

Paul compares himself to an athlete running a race. He no longer considers what is behind him—his lineage, his achievements, even his past mistakes—but sets his eyes upon "the heavenly call of God in Christ Jesus" (v. 14). He runs, he works, he strains in his Christian faith because of grace. Like an expert runner, we set our eyes on Christ, the finish line, and strain with everything we have to run toward him. Because Christ has already made us his own (v. 12), we can run confidently and with even more passion. Because we know that we belong—body and soul, in life and in death—to our faithful savior Jesus Christ, we can now be wholeheartedly willing and ready from now on to live for him.

When we belong to Jesus, we are free to live for him. We are free to run, not to earn our place, but because our place has already been earned by Jesus Christ.

Prayer: *With your help I can advance against a troop; with my God I can scale a wall.* (Psalm 18:29 NIV)

The Reigning & Returning King—Lord's Day 19—Thursday

Read: Revelation 20:11–15
"Christ will cast all his enemies and mine into eternal condemnation"

WRITING MAKES PERMANENT WHAT could easily be forgotten. We put up sticky notes, write dates on the calendar, and send emails. All so that we can remember.

At the final judgment, books are opened. These books contain the record of what we have done and left undone, and the truth will be told. Nothing will be forgotten. The protests silenced, the people shoved to the side, and the oppression considered so acceptable will finally be heard and judged. The times we walked away, turned our backs, and chose to serve ourselves will be named. All the good deeds no one saw will be revealed, but also the sins we thought no one knew or that were hidden only in our hearts will be laid bare.

Another book will also be opened: the lamb's book of life. To have your name written in this book is to have eternal life. Without it, we get what our sins deserve—eternal death. Either we will stand at the judgment on the strength of our works, or we stand on the strength of Christ's. It is only through faith in Jesus Christ that we can be confident that our name is in his book.

Prayer: *If you, Lord, kept a record of sins, Lord, who could stand?* (Psalm 130:3 NIV)

The Reigning & Returning King—Lord's Day 19—Friday

Read: 2 Thessalonians 1:3–12
"The Good Judgment"

THE JUDGMENT OF GOD is not a popular teaching today. It seems unfair to some and vindictive to others. Yet, in the midst of these honest questions, the Bible everywhere teaches there will be a judgment, this judgment is a good thing, and not all will be saved at the judgment, but only those who know God in Christ.

For the early church, judgment and grace were a comfort. The church endured affliction, resistance, and persecution. Paul praises the church for its faith and perseverance during these trials, comforting them by speaking of the judgment of God. Even if the church is weak and suffering, God sees and will bring judgment. Now, it looks like the strong survive and the weak perish, that might makes right. One day, however, the world will reflect things from God's viewpoint, the faithful will be vindicated and those who hate God will be judged. This is a source of comfort to the church under persecution.

While some struggle to imagine God's anger and judgment, it would be worse if God was indifferent to the wickedness in the world. God cares about the suffering of his people and is a God who will uphold justice at his coming.

Prayer: *The Lord is known by his acts of justice; the wicked are ensnared by the work of their hands.* (Psalm 9:16 NIV)

The Reigning & Returning King—Lord's Day 19—Saturday

Read: Matthew 25:31–46
"Sheep and Goats"

I ONCE SAW A shepherd herding a mixed flock of sheep and goats. The sheep immediately followed his voice and walked where the shepherd led. The goats, however, refused to follow the path. They would wander up and down the side of the hill, each one picking its own path and trusting its own sense of the best way to get to their destination.

Behind Jesus' parable is the difference between sheep and goats. Sheep follow the voice of the shepherd, but goats go their own way. Jesus speaks of the final judgment as a separation of a mixed flock. The sheep will be led into eternal life, while the goats will face eternal judgment. For both, the king will refer to their treatment of the least of the brothers (Christians). For as they treat the brothers, they have treated Christ who sent them. The sheep fed, welcomed, clothed, and visited the brothers, while the goats did not.

Sheep listen to the shepherd's voice, obey his call, and "love one another as I [Christ] have loved you" (John 15:12). Goats believe their way is best and refuse to walk in the way of the Good Shepherd. Jesus reveals the final end for both.

Prayer: *For he is our God and we are the people of his pasture, the flock under his care. Today, if only you would hear his voice.* (Psalm 95:7 NIV)

The Holy Spirit—Lord's Day 20—Sunday

Q53. What do you believe concerning "the Holy Spirit"?
A. First, that the Spirit, with the Father and the Son is eternal God.

Second, that the Spirit is given also to me, so that, through true faith, he makes me share in Christ and all his benefits, comforts me, and will remain with me forever.

MOST CHRISTIANS DO NOT bat an eye at the claim that "the Spirit, with the Father and the Son, is eternal God." We sing "Come, Holy Ghost" and pray to God—Father, Son, and Holy Spirit. It is the clear proclamation of scripture, the clear confession of the creed, and the clear teaching of the Heidelberg Catechism that the Holy Spirit is, indeed, eternal God. The Spirit was active at creation, is worshipped as God in both Old and New Testaments, and does what only God can do. The Spirit is co-equal and co-eternal with the Father and the Son. The Spirit is God from the beginning, equal in power and majesty to the Father and the Son. There was never a point where there was the Father and Son without the Holy Spirit.

"The Holy Spirit is God" makes a deep impact on Christian faith. It is not a matter of abstract doctrine. For it is God the Holy Spirit that is given to us, dwelling in us, and uniting us to Christ so we share in his benefits. We cannot be saved or experience new life apart from the work of the Spirit. The Holy Spirit is God himself that comes to us, comforts us, and remains with us forever.

Prayer: *LORD Almighty, blessed is the one who trusts in you.* (Psalm 84:12 NIV)

The Holy Spirit—Lord's Day 20—Monday

Read: Acts 2:1–12

"In our own tongues"

EVERY COUPLE OF YEARS, our family travels to the Netherlands to visit my wife's family. When we gather to read the Bible, it is always read in Dutch, the language of their hearts. In the same language they learned to say "Vader en moeder," (father and mother) they say "onze vader" (our Father) to the one, true God.

The Holy Spirit enables us to hear God in our own languages. On Pentecost, the Father poured out the Holy Spirit upon his people. When the Spirit came, it made the gospel available to people in the language of their hearts. "All of them were filled with the Holy Spirit and began to speak in other languages, as the Spirit gave them ability" (v. 4). The crowds who gathered proclaimed, "in our own languages we hear them speaking about God's deeds of power" (v. 11). The Spirit worked through the apostles so that these people could hear of God's salvation in the language of their hearts.

Whenever we hear about God in our own language, it is a pentecostal moment. Because God sent his Spirit, you do not need to learn another language to understand God. The next time you read the Bible in English, give praise for the work of the Holy Spirit.

Prayer: *The earth is filled with your love, LORD; teach me your decrees.* (Psalm 119:64 NIV)

The Holy Spirit—Lord's Day 20—Tuesday

Read: John 15:26–16:15

"Discomfort in the Spirit"

NO ONE IS LEFT the same by the coming of the Holy Spirit. The Holy Spirit is a comfort to believers, but is uncomfortable to the world. The Holy Spirit is the spirit of truth, which leads the church into all truth. The Holy Spirit takes the Word of Christ and declares it to the church. God the Holy Spirit has come upon the church and will lead the church in glorifying Jesus. All of this is a comfort to the church as it faces trials, rejection, and persecution. However, the Holy Spirit also disrupts the world. The Holy Spirit will convict the world "about sin and righteousness and judgment" (16:8). The presence of the Holy Spirit is the proclamation and promise of God's judgment against sin. Therefore, it is no surprise that the world does not want to listen to the Spirit and even hates those who are filled with the Holy Spirit.

The coming of the Holy Spirit leaves no one unchanged. Those who belong to Christ by faith receive the Holy Spirit and are led into the truth to glorify Christ. Those who do not are convicted of their sin and either repent or are hardened in their rejection. No one is left the same.

Prayer: *Create in me a pure heart, O God, and renew a steadfast spirit within me.* (Psalm 51:10 NIV)

The Holy Spirit—Lord's Day 20—Wednesday

Read: Genesis 1:1–3
"The Spirit at Creation"

WHEN MOST CHRISTIANS THINK of the Holy Spirit, we think of Pentecost. We think of the Spirit descending from on high in a mighty rushing wind and tongues of fire on the heads of the members of the church gathered in the temple. However, the Spirit's work in the world begins not at Pentecost, but at creation.

From the very opening of the Bible, we see the Holy Spirit at work with the Father and the Son. In the act of creation, we already see the whole Godhead at work—Father, Son, and Holy Spirit. We see God the Father almighty, creator of heaven and earth, "In the beginning God created the heavens and the earth" (v. 1). We see God the Son, the Word, as the world is spoken into existence. "Then God said, "Let there be light"; and there was light" (v. 3). God the Holy Spirit is also there at creation, hovering over the waters (v. 2). The Father creates the world in the Son by the Spirit.

The Holy Spirit not only creates the church, but was at work in creating the world. The same Spirit at work in the original creation is at work in us in the new creation.

Prayer: *The voice of the LORD is over the waters; the God of glory things, the LORD thunders over the mighty waters.* (Psalm 29:3 NIV)

The Holy Spirit—Lord's Day 20—Thursday

Read: Ezekiel 11:14–25
"Hearts of flesh"

"I'M DONE WITH HUMANITY today." The shuttle driver's statement stunned my friend as he rode to his hotel. He could not make himself love the people around him anymore. Whatever happened that day had left the driver with thin skin and a hard heart.

The Spirit's work is as wide as creation, but also as personal as the human heart. While Israel was in exile, God made a promise. The people will be gathered and brought back into the land of Israel, but they will also be changed. Their hearts will be made new. Previously, their hearts had been like stone, resistant to the leading of the LORD. Now, the LORD will give them new hearts and a new spirit to walk in God's ways. The Spirit takes a heart of stone and gives a heart of flesh, dwelling in their hearts. The work of the Holy Spirit is as personal as changing the human heart.

We can only have a soft heart if our hearts have been changed by the Holy Spirit. The promise made long ago to Ezekiel is for us, that the Spirit of God will turn our hearts of stone into hearts of flesh, so that we can walk in God's ways, including loving our neighbor.

Prayer: *Turn my hearts toward your statutes and not toward selfish gain.* (Psalm 119:36 NIV)

The Holy Spirit—Lord's Day 20—Friday

Read: Galatians 3:10–14
"What is his is ours"

"WHAT'S MINE IS YOURS; what's yours is mine." A man and a woman become husband and wife. Two become one flesh, one family. Suddenly, whatever money or property the one had is now given to the other. Whatever debt or troubles the one had is assumed by the other.

In Galatians 3, Paul tells us of this wonderful exchange between Christ and his bride, the church. The bride, representing the church, brings nothing to the marriage. We have no righteousness or good deeds to offer. Worse than that, we come with incredible debt, a curse. But on the cross, Jesus took his bride's debt and paid it himself. Jesus has everything—perfection, righteousness, holiness—and he gives it all to his bride. He takes what is ours, and we receive what is his. This is the glorious exchange between Christ and his bride.

But how do we receive the benefits of Christ? We receive the gift of the Spirit. As Paul says, "that we might receive the promise of the Spirit through faith" (v. 14). We receive all the good things that come from Christ when the Spirit unites us to him. What is his is ours and what is ours is his by the work of the Holy Spirit through faith.

Prayer: *Show us your unfailing love, LORD, and grant us your salvation.* (Psalm 85:7 NIV)

The Holy Spirit—Lord's Day 20—Saturday

Read: Romans 5:1–11
"Accomplished & Applied"

ROMANS 5 TELLS THE beautiful reality of the gospel. Christ died to save sinners. The Son of God went to the cross, not for the good or the godly, but for the ungodly. As verse 8 says, "God proves his love for us in that while we still were sinners Christ died for us."

But how do I know this is for me? God pours his love into our hearts by the Holy Spirit (v. 5). The Holy Spirit takes the love of God made manifest on the cross and pours it into our hearts. The Spirit takes what is true, that Christ died to save sinners, and declares that it is true for me. I can know that the love of God for sinners is a love for me because the Holy Spirit has poured God's love into my heart. If we have received the Holy Spirit, then we can know what Christ did, he did for us.

Jesus Christ accomplished salvation once for all on the cross. Everything we need, Jesus has done for us. Yet, it is the Holy Spirit's work to take what Christ has done and apply it to our lives, pouring God's love into our hearts as we trust in Christ.

Prayer: *Let the morning bring me word of your unfailing love, for I have put my trust in you.* (Psalm 143:8a NIV)

Q54. What do you believe concerning "the holy catholic church"?

A. I believe that the Son of God
  through his Spirit and Word,
  out of the entire human race,
  from the beginning of the world to its end,
  gathers, protects, and preserves for himself
  a community chosen for eternal life
  and united in true faith.
  And of this community I am and always will be
  a living member.

Q55. What do you understand by "the communion of saints"?

A. First, that believers one and all,
  as members of this community,
  share in Christ
  and in all his treasures and gifts.
  Second, that each member
  should consider it a duty
  to use these gifts
  readily and joyfully
  for the service and enrichment
  of the other members.

Q56. What do you believe concerning "the forgiveness of sins"?

A. I believe that God, because of Christ's satisfaction,
  will no longer remember
  any of my sins
  or my sinful nature
  which I need to struggle
  against all my life.
  Rather, by grace
  God grants me the righteousness of Christ
  to free me forever from judgment.

WORDS CAN BECOME WEAPONS. Words that should unite us, that should define our shared life, are used to draw lines, divide, and separate.

The word "Catholic" has been weaponized. From very early on, the church confessed itself as the "holy catholic church." "Catholic" is a word that simply means "universal." To say you believe in the "holy catholic church" is to say that Christ has only one body, the church, not multiple bodies in multiple countries. It is a claim about the unity of the church as it belongs to Jesus Christ.

At the time of the reformation, the word "catholic" became a weapon of Rome against the Reformers. Rome was the "Catholic" church (with a capital-C), the true church, while Protestants were seen as separate, as those cut off from the true church of Christ. By contrast, many Protestants fought back, claiming their denominations to be the "true catholics."

However, "catholic" is a word that belongs to all Christians. There is only one church, spread out across the whole world. The church is catholic because the Son has gathered, out of the whole world, only one community for eternal life, the church. As Jesus said, "there will be one flock, one shepherd" (John 10:16).

Prayer: *How good and pleasant it is when God's people live together in unity.* (Psalm 133:1 NIV)

The Community of the Church—Lord's Day 21—Monday

Read: 1 Peter 2:1–10
"Sainthood"

AFTER MOTHER TERESA'S DEATH, her private diaries were published. She had spent her life serving the poor in Calcutta, India. Yet, her diaries revealed a woman who doubted and struggled with a sense of God's absence. They revealed a very human woman of faith. To many, this saintly woman didn't seem very saint-like.

What does it mean to be a saint? Most of us probably don't feel very saintly much of the time, but if God has rescued you from sin, you are a saint. Holiness is not on the entrance exam into sainthood, it is what happens when God makes us saints. Saints are chosen and called by God for the work of his kingdom. They are redeemed sinners, called to "proclaim the mighty acts of him who called you out of darkness into his marvelous light" (v. 9). Being a saint is being set apart by God and called to live and speak so that God is glorified and the gospel proclaimed through us.

What does it mean to be a saint? We should look less to the Mother Teresas of this world, and more to the ordinary brothers and sisters that God is building into his house. Perhaps then, we will be more ready to live out our calling as God's saints for the sake of his kingdom.

Prayer: *For the LORD has chosen Jacob to be his own, Israel to be his treasured possession.* (Psalm 135:4 NIV)

The Community of the Church—Lord's Day 21—Tuesday

Read: Ephesians 4:1–16
"Body & Boat"

THE CHURCH IS A unified body. There is one body with different parts, one church with different gifts, joined together because they are joined to the head, Jesus Christ. Cutting yourself off from the church is trying to rip apart the body of Christ. We must avoid the false purity that separates, tearing the body of Christ into pieces.

The church is also a boat in a storm. If we ignore whether the boat is headed toward the rocks, or how bad the storm is raging, because all that matters is that we are all in the same boat, we court disaster. There is the temptation, knowing the high cost of division, to seek unity at all costs. We must also avoid the false unity that loses the gospel and runs the church aground.

The church has not always done this well. This is why "the holy catholic church" is something we confess in faith. The gospel unity of the church across the nations and across the ages is not something we see with our eyes, but something we believe because of Jesus Christ. It is something perceived only through the eyes of faith.

Prayer: *I will say of the LORD, "He is my refuge and my fortress, my God, in whom I trust."* (Psalm 91:2 NIV)

The Community of the Church—
Lord's Day 21—Wednesday

Read: 1 Corinthians 12:12–31
"One Body"

I ONCE BROKE MY big toe. Afterward, my balance was off; I stumbled and ached. The big toe is an important part of the body, even if it doesn't get all the glamor. When it hurts, the whole body is affected.

The church is like a human body. Just as our body is made up of many parts which are organically connected together, the church is made up of many members that are united together by the Spirit as they are united to Christ, the head of the church. Each part, each person may have a specific gift, specific calling, or specific role in the church, but all are important. Every member of the church is significant. Whether our gift is exercised visibly or behind the scenes, each of us has gifts that matter. More than that, what happens to one part of the body impacts all of it. When one part of the church is hurting, the whole body of Christ suffers. Our joys, our honor, and our suffering is shared in the body.

Whether a toe or an eye, each part of the body matters. The same is true in the church. United to Christ, we belong together into one global communion of saints.

Prayer: *Your love, LORD, reaches to the heavens, your faithfulness to the skies.* (Psalm 36:5 NIV)

The Community of the Church—Lord's Day 21—Thursday

Read: Hebrews 11:1—12:3
"Communion of Saints"

WE, AS A CULTURE, have a difficult time learning from the past. We feel the need to find our own way and learn everything for ourselves. While Christians do set our eyes on toward the future, we are a people rooted in the past—in God's faithfulness and God's promises. We do not need to "figure out these things for ourselves."

We do not make our own faith in God. Our faith goes back to Abel, Noah, and Abraham, was passed down to Isaac, Jacob, and Joseph and his brothers, and was carried by Moses and the Israelites in the wilderness, by judges and kings, and by the everyday faithful people of God. This faith was fulfilled in Jesus Christ, "the pioneer and perfecter of our faith" (12:2). What they hoped for, but did not see, we have seen in the coming of Jesus. In the Christian faith, we are not forging our own path, but joined with all the saints in the one faith in Jesus Christ.

We are connected to a deeper and longer story than our own. We belong to a people, a communion of saints, stretching back to the garden of Eden and stretching forward all the way into the new creation.

Prayer: *One generation commends your works to another; they tell of your mighty acts.* (Psalm 145:4 NIV)

The Community of the Church—Lord's Day 21—Friday

Read: 1 John 1:5—2:2

"Forgiveness of Sins"

WORDS MATTER. PHRASES LIKE "I love you," "I forgive you," "It's over," or even "I hate you" make a difference not just for a moment, but often for a lifetime. Words matter and some words can change the world.

One of these big words is "forgiveness." In Jesus' completed work on the cross, he not only dies in our place, but we receive forgiveness. Forgiveness includes the idea of a debt that has been paid, and of being released from the consequences of that unpaid debt. When you forgive your friend for their misspoken word, your neighbor for being rude, or the stranger for cutting you off, you are letting go of what they might legitimately owe you. You are saying they do not have to make up for what they did, to make it right, or to fix what went wrong. You are freeing them from that debt.

Forgiveness can be hard. At times, we want to hold on grudges, to make the other person pay, or at least suffer a little so that they feel bad and apologize. Yet, forgiveness is a word that changes the world.

Prayer: *Blessed is the one whose transgressions are forgiven, whose sins are covered.* (Psalm 32:1 NIV)

The Community of the Church—Lord's Day 21—Saturday

Read: Romans 7:15—8:4

"Forgiveness and Struggle"

WHY DID I DO that? You know that you should be patient with your sister, but find angry words pouring out of your mouth. You said you would get up to spend time with God, but your hand still hits the snooze button.

We all face the struggle between what is right and what we end up doing. In Romans 7, Paul confesses not to understand his own actions. He wants to do what is good, but ends up doing what he hates. He describes his desires as being at war inside of him and feeling captive to the desire to do evil. Who will rescue him? How can we be rescued from our sin and our sinful desires? "Thanks be to God through Jesus Christ our Lord!" (7:25). "There is therefore now no condemnation for those who are in Christ Jesus" (8:1).

We all struggle with sin, but Jesus Christ has rescued us from it. To say we believe in "the forgiveness of sins" is not to deny our struggle, but to trust in the forgiveness of Christ that is stronger than any power that wars within us. What we could not do, Christ has done for us, setting us free.

Prayer: *Keep me free from the trap that is set for me, for you are my refuge.* (Psalm 31:4 NIV)

Q57. How does "the resurrection of the body" comfort you?

A. Not only will my soul
  be taken immediately after this life
  to Christ its head,
  but also my very flesh will be
  raised by the power of Christ,
  reunited with my soul,
  and made like Christ's glorious body.

Q58. How does the article concerning "life everlasting" comfort you?

A. Even as I already now
  experience in my heart
  the beginning of eternal joy,
  so after this life I will have
  perfect blessedness such as
  no eye has seen,
  no ear has heard,
  no human heart has ever imagined:
  a blessedness in which to praise God forever.

CHRISTIANITY CONTAINS AN ASTOUNDING promise: resurrection and eternal life. Those who die in the LORD will be raised at the trumpet's sound and enter into the heavenly city. It is a promise of a future where God will dwell among us and we will live forever in his presence, praising his name.

However, this promise already touches our present. We have not yet tasted all the blessedness of life with God, but we "already now" experience the "beginning of eternal joy." Resurrection joy already breaks in to the present for those who believe in Jesus.

This promise—both now and the future—is centered in Jesus Christ. The breaking of the chains of death, the undoing of its power, the bringing of the dead back to life, this is all found in Jesus Christ. Those who die believing in Jesus will live again. Those who live believing in Jesus will not be overcome by death. Death will not be a barrier to the life-giving power of Jesus. Those who believe in Jesus Christ will not only experience physical resurrection at the return of Jesus Christ, but experience spiritual resurrection from dead in sin to being alive in Christ.

Prayer: *Our God is a God who saves; from the Sovereign LORD comes escape from death.* (Psalm 68:20 NIV)

Resurrection & Life Everlasting—Lord's Day 22—Monday

Read: John 11:17–26
"Do you believe this?"

AT SOME POINT BEFORE every funeral, I stop and take a breath. Do I believe this? Do I believe that Jesus Christ raises the dead? Do I believe that he truly gives eternal life to those who have faith in him?

"Jesus said to her, 'I am the resurrection and the life. Those who believe in me, even though they die, will live'" (v. 25). Even before his own resurrection, Jesus proclaims the final resurrection to eternal life finds its beginning, its center, and its fulfillment in him. Martha believed that the presence of Jesus could have saved her brother and now Jesus stands before her and proclaims that not even death can stop his saving power.

Do you believe this? Yes, Lord.

At a funeral, Christians proclaim the hope of the resurrection, the hope that is found only in Jesus Christ, the hope of all the saints who have died in the faith. What Jesus said to Martha is true, and there is no better word in the face of death than that Jesus Christ is risen from the grave and those who believe in him will also be raised to eternal life.

Prayer: *Precious in the sight of the LORD is the death of his faithful servants.* (Psalm 116:15 NIV)

Resurrection & Life Everlasting—Lord's Day 22—Tuesday

Read: 1 Corinthians 15:12–28
"Resurrection of the Body"

EVERYTHING HANGS ON WHETHER Jesus Christ rose from the dead. If Easter is a myth, the whole Christian faith falls apart. However, if it is true Jesus rose from the dead, nothing will ever be the same.

If Jesus Christ has been raised from the dead, then I will be raised with him. Paul proclaims that Jesus Christ is the "first fruits of those who have died" (v. 20). First fruits means that there is the promise of more to come. Through Jesus, resurrection has entered into a world of death, the power of death has been overcome. At Christ's return, all who believe in him will rise with him. Christ will crush all the powers that opposed the kingdom of God including death itself. At that time, as the catechism says, "my very flesh will be raised by the power of Christ" (Q57).

There is no "if" when it comes to the resurrection of Jesus Christ. Scripture boldly proclaims, "But in fact Christ has been raised from the dead" (v. 20). Jesus' resurrection means the promise of my resurrection on the last day. Because Jesus has been raised, we proclaim our belief in the "resurrection of the body," of all who belong to Jesus Christ.

Prayer: *He sent out his word and healed them; he rescued them from the grave.* (Psalm 107:20 NIV)

Resurrection & Life Everlasting—
Lord's Day 22—Wednesday

Read: Revelation 20:11–15
"The General Resurrection"

ON THE LAST DAY, all the dead will be raised. Scripture focuses on the resurrection of the faithful to life everlasting in the presence of God, but we are told to expect that all the dead will be raised to life on the last day.

We will all stand judgment. All—the faithful and unfaithful, the just and the wicked, those who trust in Christ and those who persecuted his church—will have to stand before the King on the throne. Books will be opened. Those sins no one saw, no court ever tried, or never saw the light of day, were seen by God. Death and Hades itself will be overthrown and judged, tossed in the lake of fire.

This judgment causes us to tremble. None of us can stand on our own under this judgment. Yet, the judgment is not overwhelming for those who trust in Christ. We will stand at the judgment, not by our goodness, but by Christ's righteousness. Those who stand on their own will fall. "Anyone whose name was not found written in the book of life was thrown into the lake of fire" (v. 15). In Christ, we enter into eternal life. Apart from Christ, we join Death in the judgment.

Prayer: *Kiss his son, or he will be angry and your way will lead to your destruction.* (Psalm 2:12a NIV)

Resurrection & Life Everlasting—Lord's Day 22—Thursday

Read: Revelation 21:1–8
"Longing for Home"

AFTER MOVING, MY YOUNG son would often look at me and say, "I want to go to our Iowa home." Even though we knew that Canada would be our new home, it didn't stop us longing for home.

Underneath that longing for home, whether in Ontario or Iowa, is the longing for our true home. We were made for life with God. Revelation 21 tells us that, by faith in Christ, one day we will be brought home. "See, the home of God is among mortals. He will dwell with them; they will be his peoples, and God himself will be with them" (v. 3). One day, God will make his home among us, and we will make our home in him. The holy city, the New Jerusalem, dressed like a bride, will be wed with the bridegroom, Jesus Christ. There will be a wedding feast of celebration, for we will be finally home. Heaven is our true home, life before the face of God.

Since the Fall in the Garden, all of humanity has been living away from home, away from God. But God promises that those who belong to him by faith will be brought home when God's home comes to earth.

Prayer: *One thing I ask from the LORD, this only do I seek: that I may dwell in the house of the LORD all the days of my life.* (Psalm 27:4a NIV)

Resurrection & Life Everlasting—Lord's Day 22—Friday

Read: John 3:16–21
"Beginning of eternal joy"

ONE OF MY FAVORITE parts of making cookies is tasting the cookie dough. The cookies are always better, but it was a joy to get a little sample while I wait for the cookies to bake.

We already taste the beginnings of the joy of eternal life now. In John 3, Jesus reveals two aspects of this joy. First, we have freedom from condemnation (v. 18a). By believing in Christ, we will not be condemned at the last judgment. Like a man on trial who already knows the verdict, we can live with joy and freedom, knowing that we will be declared innocent because of Jesus Christ. Second, we have the peace of walking in the light (v. 21). People who live in the shadows always fear being found out. They live in constant anxiety and worry that they will be exposed for who they are. When we know we belong to Christ, we can let ourselves and our deeds be seen—not to boast, but to glorify God.

One day we will fully experience the joy of eternal life. But even now, we experience the beginnings of that joy. Today we get a taste, but one day we will get a feast.

Prayer: *The Lord has done great things for us, and we are filled with joy.* (Psalm 126:3 NIV)

Resurrection & Life Everlasting—Lord's Day 22—Saturday

Read: Isaiah 64:1–4
"The Coming of God"

"O LORD, HASTE THE day when the faith shall be sight, the clouds be rolled back as a scroll." In writing "It is well with my soul," Horatio Spafford was inviting us to long for the day of the Lord to come soon.

God's coming will be jarring. It will be more like a violent thunderstorm than soft, gentle rain. Isaiah describes it like heaven being torn open, the mountains shaking so that they almost fall apart, like fire consuming brushwood or causing water to boil. The world cannot remain as it is before the presence of the Holy One. Isaiah's description echoes the experience of Israel at Mount Sinai. There God came down upon the mountain in fire and smoke, thunder and lightning. The people were told to purify themselves for God's coming and not to touch the mountain or they will die. When God comes in power at the end of the age, it will be like God's coming on Sinai, which left neither the mountain nor the people unchanged.

Spafford and Isaiah were singing a similar song when the former wrote, "O Lord, haste the day," and the latter, "O that you would tear open the heavens and come down" (v. 21). Together, they wish for that day to come soon, because it will be the day we will see God.

Prayer: *Tremble and do not sin; when you are on your beds, search your hearts and be silent.* (Psalm 4:4 NIV)

Righteous Before God—Lord's Day 23—Sunday

Q59. What good does it do you, however, to believe all this?
A. In Christ I am righteous before God and heir to life everlasting.

Q60. How are you righteous before God?
A. Only by true faith in Jesus Christ.
   Even though my conscience accuses me of having grievously sinned
   against all God's commandments, of never having kept any of them,
   and of still being inclined toward all evil, nevertheless,
   without any merit of my own, out of sheer grace, God grants and credits to me
   the perfect satisfaction, righteousness, and holiness of Christ,
   as if I had never sinned nor been a sinner, and as if I had been as perfectly obedient
   as Christ was obedient for me. All I need to do is accept this gift with a believing heart.

Q61. Why do you say that through faith alone you are righteous?
A. Not because I please God by the worthiness of my faith.
   It is because only Christ's satisfaction, righteousness, and holiness
   make me righteous before God, and because I can accept this righteousness
   and make it mine in no other way than through faith.

QUESTION 60 WAS THE question that sparked the Protestant Reformation, "How are you righteous before God?"

Martin Luther knew the weight of this question. He, like Paul before him, had gone as far as one could go trying to work his way into right relationship with God. Luther confessed sins constantly and passed all his fellow monks trying to please God, but even his best efforts were tainted by sin. Fear and anxiety wracked him until he stumbled upon Paul's teaching that we are saved by grace through faith. That is, Luther (re)discovered that salvation comes to us from Christ as a gift, not in response to any work on our part. Christ's worthiness, not ours, makes all the difference. What Christ has done is counted as ours "without any merit of [our] own, out of sheer grace" (Q60).

The Reformed share with Luther the deep, biblical conviction that we are set right with God because Christ has done all that is necessary for salvation, and all his goodness and righteousness is counted as ours when we receive it by faith. This is the heart of the Reformation: sinners stand righteous before the Father by grace through faith in Jesus Christ.

Prayer: *It is better to take refuge in the LORD than to trust in humans.*
(Psalm 118:8 NIV)

Righteous Before God—Lord's Day 23—Monday

Read: John 3:25–36
"In Christ I am righteous before God"

SOME THINGS YOU MIGHT do even if there were no benefit to them. Some of us only exercise for the good it brings, but some people enjoy it for its own sake. Friendship brings so many benefits into our lives, but we would likely want friends even apart from them. Some things, such as friendship or being healthy, are both good for their own sake and good for us.

The Christian faith is good by itself, but it is also good for us. Knowing Jesus is simply good. Yet knowing Jesus also brings wonderful and eternal blessings into our lives. As the gospel of John says, "Whoever believes in the Son has eternal life; whoever disobeys the Son will not see life, but must endure God's wrath" (v. 36). Simply being a friend of the bridegroom (Jesus) and getting to stand and hear him is enough to fill us with joy. However, we also get the wondrous benefit of being his bride. We get not only the joy of knowing Jesus, but the benefit of belonging to him as a bride—eternal life.

Knowing Jesus is a joy in itself. However, when we have faith in Christ, we receive the gift of eternal life and are, as the catechism says, "righteous before God and heir to life everlasting" (Q59). What a joyous blessing indeed!

Prayer: *You make known to me the path of life; you will fill me with joy in your presence, with eternal pleasures at your right hand.* (Psalm 16:11 NIV)

Righteous Before God—Lord's Day 23—Tuesday

Read: 1 Corinthians 1:26–31
"Christ is our Righteousness"

HOW OFTEN HAVE YOU heard someone say, "I don't mean to brag, but . . . " This "humble brag" uses words that sound humble while actually drawing attention to ourselves and our accomplishments.

From a worldly standpoint, the church is often full of misfits and outcasts, not the high rungs of society. As Paul says, "God chose what is weak in the world to shame the strong" (v. 27). Looking at themselves, none of them could boast in the presence of God. They could not boast about who they were or what they had done, because none of it could make them right before God. Instead, what we do not have, but desperately need, Christ gives to us. Wisdom—Christ has become that for us. Righteousness—Christ has lived the perfect life for us and died the perfect death for us. Sanctification—Christ works this in us by the Holy Spirit. Redemption—Christ has won this for us.

Only when we are in Christ, when we receive his gift through faith, can we return to boasting. However, this boasting looks entirely different. Instead of boasting of our virtues or accomplishments, we boast of Jesus Christ and what he has done.

Prayer: *He raises the poor from the dust and lifts the needs from the ash heap.* (Psalm 113:7 NIV)

Righteous Before God—Lord's Day 23—Wednesday

Read: Deuteronomy 9:1–12
"Without any merit of my own"

SEEING THE LOOK ON someone's face when you give them a gift they will cherish is priceless. However, what if after giving them a wonderful gift, they turned around and told everyone they had earned it, worked and paid for it themselves?

Moses warns the Israelites not to treat God's gift as if they had earned it. After forty years in the wilderness, God promised that he would bring Israel into the land he had promised them, he would drive out the people living there, and they would occupy the land. However, he warned them not to begin believing that the LORD gave them the land because of how good they were. On the contrary, they were a stubborn and rebellious people, undeserving of the land. They would get the land without any merit of their own. It was because of God's goodness, not Israel's, that they would live in the promised land.

Like Israel, we should not treat God's gift of salvation as if we have earned it. We, too, are a stubborn and rebellious people, turning away from God and going our own way. Yet, it is because of God's goodness, without any merit of our own, that we can inherit the promise of eternal life.

Prayer: *He provided redemption for his people; he ordained his covenant forever—holy and awesome is his name.* (Psalm 111:9 NIV)

Righteous Before God—Lord's Day 23—Thursday

Read: 2 Corinthians 5:17–21
"God grants and credits to me"

A COUPLE YEARS AGO, the NBA vetoed a potential trade deal because it was deemed unfair. The trade wasn't equal. One team was getting a much better deal than the other. Even though both teams agreed to the deal, the trade was not allowed.

In salvation, an exchange takes place between Christ and those who belong to him that is entirely in our favor. We receive what Christ has earned and deserves. Christ takes on himself what we have earned and deserve. He takes all that we were—sin, death, unrighteousness—and gives us all that he is—holiness, life, and righteousness. By being united to Christ, we are made new creations. The old life, the old self, with its sinful desires and its justifiable end in death has itself been put to death. In its place, Christ has given us new life in him. Where before there was enmity between us and God, now there is reconciliation. Where before there was a gulf of sin separating us from God, now we have been brought near through the blood of Christ.

Christ gets our sin, we get his righteousness. It is counted as ours and given to us. He willingly takes on this exchange for us.

Prayer: *Yet he saved them for his name's sake, to make his mighty power known.* (Psalm 106:8 NIV)

Righteous Before God—Lord's Day 23—Friday

Read: Acts 16:25–34

"Accept this gift with a believing heart"

"It cannot be that simple," the jailor must have thought. One moment his life was over, the next he was told all he had to do to be saved was believe in the Lord Jesus. Surely something as great as salvation would take more work on his part.

Yet, it was as simple as accepting Christ with a believing heart. Imprisoned, Paul and Silas were praying and singing. The ground shook, the chains fell off, and the prison doors were opened. Letting prisoners escape was a death sentence for the guards, so the jailor draws his sword. When Paul stops him, telling him none have escaped, the man is stunned. "What must I do to be saved?" Saved from a death sentence, a deeper salvation is promised to him. He must place his trust in the Lord Jesus. This will bring salvation to him personally and spill over into his household.

"It cannot be that simple." Yet, we are saved just like a jailor. It is not something we achieve, but something we receive. Salvation will change every nook and cranny of our lives, but it is as simple as Paul says, "Believe on the Lord Jesus, and you will be saved" (v. 31).

Prayer: *Truly may soul finds rest in God; my salvation comes from him.* (Psalm 62:1 NIV)

Righteous Before God—Lord's Day 23—Saturday

Read: Romans 4:1–15

"Righteous will live by faith"

In Genesis, God makes incredible promises to Abraham. The Lord promises to be his God, to be his shield and protector, to bless those who bless him and curse those who curse him, to give him a people and a place, and to bless all the nations through him.

What type of blessing was given to Abraham, work or faith? When we work at a job, there is a reward, we receive wages. We work, we earn what we get. But then there are gifts. We do not earn gifts, we receive them by faith. Abraham received the blessing of God by faith, not by work. He received it before he had done anything, including circumcision. It was before anything that could be considered a work, any action that could be said to "deserve" the blessing. Instead, we hear that, "Abraham believed God, and it was counted to him as righteousness" (v. 3). Abraham's blessing was by faith.

We receive the blessing of Abraham the same way. The work of Christ that sets us right with God—the fulfillment of God's promise to Abraham—is something we do not earn, but receive. It is not the wages we receive for our efforts, but the free gift of God in Jesus Christ.

Prayer: *Save us and help us with your right hand, that those you love may be delivered.* (Psalm 60:5 NIV)

Gift of Grace—Lord's Day 24—Sunday

Q62. Why can't our good works
   be our righteousness before God,
   or at least a part of our righteousness?
A. Because the righteousness
   which can pass God's judgment
   must be entirely perfect
   and must in every way measure up to the divine law.
   But even our best works in this life
   are imperfect
   and stained with sin.

Q63. How can our good works
   be said to merit nothing
   when God promises to reward them
   in this life and the next?
A. This reward is not earned;
   it is a gift of grace.

Q64. But doesn't this teaching make people indifferent and wicked?
A. No.
   It is impossible
   for those grafted into Christ through true faith
   not to produce fruits of gratitude.

QUESTION 64 ADDRESSES THE fear that teaching grace is dangerous. If we hear that we are saved by grace through faith, apart from our works, maybe we will believe our actions do not matter and will live selfishly and sinfully. Israel often presumed upon their special relationship to God and were both indifferent and wicked. Paul had to refute both those who thought grace meant they could do whatever they wanted (the Corinthians) and those who tried to respond to "the problem of grace" by adding rules and regulations to Christianity (the Galatians). This fear rears its head every time the teaching of God's grace is recovered and taught with boldness.

However, the solution is to truly understand God's grace. As the catechism says, "It is impossible for those grafted into Christ through true faith not to produce fruits of gratitude" (Q64). When we have been saved by grace, then nothing will be the same for us. When we have been filled with the Holy Spirit and behold Christ *for us*, then we will be *for Christ* with all that we are. The solution to misused grace is not less grace, but deeper grace, transforming grace, God's grace in Jesus Christ.

Prayer: *For you, LORD, have delivered me from death, my eyes from tears, my feet from stumbling, that I may walk before the LORD in the land of the living.* (Psalm 116:8–9 NIV)

Gift of Grace—Lord's Day 24—Monday

Read: Isaiah 64:6–7
"Stained with sin"

WHEN I WORK OUTSIDE in our garden, I often come inside with my hands covered in mud. Everything I touch gets muddy. If I tried to put away the clean dishes, they would end up dirty in the cupboard. If I tried folding laundry, the clothes would be dirty in the dresser. Because my hands were dirty, everything I did, even good things, was contaminated.

The prophet Isaiah tells us that, because of our sin, even our righteous deeds are like filthy rags. It is like our hands are contaminated by sin and everything we touch is affected. The stain of our sinful hands and sinful hearts touches everything we do, even our best works, our best thoughts, feelings, and actions. As Isaiah reminds us, this plight affects all of us and all of our deeds (v. 6).

Why can't our righteous deeds count as a part of our righteousness before God? They have been contaminated by sin. We need a righteousness that will not be corrupted by our sin, but will cleanse us from our sin. In other words, we need the righteousness of Jesus Christ. We need his perfect life and his perfect works, because nothing we offer in ourselves is clean.

Prayer: *All have turned away, all have become corrupt; there is no one who does good, not even one.* (Psalm 14:3 NIV)

Gift of Grace—Lord's Day 24—Tuesday

Read: Luke 17:1–10
"A gift of grace"

WE HAVE A RULE: if you don't eat dinner, you don't get dessert. However, eating your dinner is not an amazing achievement, it is simply what you are supposed to do. You should eat it because it is good for your body, not because of any reward.

When we serve God and others, our actions may be good (in a limited sense), but they do not "deserve" rewards from God. Jesus recalls the relationship of a master to his hired servant. "Do you thank the slave for doing what was commanded? So you also, when you have done all that you were ordered to do, say, 'We are worthless slaves; we have done only what we ought to have done!'" (vv. 9–10). A man expects those working for him to do their job without the promise of extra bonuses. In the same way, God calls for our obedience without any special reward.

We can be tempted to think if we do our part, God owes us a reward. We have earned dessert by eating our vegetables. However, Jesus reminds us that this is not how it works. Obedience is good, but it is simply what is expected. It does not earn rewards. All that we receive is a gift of grace.

Prayer: *You are good, and what you do is good; teach me your decrees.* (Psalm 119:68 NIV)

Gift of Grace—Lord's Day 24—Wednesday

Read: Matthew 5:1–12
"When God promises to reward them"

THE FAMOUS GERMAN ATHEIST, Friedrich Nietzsche railed against Christianity, in part, because of Jesus' beatitudes. Jesus' favor and blessing of the weak was offensive to everything he knew to be true about the world and how it worked.

Jesus' Sermon on the Mount begins with blessing. Nine times he says, "Blessed." This blessing is not earned, but simply a gift. But this blessing goes to ones we would not expect. God's blessing rests first on those despised by the world. Blessed are the poor in spirit, those who mourn, and the meek. Not blessed are the strong, the go-getters, the ones who take what they need and get what they want their own way. Blessed are the merciful, not the cutthroat. Jesus calls blessed what the world sees as weakness.

For everything he got wrong, Nietzsche understood that Christians, in holding fast to Jesus' words, were an affront to the world. Grace is always offensive to a world that runs on rewards, but grace to the least and lowest is doubly offensive to a world that runs on power. Christians live belonging to a king who freely pours out blessing on the meek, the merciful, and the mourning.

Prayer: *You save the humble but bring low those whose eyes are haughty.* (Psalm 18:27 NIV)

Gift of Grace—Lord's Day 24—Thursday

Read: Matthew 7:15–20
"Fruits of thankfulness"

HOW DO YOU TELL counterfeit money from real money? When you've seen and felt the real stuff all day, the fakes jump out at you. Even before you could check the microprinting, you can sense that something is off. Handling the real thing helps root out a counterfeit.

Jesus warns his disciples they will encounter false teachers. They look and talk like they know Jesus, but their lives give evidence (fruit) they do not. Does their life and teaching encourage others to love God and to love neighbor? Does their life and teaching point to Jesus, the Word made flesh, who died and rose again for our salvation? Jesus says we will know them by their fruits. By the same token, we will know true teachers by their fruit. Those who know and belong to Christ will live in ways that show it. They will bear good fruit.

Being immersed daily in the word of God primes us to be able to spot a fake. When we have handled the real deal, when we have been with Jesus, anything else that tries to sound like our Lord is going to ring false in our ears.

Prayer: *Blessed is the one who does not walk in step with the wicked, or stand in the way that sinners take, or sit in the company of mockers.* (Psalm 1:1 NIV)

Gift of Grace—Lord's Day 24—Friday

Read: John 15:1–11
"Abide in the Vine"

A GARDENER PLANTS A vine so it will bear fruit. The branch, if it is connected to the vine, will produce leaves and flowers which will bring forth grapes. However, if that branch is cut off or removed—has lost its living connection to the vine—it withers and dies. As Jesus says, a branch bears fruit only when it is connected to the vine.

The branch must remain attached to the vine if it is going to bear fruit. It must "abide"— stay, endure, remain steadfast. It must have that living connection to the vine. The same is true of disciples with Jesus. Disciples of Jesus are to remain in living connection to Jesus Christ. Unlike the flowers which fade, our connection to Jesus Christ must endure. Like the vine, we are to draw life from him.

There is much to do in the Christian life, but none of it is possible, none of it makes sense, if we do not abide in Jesus. Apart from Christ, all the commands, all the doing will only be bad news and disappointment. However, when we abide in Jesus Christ, our lives will bear fruit—bear evidence—of his life in us.

Prayer: *That person is like a tree planted by streams of water, which yields its fruit in season and whose leaf does not wither—whatever they do prospers.* (Psalm 1:3 NIV)

Gift of Grace—Lord's Day 24—Saturday

Read: Hebrews 11:1–7
"We cannot please God apart from faith"

WHY WE DO SOMETHING matters. An action that looks loving (doing the dishes, cooking dinner, helping a stranger), done to boost our ego or reputation, instead of our out love, is evidence of something wrong. Bad motives poison even good actions.

Faith in Christ should be the motivation for our good works. Tucked in with the description of faith and examples of faith is the simple statement that "without faith it is impossible to please God" (v. 6). Faith is also a conviction, a deep-seated belief and trust in God and his faithfulness even when our eyes do not see it. Actions that look good on the outside, but are done apart from faith, are not truly good and do not please God. Faith leads to action, but action apart from faith does not please God. If we live without trust and confidence in God—without the assurance and conviction of faith—all our deeds might look good, but still fall short.

In Hebrews 11, the likes of Abel, Enoch, Noah, Abraham, Moses, and others are commended not for their righteous actions, but for their faith. This confidence and trust in God led to action, but it is their faith that was commended.

Prayer: *My soul faints with longing for your salvation, but I have put my hope in your word.* (Psalm 119:81 NIV)

Q65. It is through faith alone
     that we share in Christ and all his benefits:
     where then does that faith come from?
A. The Holy Spirit produces it in our hearts
     by the preaching of the holy gospel,
     and confirms it
     by the use of the holy sacraments.

Q66. What are sacraments?
A. Sacraments are visible, holy signs and seals.
     They were instituted by God so that by our use of them
     he might make us understand more clearly
     the promise of the gospel,
     and seal that promise.
     And this is God's gospel promise:
     to grant us forgiveness of sins and eternal life
     by grace
     because of Christ's one sacrifice
     accomplished on the cross.

Q67. Are both the word and the sacraments then
     intended to focus our faith
     on the sacrifice of Jesus Christ on the cross
     as the only ground of our salvation?
A. Yes!
     In the gospel the Holy Spirit teaches us
     and by the holy sacraments confirms
     that our entire salvation rests on Christ's one sacrifice
     for us on the cross.

Q68. How many sacraments
     did Christ institute in the New Testament?
A. Two: holy baptism and the holy supper.

DURING THE REFORMATION, ONE of the most divisive issues in the church was the nature of the sacraments. It not only divided Protestants from Rome, but Protestants from one another. The word "sacrament" comes from a latin word meaning "oath," but refers to specific Christian rites.

There was sharp disagreement between Rome and the Protestants on which rites (and how many) were to be considered sacraments. Rome argues for seven, while the majority of Protestants claimed that there were only two (baptism and the Lord's Supper) because only two could be based upon the specific command of Christ (Q68). Our forebears took the sacraments so seriously that, even within Protestants, significant disagreements on baptism and the Lord's Supper fractured the Protestant movement.

The Heidelberg Catechism works to hold three important threads together as we begin to consider baptism and the Supper. First, the sacraments do not save us, but confirm our faith. We are saved by grace through faith. Second, God truly works through the sacraments, they are not mere symbols. The sacraments are visible, tangible signs of the gospel promise. Third, the sacraments focus us on Christ and his cross. The sacraments point beyond themselves to the true substance of our faith—Jesus Christ.

Prayer: *You prepare a table before me in the presence of my enemies. You anoint my head with oil, my cup overflows.* (Psalm 23:5 NIV)

Signs & Seals—Lord's Day 25—Monday

Read: 1 Corinthians 2:10–14
"Faith comes by the Spirit"

WITH STARTING EVERY PROJECT or new school year, we take a "before" picture and then an "after" photo at the end. This allows us to look at them side-by-side and see just how much things have changed.

Before: our own wisdom is not wise enough for us to understand God. Our own human spirit cannot reach deep or far enough to comprehend God. Our own intelligence is not enough to discern the gifts of God's Spirit, but instead considers them foolish (v. 14). We cannot believe in Christ, be united to him, or receive his benefits on our own.

After: something changes when we receive the Holy Spirit. The Spirit reveals the things of God (v. 10). The Spirit gives us understanding of God (v. 12). The Spirit teaches us and enables discernment (vv. 13–14). The Spirit also bestows gifts to the church (v. 14). God the Holy Spirit enlivens, illumines, and empowers the church with knowledge, understanding, and gifts. We no longer have the spirit of the world, but the Spirit of God.

What we were before, we are no longer after receiving the Holy Spirit. It is only through the Holy Spirit that we come to know Christ and receive him by faith.

Prayer: *The LORD lives! Praise be to my Rock! Exalted be God my Savior!* (Psalm 18:46 NIV)

Signs & Seals—Lord's Day 25—Tuesday

Read: Romans 4:9–15
"Visible signs and seals"

THE CATECHISM CALLS THE sacraments "signs and seals." This comes from Romans 4:11, where Abraham "received the sign of circumcision as a seal of the righteousness that he had by faith while he was still uncircumcised" (v. 11). Circumcision is both a sign and a seal.

The sacraments are signs of the promise of God. A sign points to something. The water, bread, and cup point to the gospel promise, just as circumcision pointed Abraham to the promised inheritance received through faith (v. 13). The sacraments of baptism and the Lord's Supper are signs of the promise of gospel.

The sacraments also seal the gospel promise as being for us. Like a wax seal on a letter that confirms the identity of the sender or the brand on a steer that showed who it belonged to, circumcision was a seal marking that God's promise was for you who received the sign of the covenant. In a similar way, baptism and the Lord's Supper confirm that the gospel promise is, in fact, for us.

As signs and seals, the sacraments point us clearly to the gospel promise—forgiveness of sins and eternal life—and proclaim that this promise is for you.

Prayer: *I will sing the Lord's praise, for he has been good to me.*
(Psalm 13:6 NIV)

Signs & Seals—Lord's Day 25—Wednesday

Read: 1 Corinthians 10:1–13
"Where have I seen this before?"

PASSING THROUGH WATER FROM bondage into freedom. Eating bread that comes as God's gift. Drinking what God himself poured out. Where have we seen this before? Inspired by the Spirit, Paul connects the experience of Israel in the wilderness with the experience of the church in the sacraments.

The people of Israel passed through the waters of the Red Sea, leaving the bondage of Egypt and entering the freedom of the wilderness with God. Paul calls this a baptism into Moses. In a similar way, Christians pass through the waters of baptism, leaving the bondage of our old life of sin and entering into the wilderness of discipleship. This is baptism into Christ.

God sustained Israel through manna from heaven and water from the rock. Paul tells us that the rock from which the water came was Christ. Christians too are nourished by God, eating spiritual food and drinking spiritual drink at the Lord's Supper.

Christ gave us baptism and the Lord's Supper as gifts to the church. Yet, these practices connect back to all that God has done before in redeeming, delivering, and providing for his people.

Prayer: *to him who led his people through the wilderness, His love endures forever.* (Psalm 136:16 NIV)

Signs & Seals—Lord's Day 25—Thursday

Read: Romans 6:1–11
"Baptized into Christ"

WHENEVER HE WAS FACING strong temptation from the devil, Martin Luther was said to respond, "I am baptized." This short phrase was a reminder of his true identity as an adopted son of God. He would claim his baptism as a sure sign that he belonged to Christ and not to Satan.

When Christians are plunged into the waters of baptism, they are joined with Christ in his death. "Do you not know that all of us who have been baptized into Christ Jesus were baptized into his death?" (v. 3). In Christ, we have died to sin and therefore should no longer go living in it. Because he was raised to life, we who have been joined to him can be certain that we will join him one day in the resurrection. Baptism places our life alongside the life of Christ, so that our old life of sin is nailed to the cross and we are now alive and free in Christ.

Our baptism should flow naturally into discipleship to Jesus Christ. Baptism not only exhibits the gift of God in Christ, but also the claim of God in Christ upon our lives—to walk in newness of life.

Prayer: *God is our refuge and strength, an ever-present help in trouble.* (Psalm 46:1 NIV)

Signs & Seals—Lord's Day 25—Friday

Read: 1 Corinthians 11:23–28
"Proclaims the Lord's Death"

WHAT HAPPENS WHEN WE break bread and drink the cup?

The Lord's Supper is, among other things, a declaration. "For as often as you eat this bread and drink the cup, you proclaim the Lord's death until he comes" (v. 26). It is a proclamation of the death of Christ. Christians break bread, just as his body was broken. Christians pour out the cup, just as his blood was poured out on the cross. Through this symbolic action, at the table Christians proclaim the central mystery of the Christian faith—that God came as the man Jesus Christ and died on the cross. At the center of the Christian faith is the death that brings life, the willing surrender that won freedom, the sacrifice that brought cleansing, and the payment that provided forgiveness. At the table, among other things, Christians proclaim the death of Christ.

This proclamation includes hope. We proclaim his death until he comes, because we believe his words when he says he will come again. At the table, we proclaim what has happened in Christ in anticipation of what will one day happen in Christ when he comes to set all things right and make all things new. We proclaim his death until he comes.

Prayer: *You are my strength, I watch for you; you, my God, are my fortress.* (Psalm 59:9 NIV)

Signs & Seals—Lord's Day 25—Saturday

Read: Matthew 28:16–20
"Baptism and Mission"

WHAT IS THE MISSION of the church? In the Great Commission, Jesus calls his church to go into all the world and make disciples of Jesus Christ—to tell the good news and call people to true faith in Jesus.

However, while certainly not less, the Great Commission includes more than this. Jesus tells his disciples to go, make disciples, baptize, and teach. Christians go and proclaim the message of the gospel so others respond in faith and teach people how to obey Christ—to walk in his ways. Mission also includes the call to baptize. Sacraments are part of the mission of the church. Tied up with the need to go (into Jerusalem, Judea, Samaria, and the ends of the earth; Acts 1:8) and the need to make disciples of all nations and teach them Christ is the call to baptize. The sacraments as a whole (and baptism in particular) are missional.

How often when we think of the mission of the Church do we think of sacraments? An ever-growing desire to share the gospel and make disciples should lead our churches to grow in their desire to participate in the sacraments as well. Only then we will be fully living out the Great Commission.

Prayer: *I will sing of the LORD's great love forever; with my mouth I will make your faithfulness known through all generations.* (Psalm 89:1 NIV)

Q69. How does holy baptism
    remind and assure you
    that Christ's one sacrifice on the cross
    benefits you personally?

A. In this way:
    Christ instituted this outward washing
    and with it promised that,
    as surely as water washes
    away the dirt of the body,
    so certainly his blood and his Spirit
    wash away my soul's impurity,
    that is, all my sins.

Q70. What does it mean
    to be washed with Christ's blood and Spirit?

A. To be washed with Christ's blood means
    that God, by grace, has forgiven our sins
    because of Christ's blood
    poured out for us in his sacrifice on the cross.
    To be washed with Christ's Spirit means
    that the Holy Spirit has renewed
    and sanctified us to be members of Christ,
    so that more and more
    we become dead to sin
    and live holy and blameless lives.

Q71. Where does Christ promise
    that we are washed with his blood and Spirit
    as surely as we are washed
    with the water of baptism?

A. In the institution of baptism, where he says:
    "Go therefore and make disciples of all nations,
    baptizing them in the name of the Father
    and of the Son
    and of the Holy Spirit."
    "The one who believes and is baptized will be saved;
    but the one who does not believe will be condemned."
    This promise is repeated when Scripture calls baptism
    "the water of rebirth" and
    the washing away of sins.

WHAT HAPPENS IN BAPTISM? There are at least four biblical images of baptism.

First, baptism is a washing. "As surely as water washes away the dirt of the body, so certainly his blood and his Spirit wash away my soul's impurity, that is, all my sins" (Q69). Our sins have stained us, made us unclean. Baptism is a sign and seal of God's promise to wash away our sins through the blood of Christ.

Second, baptism is a sprinkling of blood. The blood of a sacrificial animal was sprinkled upon the altar to atone for the sins of the people. "Christ's blood poured out for us in his sacrifice on the cross" (Q70) has paid the penalty for our sins. My baptism is the sign that Christ's sprinkled, saving blood was poured out for me.

Third, baptism is a burial and resurrection. Like Christ buried in the tomb, Christians are buried in the baptismal waters and raised to new life. We are united to Christ's death and his resurrection (Rom 6:1–11). Baptism is a sign and seal of the death of the old self and the rising to life of the new self in Christ Jesus.

Fourth, baptism is an anointing. Prophets, priests, and kings were all anointed to their calling. Baptism itself is a sign and seal of the promise of the Holy Spirit, who calls, indwells, and anoints Christians to their callings as disciples of Christ.

Prayer: *The voice of the LORD is over the waters; the God of glory thunders, the LORD thunders over the mighty waters.* (Psalm 29:3 NIV).

The Waters of Baptism—Lord's Day 26—Monday

Read: Matthew 3:11–17
"Baptism as Judgment"

EACH OF THE GOSPELS includes an account of John baptizing by the Jordan. Just as baptism is at the beginning of the Christian life, baptism was at the beginning of Jesus Christ's ministry.

According to John, Jesus brings a baptism much greater than his. Baptism into Jesus Christ is a form of judgment. Jesus does not simply baptize with water, but with Holy Spirit and fire. In Christian baptism, water is joined with Spirit and fire. Baptism is more than our act of repentance, it involves the work of the Holy Spirit coming with fire to burn away the impurities in us. Baptism declares judgment on sin and the death of the old self. Like the waters of the flood, the waters of baptism involve cleansing judgment and new life on the other side.

Jesus brings a greater baptism, but he also entered into baptism for us. Jesus, who never sinned, entered into the waters, and took on a baptism of sinners for us. Jesus, who never needed to repent, perfectly repented on our behalf. When we are baptized into Christ and trust in his name, we share even in his perfect repentance for us.

Prayer: *I will be glad and rejoice in your love, for you saw my affliction and knew the anguish of my soul.* (Psalm 31:7 NIV)

The Waters of Baptism—Lord's Day 26—Tuesday

Read: 1 Peter 3:18–22
"Baptism saves you"

ONE OF THE MOST popular bible stories for children is Noah, the flood, and all those cute animals. However, at its heart, this is a story of judgment and death, of cleansing and new life.

1 Peter reveals the deep connection between salvation in Christ, baptism, and Noah. At the time of Noah, there was a flood of judgment and God saved a small remnant in the ark. God was patient, but many did not obey. Only the few in the ark were saved. In baptism, we are saved from judgment by passing through the waters, resting safe in the ark of Christ, our consciences cleansed before God. God's judgment on sin, provision of salvation through water, and new creation on the other side all point ahead to God's great work of salvation in Christ.

Baptism, like the flood, points us to God's promise to save, even as it immerses us in God's judgment on sin. In this way, our baptism should lead us to cling more firmly to Christ, who "suffered for sins once for all, the righteous for the unrighteous, in order to bring you to God" (v. 18).

Prayer: *Do not let the floodwaters engulfs me or the depths swallow me up or the pit close its mouth over me.* (Psalm 69:15 NIV)

The Waters of Baptism—Lord's Day 26—Wednesday

Read: Ezekiel 36:22–32
"Sprinkle Clean Water"

WHY DO SOME CHURCHES sprinkle water at baptism instead of pouring it or immersing?

Sprinkling of water is an image of cleansing. In Ezekiel 36, God proclaims his people are unclean. They have dishonored his name and walked in the ways of wickedness. However, God will act for the sake of his own name and will display his holiness before the eyes of his people and among the nations. God will sprinkle clean water on his people and make them clean. He will give them a new heart of flesh to replace their old heart of stone and put a new spirit within them. The language of sprinkling points back to the priests sprinkling blood to atone for the sins of the people. By sprinkling blood the people were cleansed from their sins.

The whole sacrificial system, as well as the sprinkling of water in Ezekiel 36, points ahead to the work of Jesus on the cross. It is his blood that makes us clean. This promise is held forth in baptism, where "as surely as water washes away the dirt of the body, so certainly his blood and his Spirit wash away my soul's impurity, that is, all my sins" (Q69).

Prayer: *Wash away all my iniquity and cleanse me from my sin.* (Psalm 51:2 NIV)

The Waters of Baptism—Lord's Day 26—Thursday

Read: Mark 16:9–20
"The one who believes and is baptized will be saved"

CAN YOU BE SAVED if you have never been baptized? The simple answer is "yes," but perhaps this is the wrong question.

Baptism and belief are meant to be together in the mature Christian life. Jesus institutes baptism as central to the mission of the church. Those who go forth to proclaim the good news, whose ministry will be accompanied by signs, will go out and baptize. When belief and baptism are found together, there will be salvation. Where there is no belief, there is only condemnation. Whether, as in the case of infants, baptism comes prior to belief or, in the case of adult converts, belief comes prior to baptism, belief in Jesus Christ and baptism into the name of the Father, Son, and Holy Spirit go together. Baptism calls us to believe in Jesus Christ. Apart from faith in Christ, there is only condemnation.

Christ gave us baptism as the sacrament of initiation into the Christian life. It is a mark that God's promises are for us, that we have been claimed by God, and that this claim upon our lives calls us to faith in Christ and to faithfully walk with him all of our days.

Prayer: *Our God is a God who saves; from the Sovereign LORD comes escape from death.* (Psalm 68:20 NIV)

The Waters of Baptism—Lord's Day 26—Friday

Read: Hebrews 12:18–24
"Sprinkled Blood of Christ"

How can we come into the presence of God? Israel came trembling before the LORD at Mount Sinai. God descended with thunder and trumpets and the mountain was covered in fire and smoke. So holy was the LORD that they could not even touch the mountain, lest they die. It is awesome and dangerous to come before the LORD.

We come before the same God that Israel did at Sinai. We do not come physically to a mountain that can be touched, but to the heavenly Jerusalem. However, we come in Jesus Christ, whose blood was sprinkled on the altar to make us righteous. Abel's blood cried out to God from the ground, but the blood of Christ speaks the better word. The blood of Christ cries out from the cross that our sins have been paid for, and we can approach the mountain of the LORD, the holy presence of God, without dying, for Christ has already died in our place.

The waters of baptism hold forth the promise of the blood of Christ. As we are sprinkled with water, so we hold fast to the promise that Christ's blood has been sprinkled upon us that we might stand one day in the heavenly Jerusalem.

Prayer: *Lord, I love the house where you live, the place where your glory dwells.* (Psalm 26:8 NIV)

The Waters of Baptism—Lord's Day 26—Saturday

Read: 1 Corinthians 6:9–11
"You were washed"

"Just because you keep saying it louder does not make it true." When our children are not getting the answer they want, it is common for them to keep repeating themselves louder. They seem to believe that by speaking louder, it will somehow change the truth.

Our culture can get loud repeating what it believes to be true. However, Scripture reveals that what we do with what belongs to the Lord (our bodies), what belongs to our neighbor, and what we worship has significant consequences, even excluding us from inheriting the kingdom of God. Read 1 Corinthians 6:9–11 again. Many who join the church used to do all these things. But not anymore. Something changed. Something was done for them, to them, and in them so that they no longer walk in these ways, but walk in the way of the LORD.

You were washed, sanctified, and justified. God, by the Spirit, makes you holy (sanctification). God, in the name of Jesus, has declared you innocent and righteous (justification), and God, in baptism, has claimed you and cleansed you (washed). No matter how loudly the world shouts about the "best way to live," remember who you were and now who you are in Christ.

Prayer: *See if there is any offensive way in me, and lead me in the way everlasting.* (Psalm 139:24 NIV)

Included in the Covenant—Lord's Day 27—Sunday

Q72. Does this outward washing with water itself wash away sins?
A. No, only Jesus Christ's blood and the Holy Spirit
    cleanse us from all sins.

Q73. Why then does the Holy Spirit call baptism
    the water of rebirth and the washing away of sins?
A. God has good reason for these words.
    To begin with, God wants to teach us that
    the blood and Spirit of Christ take away our sins
    just as water removes dirt from the body.
    But more important,
    God wants to assure us, by this divine pledge and sign,
    that we are as truly washed of our sins spiritually
    as our bodies are washed with water physically.

Q74. Should infants also be baptized?
A. Yes.
    Infants as well as adults are included in God's covenant and people,
    and they, no less than adults, are promised
    deliverance from sin through Christ's blood
    and the Holy Spirit who produces faith.
    Therefore, by baptism, the sign of the covenant,
    they too should be incorporated into the Christian church
    and distinguished from the children of unbelievers.
    This was done in the Old Testament by circumcision,
    which was replaced in the New Testament by baptism.

FROM THE CALL OF Abraham, God has been in the business of forming and saving a family. While this salvation project was about individuals, we are saved into the family of God in Christ.

At times this new family will cut across our natural families. Jesus tells us that his coming will divide brothers and put parents one against the other. The gospel redefines family through baptism. In a very real sense, water (baptism) is more significant than blood (birth).

However, the family of God both cuts across our natural families and includes them. God called Abraham to circumcise his son, marking him as part of God's covenant people, proclaiming the covenant promises are for him. Similarly, children of believing parents receive the covenant sign, baptism, to proclaim that the gospel promises are for them and they are included in the covenant community.

At times, God saves us out of our existing families by calling us to cling to Christ even when all others reject him. At times, God saves our families by baptizing our children and raising one generation to call to the next and proclaim the good news of salvation through faith in Christ. At all times, God saves us into a new family, the church.

Prayer: *I spread out my hands to you; I thirst for you like a parched land.* (Psalm 143:6 NIV)

Included in the Covenant—Lord's Day 27—Monday

Read: Colossians 2:11–13
"Circumcision & Baptism"

SHOULD CHRISTIANS BE CIRCUMCISED? Maybe. The early church struggled with this question and, inspired by the Spirit, never made circumcision a requirement for entry into the church. If a man was already circumcised, that was fine, but if not, that was fine as well. Should Christians be baptized? Absolutely.

Baptism replaces circumcision as the sign and seal of membership in the covenant community. When we are baptized into Christ, we are buried with him, and our flesh is cut off in a spiritual circumcision. In baptism, we die in order to be brought into the community of God. Baptism is a dying and cutting off and a raising to new life with Christ. What circumcision did in the old covenant was fulfilled in the cross of Christ, where he was cut off that we might be brought in. The rite of circumcision with its physical cutting and removal is replaced in the new covenant by baptism, with its washing joining us to the circumcision of Christ.

When we are baptized, we are brought into the community of God's people. "God wants to assure us, by this divine pledge and sign, that we are as truly washed of our sins spiritually as our bodies are washed with water physically" (Q73).

Prayer: *Open my lips, Lord, and my mouth will declare your praise.*
(Psalm 51:15 NIV)

Included in the Covenant—Lord's Day 27—Tuesday

Read: Genesis 17:9–14; Acts 2:37–39
"Who shall be marked?"

WHO IS MARKED BY circumcision as belonging to this covenant, as being in relationship with God? Infants and outsiders.

Infants are the first group to be circumcised. Before the child could speak, before it could lift up its head, before it could even remember the circumcision taking place, the child was marked as belonging to God. Before the child could choose God, it was already chosen. Before it could even begin to love God, it was loved by God.

The second group to undergo circumcision were outsiders. These are Gentiles, non-Jews. God intended that people who are not physical descendants of Abraham would be brought into the covenant. These Gentile outsiders would be marked as belonging to God, as one of his people forever.

Now consider Acts 2. At the word of the gospel, hearts were cut—circumcised. In response, they were told to be baptized. They were told that the promises of God—the promise of forgiveness and relationship with God—is for you, your children, and all who are far off. Infants and outsiders. At Pentecost, we see the promise of God made all the way back in Genesis 17 being fulfilled by the giving of the spirit and the waters of baptism.

Prayer: *For he remembered his holy promise given to his servant Abraham.* (Psalm 105:42 NIV)

Included in the Covenant—Lord's Day 27—Wednesday

Read: Revelation 7:9–14
"Washed"

STAINS ARE TOUGH TO get out. Spray on stain remover, wash with special detergent, and some stains simply will not get out. Christians await a heavenly wedding banquet where we come dressed in white, ready to celebrate with Jesus. However, all our clothes are stained and we cannot get the stain out.

It is only the blood of Christ that can make us clean. John receives a vision of the great multitude of saints praising God. Everyone is robed in white. When John is asked who they are, the elders says, "These are they who have come out of the great ordeal; they have washed their robes and made them white in the blood of the Lamb" (v. 14). Not just any washing will do. Those who stand praising before the throne of God for all eternity will be those whose robes have been made white in the blood of the Lamb, Jesus Christ.

Do you want to be clothed in white on that great and glorious day? While some methods may help get dress clothes clean, the stain of our sins comes out with only one remedy: the blood of Christ. If we trust in him, there is no stain too deep that he will not remove.

Prayer: *Hide your face from my sins and blot out my iniquity.*
(Psalm 51:9 NIV)

Included in the Covenant—Lord's Day 27—Thursday

Read: Galatians 3:23–29
"Put on Christ"

IF WE SEE SOMEONE in a police uniform, hospital scrubs, or even a clerical collar, we probably know what they do for a living. Once they put on the uniform, they must act in a way appropriate with what they wear. We know who they are by what the wear.

In baptism, you have "clothed yourselves with Christ" (v. 27). This is both a gift and a calling. First, we are given the gift of a new identity in Christ. When we are baptized, we are now "in Christ." This identity runs deeper than the doctor who puts on hospital scrubs. It runs to the very core of who we are. Second, we are called to live differently because we have been clothed with Christ. Just as the doctor or police officer must act appropriately when they are wearing their uniforms, putting on Christ means living a certain way of life. Our actions and our heart should be shaped by Christ, what he has done for us and his way in the world.

Every morning, we get out of bed and get dressed. In baptism, we have already been clothed with Christ. Let us now live into the clothes we have been given.

Prayer: *It is God who arms me with strength and keeps my way secure.*
(Psalm 18:32 NIV)

Included in the Covenant—Lord's Day 27—Friday

Read: Matthew 19:13–15
"Let the little children come"

BECOMING A FATHER WAS scary. I didn't know how to do it. The task seemed so large and my son so small. Yet, the best advice I ever received was "bring your kids to Jesus." However I may struggle in being a father, I know where to bring my children.

Jesus wants little children to be brought to him. Parents were bringing their children to Jesus so that he would lay his hands on them and pray. However, the disciples began to chastise the parents. The disciples were setting up barriers to keep the children from Jesus. Yet, Jesus rebukes the disciples, not the children. "Let the little children come to me, and do not stop them" (v. 14). The parents had the right idea: "bring your kid to Jesus." For, Jesus says, the kingdom of heaven belongs to little children like them.

Godly parents desire for their children to come to Jesus. One of the ways they come is in baptism. Jesus takes even the littlest children, lays his hands on them, claims them, and promises them forgiveness through the blood of Christ. Jesus says "Let the little children come to me," so we offer our children in baptism.

Prayer: *For you created my inmost being; you knit me together in my mother's womb.* (Psalm 139:13 NIV)

Included in the Covenant—Lord's Day 27—Saturday

Read: Acts 16:25–43
"The Whole Household"

IN ACTS 2:39, PETER claims "the promise [of the gospel] is for you, for your children, and for all who are far away, everyone whom the Lord our God calls to him." God calls Jews to faith in Jesus Christ ("the promise is for you") and Gentiles ("those who are far away"), but what about children?

In Acts 16, the jailor's whole household was baptized. An earthquake shook the prison where Paul and Silas were chained, freeing the prisoners. Thinking they had escaped, the jailor planned to kill himself. Paul stopped him, and the jailor asked, "What must I do be to saved?" Paul and Silas answered, "Believe on the Lord Jesus, and you will be saved, you and your household" (v. 31). They shared the good news with those who were in the jailor's house, and the whole family was baptized. That family would have included children. Because the jailor believed, his children were included in the promise of baptism.

God works not only to save individuals, but to save whole households. In this way, God fulfills what was promised through Peter, that the promise was not just for the adults who receive it, but for their children as well.

Prayer: *Look to the Lord and his strength, seek his face always.* (Psalm 105:4 NIV)

Q75. How does the holy supper remind and assure you that you share in Christ's one sacrifice on the cross and in all his benefits?

A. In this way:

Christ has commanded me and all believers
to eat this broken bread and to drink this cup
in remembrance of him.
With this command come these promises:
First,
as surely as I see with my eyes
the bread of the Lord broken for me
and the cup shared with me,
so surely
his body was offered and broken for me
and his blood poured out for me
on the cross.
Second,
as surely as
I receive from the hand of the one who serves,
and taste with my mouth
the bread and cup of the Lord,
given me as sure signs of Christ's body and blood,
so surely
he nourishes and refreshes my soul for eternal life
with his crucified body and poured-out blood.

Q76. What does it mean to eat the crucified body of Christ and to drink his poured-out blood?

A. It means

to accept with a believing heart
the entire suffering and death of Christ
and thereby
to receive forgiveness of sins and eternal life.
But it means more.
Through the Holy Spirit, who lives both in Christ and in us,
we are united more and more to Christ's blessed body.
And so, although he is in heaven and we are on earth,
we are flesh of his flesh and bone of his bone.
And we forever live on and are governed by one Spirit,
as the members of our body are by one soul.

**Q77. Where does Christ promise
to nourish and refresh believers with his body and blood
as surely as they eat this broken bread
and drink this cup?**

A. In the institution of the Lord's Supper:
>"The Lord Jesus on the night when he was betrayed
>took a loaf of bread, and when he had given thanks,
>he broke it and said,
>"This is my body that is [broken*] for you.
>Do this in remembrance of me."
>In the same way he took the cup also, after supper, saying,
>"This cup is the new covenant in my blood.
>Do this, as often as you drink it, in remembrance of me."
>For as often as you eat this bread and drink the cup,
>you proclaim the Lord's death until he comes."
>This promise is repeated by Paul in these words:
>"The cup of blessing that we bless,
>is it not a sharing in the blood of Christ?
>The bread that we break, is it not a sharing in the body of Christ?
>Because there is one bread, we who are many are one body,
>for we all partake of the one bread."

JESUS DIED FOR THE sin of the world, to rescue his people, and to redeem all creation, but how do I know he died *for me*?

Do you see the bread broken and given to you? Do you see the cup poured and shared with you? Just as God gives the gift of the bread and cup to you at the Supper, Christ gave himself for you on the cross. As personally as you eat and drink, so personally did Christ die for you. In this way, eating and drinking at the Supper is a deeply personal assurance of the gospel being good news for you.

However, the supper is also much bigger than a personal experience. At the Supper, the Church eats and drinks together. Jesus did not command us to eat and drink alone, but together as his body. It is not just a personal meal, but a church meal. It is a meal eaten together by people who, because of Christ's death and resurrection, have become a whole new community, a people whose citizenship is in heaven. In eating this meal, we are bound to Christ and bound together as well.

Prayer: *You, LORD, are forgiving and good, abounding in love to all who call to you.*
(Psalm 86:5 NIV)

The word "broken" does not appear in the NRSV text, but it was present in the original German of the Heidelberg Catechism

His Body & Blood—Lord's Day 28—Monday

Read: Luke 22:1–23
"Body Broken"

AT THE LAST SUPPER, Jesus gave thanks, broke bread, and gave it to his disciples. In these three actions, he was not only telling us how to eat the Lord's Supper, but was proclaiming his upcoming death. First, Jesus gave thanks. The bread was both a gift from God and offered back to God. Jesus himself, on the cross, was both God's gift to us and a perfect offering of thanksgiving and obedience to God. Second, Jesus broke the bread. While none of his bones were broken, Jesus was whipped, beaten, spat upon, and pierced for us. Jesus' body was broken for us on the cross. Third, the bread was given to the disciples. Jesus suffered not for himself, but to give himself for the salvation of sinners. He gave himself on the cross for us.

Whenever we come to the table and give thanks, we remember that Jesus was both the gift to us and offered himself to God for us. Whenever we come to the table and break the bread, we remember that Jesus' body was broken for us on the cross. Whenever we come to the table and receive the bread, we remember that Jesus gave himself to us, for us.

Prayer: *Who is like you, LORD God Almighty? You, LORD are mighty, and your faithfulness surrounds you.* (Psalm 89:8 NIV)

His Body & Blood—Lord's Day 28—Tuesday

Read: Matthew 26:17–30
"Cup of the Covenant"

WHY BREAD AND A cup? The bread was broken and given, just as Christ's body was broken and given for the salvation of sinners. Why then does Jesus also call us to drink from a cup?

First, Jesus calls the cup "the blood of the covenant." Jesus' blood on the cross establishes the relationship (covenant) between God and redeemed sinners. Second, the cup is poured out for many for the forgiveness of sins. Jesus establishes our relationship with God and accomplishes our forgiveness by pouring out his blood. The forgiveness and the covenantal relationship with God go hand-in-hand. Third, Jesus will not drink the cup again until he drinks it with his disciples in the Father's kingdom. The cup points ahead to the final redemption that will arrive when Christ returns and his kingdom is fully established.

Why bread and cup? The cup at the Supper draws together our past (forgiveness), present (relationship), and future (kingdom) redemption, showing forth the whole beauty of the gospel. Whenever we drink the cup, we remember Christ has established our covenantal relationship with God, has forgiven us our sins, and has promised to return in his glorious kingdom.

Prayer: *I will lift up the cup of salvation and call on the name of the LORD.* (Psalm 116:13 NIV)

His Body & Blood—Lord's Day 28—Wednesday

Read: John 6:35-40
"What truly satisfies"

CANADIANS EAT MORE KRAFT Dinner per capita than any country in the world. Yet, no matter how much Kraft Dinner you eat, you will get hungry later. Then if you eat another box, you will still get hungry again.

When the crowds came looking for Jesus, they came looking for food. Jesus' response tells us they were not asking for too much, but for too little. They were demanding more of the same, more of what they already knew, had already tasted. They were asking for bread, when Jesus was giving them himself. Jesus said to them, "I am the bread of life. Whoever comes to me will never be hungry, and whoever believes in me will never be thirsty" (v. 35). What we truly hunger for is Jesus. What we need is him to give us himself that we may feast upon him and be truly satisfied.

Eat bread and you will get hungry again. Fill your life with distraction or accolades and it will never be enough, the hunger will keep coming back. In essence, Jesus is saying, "Come to me, and I will give you myself. Come to me, and I will give you life—life that lasts into eternity."

Prayer: *You, God, are my God, earnestly I seek you; I thirst for you, my whole being longs for you, in a dry and parched land where there is no water.* (Psalm 63:1 NIV)

His Body & Blood—Lord's Day 28—Thursday

Read: John 6:41-59
"Eating and Drinking"

FOR FORTY YEARS, GOD provided daily bread for the Israelites, known as manna. Though the bread was miraculous and kept them fed in the desert, all the people whom God led out of Egypt eventually died. However, Jesus promises to give bread that will keep us to eternal life.

Jesus invites his disciples not only to believe, but to eat. Throughout the gospels, there is the call to believe in Jesus Christ and the promise of eternal life. However, in John 6, receiving the promise of eternal life includes eating the flesh and drinking the blood of Christ. Jesus is pointing toward the Lord's Supper, where he will say of the bread, "this is my body given for you" and of the cup "this is my blood of the covenant." To eat and drink of Christ is not only to believe in him, but also to come to the feast he has provided.

When we come to the Lord's Supper, Christ truly nourishes us and refreshes us with his body and blood. Being united to Christ, we have life in us (v. 53), we have eternal life in Christ and the promise of resurrection (v. 54), and we have deep, lasting fellowship with Christ (v. 56).

Prayer: *For he satisfies the thirsty and fills the hungry with good things.* (Psalm 107:9 NIV)

His Body & Blood—Lord's Day 28—Friday

Read: 1 John 4:13–21
"Some things go together"

SOME THINGS JUST GO together. Peanut butter and jelly. Potlucks and casseroles. Macaroni and cheese.

There are aspects of the Christians life that simply go together. We cannot have one without the other. John's letter shows that having the Holy Spirit, testifying and confessing Christ, and abiding in God are all tied together. When we have the Holy Spirit, we confess wholeheartedly that Christ came as the Savior of the world. When we confess Christ, we know that God abides in us and we abide in God, which comes through the Spirit. You cannot have one without the other two. Spirit, confession, and abiding go together.

The result of these three marks is that we know the love God has for us, we have boldness on the day of judgment, and therefore we love our brothers and sisters because of the love God has poured out upon us in Jesus Christ. These too are tied together. "We love because he first loved us" (v. 19). Just as believing, having the Spirit, and abiding in Christ go together, so too do knowing God's love, being confident on the day of judgment, and loving others.

Prayer: *Let them give thanks to the LORD for his unfailing love, and his wonderful deeds for mankind.* (Psalm 107:8 NIV)

His Body & Blood—Lord's Day 28—Saturday

Read: 1 Corinthians 10:14–22
"A Meal of Sharing"

MEALS ARE ABOUT MORE than filling our stomachs. We do not sit down for Thanksgiving just because our stomachs happen to rumble on that day. A meal is a form of sharing. We become part of something by our eating.

Both the food we eat and the company we keep is part of our life with God and in the world. Jesus was regularly criticized for the company he kept at meals. In the New Testament church, what they ate and with whom they ate was one of the most counter-cultural witnesses in their world. Masters and slaves, rich and poor, Jews and Gentiles around the same table. In 1 Corinthians 10, Paul connects this well-known principle of meals as sharing with the Lord's Supper. The Lord's Supper, like all meals, is a place of fellowship and joining together. But unlike every meal, we have fellowship with the LORD at his Table.

It is not just what we eat, but with whom we eat that matters to God. At the table, he invites us to eat with him, to share in the body and blood of Christ, and be joined to Christ's body, the Church.

Prayer: *I rejoiced with those who said to me, "Let us go to the house of the LORD."* (Psalm 122:1 NIV)

Q78. Do the bread and wine become the real body and blood of Christ?

A. No. Just as the water of baptism is not changed into Christ's blood
and does not itself wash away sins but is simply a divine sign
and assurance of these things, so too the holy bread of the Lord's Supper
does not become the actual body of Christ, even though it is called the body of Christ
in keeping with the nature and language of sacraments.

Q79. Why then does Christ call the bread his body and the cup his blood,
or the new covenant in his blood, and Paul use the words,
a sharing in Christ's body and blood?

A. Christ has good reason for these words.
He wants to teach us that just as bread and wine nourish the temporal life,
so too his crucified body and poured-out blood
are the true food and drink of our souls for eternal life.
But more important, he wants to assure us, by this visible sign and pledge,
that we, through the Holy Spirit's work,
share in his true body and blood as surely as our mouths
receive these holy signs in his remembrance,
and that all of his suffering and obedience
are as definitely ours as if we personally
had suffered and made satisfaction for our sins.

DURING THE MIDDLE AGES, church services were conducted in Latin. However, some priests could not actually speak Latin, so when they led worship, they fumbled their way through the words. For instance, during the Lord's Supper, they were supposed to say, "Hoc est corpus meum" (this is my body), but it often came out sounding like "Hocus Pocus." This jumbled Latin phrase, Hocus Pocus, became associated with magic, because many people believed that something magic-like took place at the Lord's Table.

But what happens when we come to the Lord's Table? In most churches, though the details differ, words are spoken, prayers are prayed, bread is broken, a cup is poured, then the people of God are invited to eat. But what actually happens? Perhaps it is easier to start with what does not happen. The bread and wine do not change into something else. However, that is not to say that nothing happens. Christ nourishes us at the table. God truly feeds us, truly joins us to Christ, truly assures us of our belonging to him through the bread and the cup. God does all this without transforming the bread and cup at all. He does it through the work of the Holy Spirit. The Lord's Supper is not hocus pocus, but the gift of God for the people of God.

Prayer: *Blessed are those you choose and bring near to live in your courts! We are filled with the good things of your house, of your holy temple.* (Psalm 65:4 NIV)

The Bread & The Cup—Lord's Day 29—Monday

Read: Titus 3:4–7
"Real Baptism"

"It's LIKE MAGIC." THE entertainer appears to be floating. He pours a glass of water, waves his hands, and suddenly the water is transformed into something else. Magic. Is that how we should understand what is happening in baptism?

In Titus 3, we are told that God saved us through water. Water itself, even baptismal water, does not save. We are saved by the finished work of Christ, but God also says that "he saved us . . . through the water of rebirth" (v. 5). Water is an instrument in the hands of God ("by the Holy Spirit" v. 5) as a pledge of his promise to save us. God uses the simple waters of baptism to seal his promise upon us, to claim us as his own.

Baptism is not magic, but it is real. Through ordinary water, God acts in baptism to write his promise upon us, his promise to save us according to his mercy, not because of anything good we have done. God acts in baptism to pour out his Spirit upon us through Jesus Christ, so that we might become heirs of the hope of eternal life. Baptism is not magic, but it certainly is real, and the waters are an instrument in the hands of God.

Prayer: *Your righteousness, God, reaches to the heavens, you who have done great things. Who is like you, God?* (Psalm 71:19 NIV)

The Bread & The Cup—Lord's Day 29—Tuesday

Read: Mark 14:12–25
"Is"

JESUS SAID, "THIS IS my body" as he gave the bread to his disciples (v. 22). He said, "This is my blood," as he gave them the cup (v. 23). We repeat these words every time we celebrate the Lord's Supper. But what did Jesus mean? What does "is" mean?

"This is my body" means the bread exhibits Christ's body. As the catechism says, "just as bread and wine nourish the temporal life, so too his crucified body and poured-out blood are the true food and drink of our souls for eternal life" (Q79). We must truly be nourished by the flesh and blood of Christ unto eternal life. When we eat the bread and drink the cup, we are nourished by Christ. However, the bread and wine do not themselves change in any way. They never become anything but what they were before. Instead, in the meal, they become instruments by which the Holy Spirit causes us to share in and be nourished by the body and blood of Christ.

This is not an easy teaching to understand. Christians disagree what Jesus means when he says "is." While we await the day when Christ will make all things clear, let us hold our convictions with humility and grace.

Prayer: *The LORD lives! Praise be to my Rock! Exalted be God my Savior!* (Psalm 18:46 NIV)

The Bread & The Cup—Lord's Day 29—Wednesday

Read: Exodus 12:1–13
"Lord's Supper as Passover"

EVERY YEAR AFTER THAT first Passover in Egypt, God's people ate that meal together, remembering and reenacting that night. Rich in symbolism, Jesus chose that meal as the occasion for instituting the Lord's Supper.

In the Passover there was deliverance from death through the death of a perfect lamb. As God sent a final plague on Egypt, Israel took a spotless lamb, killed it, and spread its blood on the door posts. They ate lamb and bread without yeast, ready at any moment to leave. Those who rested under the bloody sign were saved. Just as the blood of a spotless lamb on the wooden doorposts caused the angel of death to pass over them, the blood of Jesus Christ on the wood of the cross frees from eternal death all who trust in him. At Passover, Jesus connects his own death to the death of the lamb and the liberation of God's people.

The Passover was a meal of joy and liberation. When we eat the bread and drink the cup of the Lord's Supper, we too participate in a meal of joy and liberation, where we proclaim that a lamb was slain to set us free, not just from Pharaoh, but from sin and death forevermore.

Prayer: *For you, LORD, have delivered me from death, my eyes from tears, my feet from stumbling.* (Psalm 116:8 NIV)

The Bread & The Cup—Lord's Day 29—Thursday

Read: Exodus 16
"Lord's Supper as Manna"

GOD FEEDS HIS PEOPLE. After leaving Egypt and crossing the Red Sea, the people of God came to the wilderness of Sin. They complained of hunger, remembering fondly their time in Egypt. They had quickly forgotten the whips of Pharaoh, their children thrown into the Nile, and God leading them out as they plundered the people, all because they were hungry. Yet, God graciously fed them. He fed the young and the old, the weak and the strong. He fed the grumblers and the mumblers. He fed the forgetful and the ungrateful. He fed and nourished sinners, every day, for forty years. There was always enough for them, including double in preparation for the Sabbath. He even gave them meat to eat when they complained of having only bread. God graciously feeds his people.

When we come to the Lord's Table, God again graciously feeds his people. The Table is set as an act of grace. Like Israel, it is not a meal we deserve, but one God graciously provides for us, nourishing and sustaining us as we walk in the wilderness. Like Israel, we who come are often weak or grumblers, and always sinners. Yet, God graciously feeds us day by day.

Prayer: *The LORD is my shepherd, I lack nothing. He makes me lie down in green pastures, he leads my beside quiet waters.* (Psalm 23:1–2 NIV)

The Bread & The Cup—Lord's Day 29—Friday

Read: Leviticus 3:1–5; 7:11–18
"Lord's Supper as Thanksgiving"

ONE OF THE SACRIFICES God gave to Israel was the Peace offering. Out of thanksgiving to God, the worshipper brought his offering, laid his hand on it, and slew it. The priest sprinkled blood on the altar and around it. The portion of the meat that belonged to God was placed upon the already burning altar. The priest took his portion (breast and right shoulder), while the worshipper took the rest home to eat with his family. The priest, the worshipper, and God (through fire) all consume the offering. The peace offering symbolized, through a meal, peace with God. It was a meal of fellowship and peace where God, priest, and worshipper eat together.

Jesus Christ fulfilled the peace offering. He is the offering itself, pouring out his life in service and thanksgiving to God. He is the priest, who serves at the altar as mediator. He is also the worshipper, placing his life on the altar in praise to the Father. At the Lord's Table, we are invited to a meal where, because of Christ's sacrifice of thanksgiving, we can celebrate our peace with God. When we leave the table, we can offer our lives as an echo of the great offering of Christ.

Prayer: *Praise the LORD. Give thanks to the LORD, for he is good; his love endures forever.* (Psalm 106:1 NIV)

The Bread & The Cup—Lord's Day 29—Saturday

Read: Exodus 24
"Lord's Supper as a Meal with God"

HOW DO YOU GET ready to sit down and eat a meal with your family? Perhaps you wash your hands, set out plates and cutlery, and open the meal with a prayer of thanks to God.

God desires to eat with his people. At the foot of Mount Sinai, God delivered the law, including the Ten Commandments. Afterward Moses, Aaron, his two sons Nadab and Abihu, and the seventy elders of Israel went up the mountain and beheld God. And then, we are told, "they ate and drank" (v. 11). When God summoned the leaders of Israel up onto Mount Sinai to come into his presence, they were to eat and drink. There was a meal up there on the mountain in the presence of God.

How would you get ready for a meal with God? Would you take the time to be washed, set the table, and offering a great prayer of thanksgiving? When we come to the Lord's Table for the Supper, we are like Moses, Aaron, and the elders, approaching the mountain for a meal with the LORD. Like the best of meals, it is a joyous event, but we should prepare our heart, our minds, and our bodies before we come.

Prayer: *Blessed are those whose strength is in you, whose hearts are set on pilgrimage.* (Psalm 84:5 NIV)

**Q80. How does the Lord's Supper
differ from the Roman Catholic Mass?**

A. The Lord's Supper declares to us
that all our sins are completely forgiven
through the one sacrifice of Jesus Christ,
which he himself accomplished on the cross once for all.
It also declares to us that the Holy Spirit grafts us into Christ,
who with his true body is now in heaven
at the right hand of the Father
where he wants us to worship him.
[But the Mass teaches
that the living and the dead
do not have their sins forgiven
through the suffering of Christ
unless Christ is still offered for them daily by the priests.
It also teaches that Christ is bodily present
under the form of bread and wine
where Christ is therefore to be worshiped.
Thus the Mass is basically nothing but a denial
of the one sacrifice and suffering of Jesus Christ
and a condemnable idolatry.]

Q81. Who should come to the Lord's table?

A. Those who are displeased with themselves
because of their sins,
but who nevertheless trust
that their sins are pardoned
and that their remaining weakness is covered
by the suffering and death of Christ,
and who also desire more and more
to strengthen their faith
and to lead a better life.
Hypocrites and those who are unrepentant, however,
eat and drink judgment on themselves.

**Q82. Should those be admitted to the Lord's Supper
who show by what they profess and how they live
that they are unbelieving and ungodly?**

A. No, that would dishonor God's covenant
and bring down God's wrath upon the entire congregation.
Therefore, according to the instruction of Christ and his apostles,
the Christian church is duty-bound to exclude such people,
by the official use of the keys of the kingdom,
until they reform their lives.

ONE OF THE STRENGTHS of the Heidelberg Catechism is its peaceful tone. However, Question 80 is one of the most controversial questions in the catechism. In some denominations, the second half of the answer has been removed. In others, there is a footnote explaining that this answer is a product of a particular historical period.

Why was this such an important issue when the catechism was written and should we still be concerned today? First, "Mass as sacrifice" denies the sufficiency of Christ's sacrifice, implying the cross was not enough for our forgiveness of sins. Jesus must be offered again and again on the altar. By contrast, Christ offered himself once for the sin of the whole world. No other sacrifice is needed. Second, "Mass as sacrifice" denies the finished nature of Jesus' work. Jesus' death on the cross was "once for all" both in the sense of being enough to cover sin, but also in the sense of being finished and completed. Hebrews explicitly teaches that though priests had previously offered sacrifices daily, Jesus the great High Priest offered a sacrifice once and now is seated at the right hand of the Father, his work being completed.

Though we should strive for peace with our neighbors and our brothers, there are times to engage in disagreement. There is much beauty, depth, and breadth to what God does through the sacrament of the Lord's Supper. However, it is not a re-sacrifice of Christ, for his one sacrifice on the cross is finished and enough for us.

Prayer: *Show us your unfailing love, LORD, and grand us your salvation.* (Psalm 85:7 NIV)

Coming to the Table—Lord's Day 30—Monday

Read: Isaiah 1:11–20

"Cleanse yourself"

WHAT DOES GOD DESIRE from us in order to enter his presence in worship?

Israel believed as long as they offered the right sacrifices, they could come to God in prayer and worship. Though they offered sweet smelling incense before the Lord, their lives were a stench in his nostrils. God proclaims that their hands are full of blood (v. 15) and that their incessant offerings were futile (v. 13), an abomination (v. 13), a burden to God (v. 14), and something God's soul hates (v. 14). God calls upon his people to wash themselves clean, to rid themselves of evil and do justice to the oppressed, orphan, and widow (vv. 16–17). God promises to make their scarlet sins white as snow. When our worship is sweet, but our lives a stench, we cannot come into the Lord's presence.

Christians can fall into the same delusional pattern as Israel did. We can believe that as long as we praise the Lord on Sunday, what we do Monday through Saturday does not matter. Isaiah's warning explains why churches have confession of sin prior to coming to the Lord's Table, but also why those who sin without remorse cannot come to the feast.

Prayer: *Do not hold against us the sins of past generations; may your mercy come quickly to meet us, for we are in desperate need.* (Psalm 79:8 NIV)

Coming to the Table—Lord's Day 30—Tuesday

Read: 1 Corinthians 11:17–34

"Discerning the Body"

SOMETIMES, THE ACTIONS OF the few affect everyone. It only takes one person in the family getting sick before we all have runny noses. In the church this is even more true, since we are bound together by Christ through the Spirit.

Paul is not impressed with how the Corinthians are celebrating the Lord's Supper. When they gather together, they are not truly together. They do not feast as one body in Christ. There are divisions and factions in the church, so that the unity proclaimed in the Supper seems a farce. There is inequality, such that some are rushing forward to eat, so that others go hungry. Their selfish neglect of their brothers and sisters shows "contempt for the church of God" (v. 22). Paul proclaims that their practice of the Lord's Supper is not an occasion for rejoicing, but for judgment. No true feast of God should leave one person full and another empty.

When we come to the Lord's Supper, we cannot eat without regard for our brother and sister. When we feast while our brothers and sisters go hungry, we fail to discern the body. Such an eating is not an occasion for celebration, but lament and judgment.

Prayer: *We have sinned, even as our ancestors did; we have done wrong and acted wickedly.* (Psalm 106:6 NIV)

Coming to the Table—Lord's Day 30—Wednesday

Read: Isaiah 55:1–5
"Come to the Feast"

"DINNER'S READY!" THERE IS a small scuffle over who gets what plate, but everyone is eager to eat. They come hungry and thirsty to the dinner table. Because they are hungry, they want to be there, to eat the good food, and to eat with the family.

The Lord's Table is for the hungry and thirsty. In the vision of Isaiah, he sees the thirsty, the penniless, and the hungry streaming to the LORD. They come penniless, with nothing to offer, and find themselves satisfied by the LORD. This is an image of the feast of the Lord's Table. All of us come penniless to the Table. We have nothing in ourselves to offer the Lord that we should deserve to feast with him, to be satisfied in his presence. Yet, the Lord says, "Come!" He invites us to come to him, to eat what is good, to delight in rich food, and to live.

When we come to the Lord's Table, we hear that God's feast is prepared for the hungry and thirsty. It is prepared for us, who are hungry for the presence of God, who thirst for the new heavens and the new earth, who bring nothing and receive everything.

Prayer: *Look to the LORD and his strength; seek his face always.* (Psalm 105:4 NIV)

Coming to the Table—Lord's Day 30—Thursday

Read: Colossians 3:1–4
"Where is Jesus?"

WHERE IS JESUS RIGHT now? More specifically, where is Jesus' body as you read this? One of the key differences between various branches of the Christian faith on the Lord's Supper is related to how we answer this question. Where is Jesus' body?

According to Scripture, Jesus is seated at the right hand of the Father in heaven. In Colossians 3, we are told to seek the things that are above, in heaven, not the things that are on earth. The logic goes like this: since we have been raised with Christ, our life is hidden in Christ. So, we are to fix our eyes on Christ. Christ has ascended into heaven and is seated at the right hand of the Father. Therefore, to fix our eyes on Christ, we need to look where he is. As a result, our minds should be set on heaven and on Christ who is in heaven.

At the Table, the Spirit brings us where Jesus is. The Reformed believe that we are brought into the presence of Jesus who remains at the right hand of the Father. By the power of the Spirit, we are brought "where Christ is, seated at the right hand of God" (v. 1).

Prayer: *Blessed are those you choose and bring near to live in your courts! We are filled with the good things of your house, of your holy temple.*
(Psalm 65:4 NIV)

Coming to the Table—Lord's Day 30—Friday

Read: Acts 2:42–47
"The Breaking of the Bread"

How OFTEN DO YOU have the Lord's Supper? Some churches do no more than the minimum their denomination requires out of fear that it will become less meaningful if done more frequently.

However, the Lord's Supper was practiced regularly and gladly in the early church. In Acts 2, the Church was characterized by four practices—devotion to the teaching of the apostles, fellowship, breaking of bread, and prayers. In addition to daily hearing God's word, praying, and "spending much time together" (v. 46), they broke bread—ate the Lord's Supper. This was not a casual or occasional practice, but something they were devoted to. They were committed and passionate about both the Lord's Word and the Lord's Table, both praying to Christ and feasting on Christ, both fellowship with one another and fellowship with Christ at the Table. Devoted to word, prayer, bread, and fellowship, "day by day the Lord added to their number those who were being saved" (v. 47).

As we consider our churches, how many of these four characteristics would we say our churches are "devoted to"? Hopefully, we will become as devoted to the breaking of the bread as we are to teaching of the apostles, to prayer, and to fellowship together.

Prayer: *As for me, I will always have hope; I will praise you more and more.* (Psalm 71:14 NIV)

Coming to the Table—Lord's Day 30—Saturday

Read: Hebrews 10:10–18
"Standing v. Sitting"

WHEN WE WORK ALL day, it is a relief to finally sit down. Being on our feet is a sign we are moving, working, getting things done. We sit once our work is done. Sitting is a position of rest and completion of our tasks.

Before Christ, day in and day out, the priests would offer sacrifices. They were always on their feet, always working because the sacrifices they offered were never enough. The priest "stands day after day" (v. 11) and never takes away sins. Their sacrifices pointed ahead to the one perfect sacrifice that would truly take away sins. Since Christ made that sacrifice, he can now sit down. While the priests stood day after day, Jesus is seated. He has offered himself once for all for sin, so there is no more need of an offering. There is no more need to stand, run, or work for the forgiveness of sins. Jesus has completed the work for us.

Jesus offered himself once for all and sat down. There is no need to offer more sacrifice or to offer Jesus again. Once was enough. We should rest in the finished work of our Lord and High Priest Jesus Christ, who is seated at the right hand of God.

Prayer: *Let your hand rest on the man at your right hand, the son of man you have raised up for yourself.* (Psalm 80:17 NIV)

Q83. What are the keys of the kingdom?

A. The preaching of the holy gospel
    and Christian discipline toward repentance.
    Both of them
    open the kingdom of heaven to believers
    and close it to unbelievers.

**Q84. How does preaching the holy gospel
open and close the kingdom of heaven?**

A. According to the command of Christ:
    The kingdom of heaven is opened
    by proclaiming and publicly declaring
    to all believers, each and every one,
    that as often as they accept the gospel promise in true faith,
    God, because of Christ's merit, truly forgives all their sins.
    The kingdom of heaven is closed, however,
    by proclaiming and publicly declaring
    to unbelievers and hypocrites that,
    as long as they do not repent,
    the wrath of God and eternal condemnation rest on them.
    God's judgment,
    both in this life and in the life to come,
    is based on this gospel testimony.

**Q85. How is the kingdom of heaven
closed and opened by Christian discipline?**

A. According to the command of Christ:
    Those who, though called Christians,
    profess unchristian teachings or live unchristian lives,
    and who after repeated personal and loving admonition
    refuse to abandon their error and evil ways,
    and who after being reported to the church, that is,
    to those ordained by the church for that purpose,
    fail to respond also to the church's admonitions—
    such persons the church excludes from the Christian community
    by withholding the sacraments from them,
    and God also excludes them from the kingdom of Christ.
    Such persons,
    when promising and demonstrating genuine reform,
    are received again
    as members of Christ
    and of his church.

Just because some group calls itself a church, does that make it part of the one true church of Christ? The consistent answer throughout Christian history has been "No." Though not everything a church is, certain things mark this gathered group of people as a part of the true church.

The Reformers discerned three marks of the true church: Word, Sacrament, and Discipline. First, the Word of God is plainly preached. Where the gospel of Jesus Christ is proclaimed, there is a church. No matter how much good a group accomplishes, there is no church if there is no gospel. Second, the sacraments are rightfully administered. Baptism and the Lord's Supper are signs and seals of the gospel promise. When absent or twisted, we do not have a true church. Lastly, discipline is practiced. Those called Christians, but who profess unchristian teachings or live unchristian lives, are to be corrected for their own good and the good of the church. When discipline is neglected, we lie and do not live the truth as a community. The church is marked by Word, Sacrament, and Discipline. To lose any of the three is to cease to be a true church.

There is only one true Church, the Church of Jesus Christ. In the church, Jesus Christ is held forth clothed in his gospel—the gospel proclaimed in word, signified and sealed in the sacraments, and applied through discipline. There the Church of Christ is found.

Prayer: *As the mountains surround Jerusalem, so the LORD surrounds his people both now and forevermore.* (Psalm 125:2 NIV)

The Keys of the Kingdom—Lord's Day 31—Monday

Read: Matthew 16:13–23
"Keys of the Kingdom"

WE USE KEYS TO lock and unlock doors. A key can lock a door and prevent someone from coming in, but it can also be used to unlock a door to invite someone into your home.

Peter makes a proclamation: Jesus is the Messiah, the Son of God. Jesus calls Peter blessed, saying this was not revealed to Peter by humans, but by the Father. He renames Peter, saying on the rock of Peter's confession, the church would be built. In this response, Jesus promises to give Peter the keys to the kingdom. Like keys unlocking a door, Peter's proclamation of the gospel will open the door to the kingdom for those who hear it. Like keys locking a door, the proclamation of God's word will also firmly bind those who reject Christ and refuse to turn to him in faith. The preaching of the gospel locks and unlocks the kingdom as it proclaims both the promises and judgment of God.

The church has been given the keys to the kingdom in the preaching of the gospel. When we share the good news of Jesus Christ with others, we open up to them the kingdom of God, so that they can enter in through faith in Jesus.

Prayer: *How sweet are your words to my taste, sweeter than honey to my mouth.* (Psalm 119:103 NIV)

The Keys of the Kingdom—Lord's Day 31—Tuesday

Read: John 21:1–19
"The Power of Forgiveness"

DO WE TRULY BELIEVE that being forgiven can change someone's life? As the Danish philosopher Søren Kierkegaard wondered, "But why, I wonder, is forgiveness so rare? Is it not, I wonder, because faith in the power of forgiveness is so small and so rare? . . . Yet, if you yourself have ever needed forgiveness, then you know what forgiveness accomplishes."

Peter had blown it. When Jesus said all his disciples would flee, Peter said, "Not me! I will never leave you!" Yet, three times Peter denied ever knowing Jesus. Could he still be forgiven? After Jesus rose, Peter went back to fishing and brought many of the other disciples with him. Jesus calls to Peter who rushes to shore. Just as three times Peter had denied he knew Jesus, three times Jesus asks, "Do you love me?" When Peter answers "Yes," Jesus calls Peter to feed his sheep. Peter has been restored. Jesus forgives him and again invites Peter to follow Jesus.

Proclaiming the forgiveness found in Jesus is one of the most powerful acts of the church. When we, like Peter, know we need to be forgiven, forgiveness can change our life.

Prayer: *When we were overwhelmed by sins, you forgave our transgressions.* (Psalm 65:3 NIV)

The Keys of the Kingdom—Lord's Day 31—Wednesday

Read: Matthew 18:15–20

"It's personal"

WHEN SOMEONE HURTS YOU, who do you talk to? It is best, if possible, to talk with the person directly. This avoids the dangerous sin of gossip, but also is the quickest and most loving way to deal with the problem.

When someone sins against us, Jesus tells us to begin by talking face to face, personally and privately. Sins cuts us off from each other and requires restoration. Point out the sin person to person. If they listen to you, you have regained them. However, Jesus tells us this will not always work. Then, we bring one or two others along as witnesses (often elders in the church). If this fails, the sin should be publicly addressed before the church.

In Jesus' teaching, there are two important lessons for the church. First, sin must be addressed. Jesus does not give us the possibility that we ignore or dismiss the sins done against us. It can be named and forgiven, but should not be ignored. Second, the problem of sin is serious enough we should be willing to involve others. For the sake of our brother or sister, the hurt must be healed, the sin must be covered.

Prayer: *Then I acknowledged my sin to you and did not cover up my iniquity. I said, "I will confess my transgressions to the LORD." And you forgave the guilt of my sin.* (Psalm 32:5 NIV)

The Keys of the Kingdom—Lord's Day 31—Thursday

Read: Romans 10:14–17

"Proclaiming Christ"

AT SOME POINT, SOMEONE told you about Jesus. It might have been a parent around the table, a Sunday school teacher on flannel graph, a friend over coffee, or a stranger on the street. Since the resurrected Christ first sent his apostles to be witnesses to Jerusalem, Judea, Samaria, and the ends of the earth, God has been using ordinary people to share the good news of Christ.

Romans 10 speaks of the great chain of communication that moves from the sending God to the believing heart. To call upon Christ for salvation, we must believe. To believe, we must hear. To hear, we must have someone to proclaim Christ. To proclaim Christ, there must be those who are sent. God sends, the sent proclaim, the proclamation is heard, the hearers believe, and the believers call upon Christ in faith. God sends out his messengers and the fruit is faith and salvation.

In his mysterious mercy, God chooses to use ordinary men and women to share the good news. God chooses to use people like you to share Christ with others. What a privilege! What a responsibility! What a joy! "As it is written, 'How beautiful are the feet of those who bring good news!'" (v. 15).

Prayer: *My mouth will tell of your righteous deeds, of your saving acts all day long—though I know not how to relate them all.* (Psalm 71:15 NIV)

The Keys of the Kingdom—Lord's Day 31—Friday

Read: 1 Corinthians 5:9–13
"Live like you know Jesus"

WE SHOULD NOT EXPECT people who do not know Jesus to live like they know Jesus. However, once we have come to faith in Jesus, we can be expected to live differently.

Christians have different expectations for fellow Christians than for unbelievers. We should not try to hide ourselves away from the world in a hope to stay pure. If we never spent time with immoral people, we would "need to go out of the world" (v. 10). We would need to live on another planet! The world does not know Jesus and does not live as if it does. However, we should not associate with people who call themselves Christians, but who live in obvious, unrepentant sin. These are Christians who know their sin and intentionally continue to live in it. If we know Jesus, we should live like we know him. This is not an expectation of perfection, but of integrity. As disciples, our lives should match up with the teaching of Jesus. Refusing his way, but calling him Lord, is dishonest.

We should not expect people who do not know Jesus to live like they know Jesus. However, we should expect those who bear the name of Jesus to live as if he is their true Lord and Savior. None will be perfectly holy, but we should daily strive for holiness before our holy and gracious God.

Prayer: *How can a young person stay on the path of purity? By living according to your word.* (Psalm 119:9 NIV)

The Keys of the Kingdom—Lord's Day 31—Saturday

Read: 2 Corinthians 2:1–11
"Restoring through forgiveness"

WHENEVER I HAVE TO discipline my children, I tell them, "I do not want to do this, but I am doing this because I love you." Discipline—correcting my children—is an important part of being a parent, but it is not fun. However, I do it for their sake, because I love them.

The state of the church in Corinth has been causing Paul pain. He sees the state of their moral and spiritual life and knows he must write to them. The goal of Paul's writing and anguished tears is not the sorrow and pain of the church in Corinth, but their restoration through forgiveness. He wants to test them and to call them to obedience, but also for them to love and forgive. "So I urge you to reaffirm your love for him . . . Anyone whom you forgive, I also forgive. What I have forgiven, if I have forgiven anything, has been for your sake in the presence of Christ" (vv. 8, 10). Though their relationship was strained, Paul longs for them to be forgiven.

The goal of correction should always be forgiveness and restoration. We do not correct to cause pain for its own sake, but when correction brings pain, the ultimate goal is love, restoration, and forgiveness.

Prayer: *Blessed is the one you discipline, LORD, the one you teach from your law.* (Psalm 94:12 NIV)

Q86. Since we have been delivered
    from our misery
    by grace through Christ
    without any merit of our own,
    why then should we do good works?
A. Because Christ, having redeemed us by his blood,
    is also restoring us by his Spirit into his image,
    so that with our whole lives
    we may show that we are thankful to God
    for his benefits,
    so that he may be praised through us,
    so that we may be assured of our faith by its fruits,
    and so that by our godly living
    our neighbors may be won over to Christ.

Q87. Can those be saved
    who do not turn to God
    from their ungrateful
    and unrepentant ways?
A. By no means.
    Scripture tells us that
    no unchaste person,
    no idolater, adulterer, thief,
    no covetous person,
    no drunkard, slanderer, robber,
    or the like
    will inherit the kingdom of God.

Do we need to clean ourselves before we come to Christ? Absolutely not. As the old hymn says, "if you tarry til you're better, then you'll never come at all." Christ does not save us because of our goodness, but because of his. If it was up to us, none of us would be able to come and stand in God's presence. Yet, Jesus made a way for us, "delivered us from our misery," and "redeemed us by his blood."

Can we claim Christ and then continue to live in sin? Absolutely not. Turning to Christ means turning away from all ways contrary to the kingdom of Christ. Christians will never be completely sinless in this life, but knowingly and willfully to continue in sinful behavior is incompatible with Christian faith.

The Heidelberg Catechism seeks to hold these two biblical truths together as it calls for Christians to perform good works out of gratitude to God. We do not do good works in order to be saved, but because we are saved. Good works show our thankfulness to God for all that he has given us in Christ. Conversely, the refusal to walk in the ways of Christ is a refusal of Christ.

Prayer: *I will praise the LORD all my life; I will sing praise to my God as long as I live.*
(Psalm 146:2 NIV)

Works of Gratitude—Lord's Day 32—Monday

Read: Romans 6:1–14
"Not slaves to sin, but to righteousness"

EVERYBODY SERVES SOMETHING. LOOK at where we invest our time and energy, and we will find what we serve. We were made to serve, but because of the sin of our first parents, we are born trapped into service to sin. We invest our lives serving ourselves or serving selfish ends. We are trapped under the power of sin and unable to get ourselves out.

If you were finally free from this bondage, would you just go back? No, of course not. Finally free from sin, we would never want to go back. We would want to be free. The death and resurrection of Jesus Christ has taken us from service to sin to service to God. Serving God is true freedom. Christ's death broke the power of sin over us so that we no longer need to offer our lives over to sin, but can now live for God and "present your members to God as instruments of righteousness" (v. 13).

Everybody serves something. Freedom is found in serving the LORD who does good to us in all his ways. In Christ, we no longer need to serve selfish ends that only lead to more bondage. Instead, we can serve God, where true freedom is found.

Prayer: *Rescue me, LORD, from evildoers; protect me from the violent.*
(Psalm 140:1 NIV)

Works of Gratitude—Lord's Day 32—Tuesday

Read: Matthew 5:13–16
"Let others see your good works"

JESUS CALLS THE CHURCH "salt." In Jesus' time, salt was used to preserve, to purify, and to flavor. Similarly, disciples should preserve, purify, and flavor the world around them. Crucially, they salt *the world around them*. Salt is not being salt when it's left in the shaker, but it does its best work when put in food. In the same way, the church is blessed for the sake of the world around them. We are blessed to be a blessing to others. We are the salt of the earth in order to be salt *for* the earth.

In John, Jesus says, "I am the light of the world." Yet here, he tells us, "you are the light of the world." Jesus, the true light of the world, has "lit our lamps." He made us to reflect his light to the world. Jesus says that after lighting our lamps, he is not going to put us under a bushel basket—where we cannot shine, where we won't be seen. Light is made to be seen. Jesus put us on the lamp stand. He is promising us that he will make our witness effective. He will make it so that our light goes to all in the house, to all the world.

Prayer: *I wait for your salvation, LORD, and I follow your commands.*
(Psalm 119:166 NIV)

Works of Gratitude—Lord's Day 32—Wednesday

Read: Galatians 5:13–26

"True Freedom"

WHAT IS FREEDOM FOR? We might think of being free *from* something. When I say I am free from class tomorrow, I am saying I am no longer stuck in the classroom all day. Freedom can mean nothing is holding you back, but you are free to do anything. Yet, true freedom is also freedom *for* something. Being free tomorrow afternoon also means I am free to meet with you. Freedom has a purpose. It is not about being able to do anything, but now being able to do the right thing.

We are not just freed *from* sin, death, and the devil, but now have the freedom *for* walking in the Spirit. Paul lists all we are free from including twisted and selfish sexuality, false and wicked worship, bitter and rampant conflicts, as well as a lack of self-control of our bodies, tongues, and emotions. Freedom in Jesus means no longer being stuck in that way of life. We are free *from* it. Yet, we are not freed from sin so we can live however we please. Instead, now we are free *for* "love, joy, peace, patience, kindness, generosity, faithfulness, gentleness, and self-control" (vv. 22–23). Living in freedom is not something we do only in our hearts, but also in our lives. In Christ, we have been set free from a life lived in the flesh, with all that it looks like. However, that freedom means we are now free to live in the Spirit.

Does your life show that Christ has set you free? Christian freedom is not just being free from sin, but being free to pursue righteousness and the fruit of the Spirit.

Prayer: *Redeem me from human oppression, that I may obey your precepts.* (Psalm 119:134 NIV)

Works of Gratitude—Lord's Day 32—Thursday

Read: Ephesians 5:1–12

"No inheritance in the Kingdom of God"

WHY MENTION *THESE* SINS? Because they were somehow worse than any other sins, or the only ones that matter? No. So why mention these sins? Because the world of the first century did not recognize them as sins, they needed to be named as what they are: sin.

Saying there should be "not even a hint of sexual immorality" in the church erected a standard the ordinary Greek would never have dreamed of. Moderation? Yes. Avoid extremes? Absolutely. But forbid altogether? Crazy. The Greeks and Romans had a sense of right and wrong, but one shaped by common convention, not by God.

Is our world so different? We too can be guided more by convention than God. We rightly name some actions as evil and firmly reject them, but other things, we can take it so lightly that it seems to be no sin at all. The obvious sins might not need as much attention as those that slip by unnoticed or receive praise from the wider culture.

Apart from Christ, our sins leave us hopeless and in darkness, but in Christ we find forgiveness for our smallest and deepest sins. Scripture names our sin in order to lead us to light of Christ.

Prayer: *All your words are true; all your righteous laws are eternal.* (Psalm 119:160 NIV)

Works of Gratitude—Lord's Day 32—Friday

Read: Romans 12:1–3
"Living Sacrifices"

GROWING UP, MEAT CAME from the grocery store. I never thought about an animal dying so I could eat. I knew it in my head, but felt quite removed from the whole process.

When we hear the phrase "offer yourselves as living sacrifices," we are often so removed from the process that something is lost. What happened when animals were sacrificed and how might it connect to "living sacrifices"? First, the animal was killed, its life offered completely. As living sacrifices, we are to offer our lives completely to God. Afterward, the animal is cut up, separated into pieces, and part (or all) of it is placed on the altar and consumed by fire. The offering is turned into smoke that comes before the presence of the LORD. Christians hear the Word of the Lord, which is sharper than any two-edge sword. By God's Word and Spirit we are cut apart and transformed, then brought up into the presence of God. This is the life of worship: offering, cut apart by the word, transformed by the Spirit, and then brought into the presence of God.

Presenting our bodies as a living sacrifice will change us. By Word and Spirit we will not be the same after the offering.

Prayer: *Turn my eyes away from worthless things; preserve my life according to your word.* (Psalm 119:37 NIV)

Works of Gratitude—Lord's Day 32—Saturday

Read: 1 Peter 2:11–12
"Honorable Conduct"

NOT EVERYONE WILL ALWAYS like us. Jesus tells his disciples that they will be persecuted and hated because of their association with him. The book of Acts shows the truth of what Jesus said, and the letters of the New Testament include encouragement to believers who are hated and facing persecution. However, if we are disliked, let it never be because of our bad behavior. "Conduct yourselves honorably among the Gentiles" (v. 12). We must act with integrity, honesty, and honor in all we do. Our life may be a form of witness to the world: "they may see your honorable deeds and glorify God" (v. 12). At the very least it will mean that when people reject us, it will be because of Christ, not because we deserve it.

The way we live can never substitute for proclaiming the message of Jesus Christ. Yet, an honorable and upstanding life is a part of the witness we have in the world. When people do reject us, it should cause us first to take a look at our lives and whether we are acting honorably.

Prayer: *Then I will teach transgressors your ways, so that sinners will turn back to you.* (Psalm 51:13 NIV)

Q88. What is involved in genuine repentance or conversion?

A. Two things:

> the dying-away of the old self,
> and the rising-to-life of the new.

Q89. What is the dying-away of the old self?

A. To be genuinely sorry for sin

> and more and more to hate
> and run away from it.

Q90. What is the rising-to-life of the new self?

A. Wholehearted joy in God through Christ

> and a love and delight to live
> according to the will of God
> by doing every kind of good work.

Q91. What are good works?

A. Only those which

> are done out of true faith,
> conform to God's law,
> and are done for God's glory;
> and not those based
> on our own opinion or human tradition.

THE FIRST OF MARTIN Luther's Ninety-Five Theses that sparked the Protestant Reformation was "When our Lord and Teacher Jesus Christ said, 'Repent, etc.,' he meant that the entire life of believers be a life of repentance." Luther later remarked that people typically go through three conversions: the conversion of the heart, mind, and wallet. We first surrender our hearts to Christ, then our minds, before finally surrendering our wallets. Repentance is not a one-time event, but should characterize the life of the Christian.

The word "repentance" carries the sense of stopping and turning in the opposite direction. The Heidelberg Catechism (following Scripture) calls this a type of death. We stop living that old life. Genuine repentance calls for "the dying-way of the old self." But because repentance is not just stopping, but turning around, it also includes "the rising-to-life of the new." Repentance is the end of life in ourselves and the beginning of life in God.

The catechism places repentance in the section on Gratitude. Repentance is not optional, but neither is it the grounds of our acceptance before God. We trust in the finished work of Christ. Repentance involves the steady, daily surrender of our hearts, our minds, and even our money and possessions to Jesus.

Prayer: *I say to the LORD, "You are my God." Hear, LORD, my cry for mercy.* (Psalm 140:6 NIV)

The Life of Repentance—Lord's Day 33—Monday

Read: Ephesians 4:17–24
"Putting off the old self"

SOMETIMES YOUNG MEN DO a "sniff test" of discarded clothing. Running late for class, you glance at the dirty clothing around your room, find the cleanest looking shirt, smell it, and if it isn't too bad you slip it on and get going. Mothers everywhere cry out, "You have clean clothes, why aren't you wearing them?"

Having come to faith in Christ, the Ephesians had taken off their old way of living and put on the new clothes of life in Christ. Yet life became difficult and the next thing they know they are looking on the floor, sniffing those old clothes, considering those old ways of sin and then slipping that dirty shirt on again and walking out into the world.

Do we ever find ourselves looking back at those old temptations, checking them out then putting them on again? We've all done the sniff test with our sins, we've all turned back and grabbed that old dirty shirt off the floor and put it on. The command is this: put off that old stuff, trash it and clean out the closet, no longer make it a part of your wardrobe. Instead, put on the clean new clothes you have been given by Jesus.

Prayer: *You turned by wailing into dancing; you removed my sackcloth and clothed me with joy.* (Psalm 30:11 NIV)

The Life of Repentance—Lord's Day 33—Tuesday

Read: 2 Corinthians 7:9–13
"Godly Repentance"

MY DAUGHTER SAID SHE was sorry only after I took away her favorite doll as a punishment. Is she actually sorry she hurt her brother or only sorry her doll is taken away? In other words, is she sorry for what she did or sorry she is suffering the consequences?

There is a difference between godly grief and worldly grief. Worldly grief is feeling sorry for ourselves. We may feel some remorse or sorrow over what we have done, but we are really sorry that we are experiencing negative consequences for our actions. Worldly grief has one by-product: death (v. 10). It does not truly lead us to turn from sin and cling to Jesus and so leaves us spiritually dead. Godly grief is sorrow for our sins themselves and how they have offended the honor of God. This grief "produces a repentance that leads to salvation" (v. 10). It fills us with an eagerness to be cleared of wrongdoing and a disgust at our sin. The difference between being sorry for ourselves and sorry for our sin (worldly grief and godly grief) is the difference between death and life.

Whenever we fall into sin, we should take a moment to examine our hearts. Why are we sorry? Then we should turn away from our sin in repentance and toward Jesus Christ who gives us grace.

Prayer: *My sacrifice, O God, is a broken spirit; a broken and contrite heart you, God, will not despise.* (Psalm 51:17 NIV)

The Life of Repentance—Lord's Day 33—Wednesday

Read: Psalm 51

"Repentance, Forgiveness, Restoration"

WHEN DAVID'S SIN SEEMS finally buried, the prophet Nathan shows up at his doorstep. After hearing the prophet's story, David seethes, "as the Lord lives, the man who has done this deserves to die" (2 Samuel 12:5). "You are the man" (2 Samuel 12:7), Nathan says. David's response to his recognition of his sin is the prayer of Psalm 51.

The whole world may think we are doing fine, but we are broken and simply cannot fix ourselves. David knows this about himself: "Wash me. Cleanse me. Purge me. Blot out my transgressions." He knows what he needs and where to go: "Create in me a clean heart, O God, and put a new and right spirit within me" (v. 10). David is saying, "God, I can't do it. If I'm ever to have a clean heart, ever to be cleansed, ever to be whole and holy, you need to do it." "Against you, you alone, have I sinned, and done what is evil in your sight" (v. 4), and you alone can cleanse, forgive, and restore me.

Psalm 51 draws us into the larger story of God's redemption. Through Jesus, God has provided for our cleansing, our purging, our washing, our forgiveness and new life through the cross.

Prayer: *Hide your face from my sins, and blot out all my iniquity.*
(Psalm 51:9 NIV)

The Life of Repentance—Lord's Day 33—Thursday

Read: Ezekiel 37:1–14

"The rising-to-life of the new"

DISCIPLESHIP INVOLVES DYING. BORN in sin, our natural desires are bent away from God. Growing in Christ includes putting to death all those old ways, desires, and habits. We die to our old self. However, the goal of the Christian life is not death.

God brings the dead to life. In the days of Ezekiel, the people of Israel seemed all but dead. They had sinned so grievously that they had been stripped away, cut off from the land, and taken into Babylon. God sent Ezekiel to a valley of dry bones to prophesy. God put sinews, flesh, and skin on those dead bones and breathed into them the breath of life. In the same way, God will revive the people of Israel, bringing the dead nation back to life.

God does the same to us. Our dry bones are being given sinews, flesh, and skin, that we might no longer live for ourselves, but for God. What God will one day do to our physical bodies (resurrection), he already begins to do now in our spirit, bringing those dead in sin to be alive in Christ. The goal of the Christian life is life. Dying to sin ends in fullness of life.

Prayer: *But God will redeem me from the realm of the dead; he will surely take me to himself.*
(Psalm 49:15 NIV)

The Life of Repentance—Lord's Day 33—Friday

Read: Romans 6:1–11
"Dead to sin, Alive to God"

IN SOME SENSE, CHRISTIANS are always dead and alive. We are constantly dying to sin. We are also being raised to new life, finding joy in God, longing to serve him, and loving our neighbor.

Christians are both dead and alive because we have been joined to Jesus Christ. Jesus was crucified. Our old self, our old way of life, has been nailed to the cross with him. Jesus has died. We have died with him and our slavery to sin has ended. Jesus was buried. We were buried with him in baptism. He was raised. We have been raised with him, set free from bondage to sin to walk in newness of life. The key moments of Christ's passion—crucifixion, death, and burial—were all for us. His death changes who we are. The most important death of our life we have already died in Jesus. In the same way, his resurrection changes who we are. Life, freedom, and victory were accomplished when Jesus rose and we are raised with him.

What Jesus Christ has done changes who we are. We are dead and alive. The whole of our selves has died with Christ and the whole of our selves has been raised with him.

Prayer: *Direct my footsteps according to your word; let no sin rule over me.* (Psalm 119:133 NIV)

The Life of Repentance—Lord's Day 33—Saturday

Read: Ephesians 2:1–10
"Dead in Trespasses, Raised with Christ"

THE DEAD STAY DEAD. Whenever a story speaks of the dead walking, we recognize it as unnatural, even classify it as horror. Because it's the way the world works—the dead stay dead.

However, the dead come to life when God is at work. Those dead in sin are raised with Christ. Apart from him, we remain lifeless, hopeless, and trapped in sin. "For by grace you have been saved through faith, and this is not your own doing; it is the gift of God" (v. 8). God pours out his life-giving grace upon us as a gift, and the call to us is to receive it in faith. Life and Salvation is grace and we receive this gift by trusting in the gift-giver—Jesus Christ. This work of grace, this power of God, this life is available for all in Jesus Christ, extended to each and every one of us and calls for our faith and trust in God's grace.

By faith in Christ, the dead do not stay dead. We receive Christ and are joined with his life. We who were dead are now made alive in Jesus Christ. God's grace is poured out to us that we might drink of it through faith.

Prayer: *Let your face shine upon your servant; save me in your unfailing love.* (Psalm 31:16 NIV)

Q92. What is God's law?
A. God spoke all these words:

> THE FIRST COMMANDMENT
> "I am the Lord your God, who brought you of the land of Egypt, out of the house of slavery, you shall have no other gods before me."
> THE SECOND COMMANDMENT
> "You shall not make for yourself an idol, whether in the form of anything that is in heaven above, or that is on the earth beneath, or that is in the water under the earth. You shall not bow down to them or worship them; for I the Lord your God am a jealous God, punishing children for the iniquity of the parents, to the third and fourth generation of those who reject me, but showing love to the thousandth generation of those who love me and keep my commandments."
> THE THIRD COMMANDMENT
> "You shall not make wrongful use of the name of the Lord your God, for the Lord will not acquit anyone who misuses his name."
> THE FOURTH COMMANDMENT
> "Remember the sabbath day, and keep it holy. Six days you shall labor and do all your work. But the seventh day is a sabbath to the Lord your God; you shall not do any work—you, your son or your daughter, your male or female slave, your livestock, or the alien resident in your towns. For in six days the Lord made heaven and earth, the sea, and all that is in them, but rested the seventh day; therefore the Lord blessed the sabbath day and consecrated it."
> THE FIFTH COMMANDMENT
> "Honor your father and your mother, so that your days may be long in the land the Lord your God is giving to you."
> THE SIXTH COMMANDMENT
> "You shall not murder."
> THE SEVENTH COMMANDMENT
> "You shall not commit adultery."
> THE EIGHTH COMMANDMENT
> "You shall not steal."
> THE NINTH COMMANDMENT
> "You shall not bear false witness against your neighbor."
> THE TENTH COMMANDMENT
> "You shall not covet your neighbor's house; you shall not covet your neighbor's wife, or male or female slave, or ox, or donkey, or anything that belongs to your neighbor."

Q93. How are these commandments divided?
A. Into two tables.

> The first has four commandments,
> teaching us how we ought to live in relation to God.

The second has six commandments,
teaching us what we owe our neighbor.

Q94. What does the Lord require
in the first commandment?

A. That I, not wanting to endanger my own salvation,
avoid and shun
all idolatry, sorcery, superstitious rites,
and prayer to saints or other creatures.
That I rightly know the only true God,
trust him alone,
and look to God for every good thing
humbly and patiently,
and love, fear, and honor God
with all my heart.
In short,
that I give up anything
rather than go against God's will in any way.

Q95. What is idolatry?

A. Idolatry is
having or inventing something in which one trusts
in place of or alongside of the only true God,
who has revealed himself in the Word.

A COUPLE MONTHS INTO dating, my wife (then girlfriend) invited me to the Netherlands to meet her extended family. I felt nervous, wanting to make a good impression. Years later, after we were married, when she suggested a similar trip, it was a completely different experience. The first time felt like I was auditioning to be part of the family, but the second time I was already in the family.

It matters when someone asks us to do something. God did not give these commandments to Israel when they were still in Egypt and say, "Keep these commandments and I will rescue you." The Ten Commandments were given to the people after God saved them from Egypt. They are still commandments. God still calls for obedience to them and it is a sin to break them. However, the context is different. We are not auditioning to be part of the family, we are already in the family.

The Heidelberg Catechism places the Ten Commandments in its teaching on gratitude. Certainly, the Ten Commandments convict us of our sin, since none of us keeps them perfectly. However, they are also instructions for how Christians are to walk in this world. Like when they were first given, the catechism places these commandments in the context of grace as part of our lived gratitude to God for redeeming us. As those brought into God's family by grace, these commandments are God's will for how we are to live in that family.

Prayer: *Let your compassion come to me that I may live, for your law is my delight.*
(Psalm 119:77 NIV)

Trusting the True God—Lord's Day 34—Monday

Read: Exodus 19
"Israel's Mission"

AT THE FOOT OF Mount Sinai, right before giving the Ten Commandments, God gave Israel her mission. Like a bride, God had carried Israel up out of Egypt and brought them to himself. Israel is to be the bride of the LORD, the one he has chosen for himself. Israel is to be "priestly kingdom" and a "holy nation" (v. 6). Priests led people in worship of God, instructed them in God's word, and by their life showed forth the character of God. The whole nation was to worship, to instruct in God's word, and to live so that the world would know the LORD. As a holy nation, Israel was set apart by God to walk in the God's ways and honoring him with their lives. Israel was also holy, set apart from the nations, with a unique place in God's world.

In 1 Peter 2:9–10, the same language of Israel's mission is applied to the church. We are to be a royal priesthood and holy nation. We are to show the world what God is like by our worship, word, and walk. It is in this context that the LORD originally gave Israel the Ten Commandments, as part of his instructions for living out their mission.

Prayer: *You are my portion, LORD; I have promised to obey your words.* (Psalm 119:57 NIV)

Trusting the True God—Lord's Day 34—Tuesday

Read: Matthew 22:37–40
"Two Tables"

WHEN ASKED FOR THE greatest commandment, Jesus gave not one, but two. This was a typical convention in Jesus' day. Everyone agreed the greatest commandment was to love the LORD. The debate concerned the second greatest commandment. In Jesus' answer, he draws together the whole teaching of the Bible and rightly summarizes the Ten Commandments.

For centuries Christians have divided the Ten Commandments along the lines of the two great commandments. We are to love God and to love our neighbor. Christians have called these the "two tables" of the Ten Commandments, though this did not correspond to the two tablets Moses took from Mount Sinai. Both those tablets had complete copies of the commandments on them. Instead, we speak of "first table" of the law, because the first four commandments help us keep the first great commandment to love God. The "second table" are the last six commandments, which deal with our relationship with our neighbor.

When Jesus gave two answers to the one question, "What is the greatest commandment?" he gave us a guide for all of God's commandments. Love of God and love of neighbor hold together all the specific instructions that God gives to us in his word, including the Ten Commandments.

Prayer: *The earth is filled with your love, LORD, teach me your decrees.* (Psalm 119:64 NIV)

Trusting the True God—Lord's Day 34—Wednesday

Read: Revelation 19:9–16
"Worship the Creator, Not Creatures"

BEHOLDING SOMETHING GLORIOUS, WE have the urge to worship. Even non-religious people feel tugged by the beauty of a sunset, the ocean, or the mountains. We see something glorious and we want to worship. This is because we were made to worship the truly Glorious One, the LORD Most High.

While we are tempted to worship creation, we are only to worship the Creator. When John was on Patmos, he came face to face with an angel of God. John then fell at his feet to worship him. However, the angel rebuked him. The angel was a servant of the LORD just like John, only the LORD himself was worthy of worship. John was to worship God, not the angel. It was then that heaven opened, and John saw the King of Kings and Lord of Lords. Then, John could bow down and worship the true King.

The great temptation of humankind is to worship creation instead of the Creator. We are tempted to bow down and place our trust in something less, something other than the one true God. No matter how beautiful, powerful, or glorious something is in creation, we should not give to it what only God deserves: our life and our worship.

Prayer: *Praise the LORD. Praise the LORD from the heavens; praise him in the heights above.* (Psalm 148:1 NIV)

Trusting the True God—Lord's Day 34—Thursday

Read: John 17:1–19
"Rightly come to know the holy true God and trust in him alone"

SAYING "NO" IS PART of being a parent. No, you cannot touch the stove. No, you cannot cross the street without me. However, every "No" also has something positive in mind for the children, such as their safety, maturity, or health.

Why did God give us the first commandment? "You shall have no other gods before me." It is not just so that we would say "no" to idols, but so that we could come to rightly know God and trust him alone. In John 17:3, Jesus says, "And this is eternal life, that they may know you, the only true God, and Jesus Christ whom you have sent." Jesus revealed the Father and when we trust in Jesus Christ, we know the Father. The goal of rejecting idols is so that we could come to know the true God, to know Jesus Christ, and have eternal life. God commands us to shun other gods for our good.

God gives us a negative command ("No idols") for the sake of a positive good (knowing God). We keep the first commandment when we put our trust nowhere else, but come to know God truly in Jesus Christ.

Prayer: *Worship the LORD in the splendor of his holiness; tremble before him, all the earth.* (Psalm 96:9 NIV)

Trusting the True God—Lord's Day 34—Friday

Read: Matthew 10:37–39
"Forsake all others"

WE HAVE AN OCCASIONAL bedtime ritual with our children. We say, "Mommy and Daddy love you so much. But who loves you even more than Mommy and Daddy?" Our kids know the answer: Jesus. Perhaps we should add a second question, "Who do you love even more than Mommy and Daddy?"

Loyalty to Jesus cuts at the very closest bonds imaginable—between parent and child. Loving your father and mother is a good thing. However, Jesus says, "Whoever loves father or mother more than me is not worthy of me" (v. 37). If forced to choose, who would we love and follow? We must be willing to sacrifice even love for our parents (or children) for the sake of Jesus. We must, then, also be willing to set aside (or relativize) all other relationships, all other people, for the sake of Jesus. This is a hard task. Jesus utters it in the same breath as "take up the cross" and "losing their life." Love of Jesus must come before all else.

In speaking of the First Commandment, the Catechism summarizes it by saying, "I give up anything rather than go against God's will in any way." If forced to choose, who would you love and follow?

Prayer: *I have sought your face with all my heart; be gracious to me according to your promise.* (Psalm 119:58 NIV)

Trusting the True God—Lord's Day 34—Saturday

Read: 1 Chronicles 16:23–34
"Idols"

YOUNG CHILDREN OFTEN TALK to their toys. They pretend the race car, or teddy bear, or doll can talk. However, even young children know the difference between playing pretend and reality. The toys cannot really talk and act.

Any so-called god other than the LORD is a dead idol. It is like a doll that cannot talk. When David brought the ark of God into Jerusalem, the people celebrated and David appointed Asaph and his family to sing the LORD's praises. They sang of the LORD who made heaven and earth, who is worthy of praise, and to whom all creation cries out in thanksgiving. In the midst of this, we hear, "For all the gods of the peoples are idols, but the Lord made the heavens" (v. 26). Biblical teaching is not that there are plenty of gods, and our God is the greatest. Instead, it is that there is only one true God, and that all others that claim to be gods are nothing but fakes.

There is no other God but the Lord. All others are fakes. The LORD made the heavens and the earth. He rescued us from sin and death. Placing our trust anywhere else is trusting not a lesser god, but a non-god, a mere idol.

Prayer: *It is better to take refuge in the LORD than to trust in humans.* (Psalm 118:8 NIV)

Images of God—Lord's Day 35—Sunday

Q96. What is God's will for us in the second commandment?

A. That we in no way make any image of God
    nor worship him in any other way
    than has been commanded in God's Word.

Q97. May we then not make any image at all?

A. God can not and may not
    be visibly portrayed in any way.
    Although creatures may be portrayed,
    yet God forbids making or having such images
    if one's intention is to worship them
    or to serve God through them.

**Q98. But may not images be permitted in churches
    in place of books for the unlearned?**

A. No, we should not try to be wiser than God.
    God wants the Christian community instructed
    by the living preaching of his Word—
    not by idols that cannot even talk.

THE FIRST COMMANDMENT IS about worshipping the wrong god or placing your trust in something else, instead of or alongside of God. That is one form of false worship. But there is another. We can enter into false worship when we worship the true God, but "worship him in any other way than has been commanded in God's word."

This is about more than just refraining from painting pictures of God and using them for worship (though that is clearly forbidden), but about desiring to have God on our terms.

We want God to be in our lives, a part of our lives, but in a way we can manage, handle, or control. This is what an idol does. It is an image of God, whether of wood or stone (or simply in our hearts) that allows us to worship and serve God how we want. An idol can be ignored, it can be manipulated, it can be put up the shelf or walked away from as we see fit. When it comes to worshipping idols, we are in control of the situation. When it stops working for us, stops providing whatever we expect, we either put this image of god up on a shelf, or change our image of god to meet our new set of expectations. Idols are a way of claiming to worship God, but still having ourselves on the throne.

Prayer: *Know that the Lord is God. It is he who made us, and we are his; we are his people, the sheep of his pasture.* (Psalm 100:3 NIV)

Images of God—Lord's Day 35—Monday

Read: Deuteronomy 4:15–24
"Beware of Making Images"

WHAT DOES GOD LOOK like? Popular culture often depicts older men with long, graying beards, but this has nothing to do with the God who reveals himself in Scripture. However tempting, depicting God will only lead us astray.

God has not revealed himself as having any form that can be depicted in creation. God reminds us, "you saw no form when the Lord spoke to you at Horeb out of the fire, take care and watch yourselves closely" (v. 15). Even fire and smoke, out of which God spoke, are not fitting images of God for our worship. All images of God are ways of making God something he is not. The LORD calls it acting corruptly (v. 16) and forgetting the covenant (v. 23). God does not look like anything in creation, so to try and depict God in any created form is to dishonor him and pretend God is something other than what he has shown himself to be.

Many Christians have rightly shared with Jews a concern about the use of images in worship. This is not a rejection of images or art, but a desire to worship God as he has revealed himself in his word: without visible form.

Prayer: *Praise the LORD, for the LORD is good; sing praise to his name, for that is pleasant.* (Psalm 135:3 NIV)

Images of God—Lord's Day 35—Tuesday

Read: Exodus 32
"Golden Calf"

WHILE VISITING MISSIONARIES IN Mexico, our group visited house churches in small mountain villages and one large catholic cathedral in the city. Though warned by our guides, we were shocked stepping into the cathedral. The seatless sanctuary was lined with statues of Jesus, Mary, and the Apostles. Blood and feathers covered the floor as a man slaughtered a chicken. The priest standing at the altar consecrating the mass. Before each of the statues were people prostrate, weeping, wailing, praying, placing offerings.

When Moses walked down the mountain, he beheld a similar scene. God's people, rescued out of Egypt by the hand of God, were worshipping a golden calf they had made. Dancing before this golden statue, they claimed to worship the LORD, who brought them out of Egypt. They claimed to be worshipping God through this golden calf, not another god. Moses names this a great sin and the LORD says it is so great that "Whoever has sinned against me I will blot out of my book" (v. 33).

God does not want us to worship him through any image. This includes golden calves or even Jesus statues. By trying to worship God through an image, we end up turning away from God himself.

Prayer: *The idols of the nations are silver and gold, made by human hands. They have mouths, but cannot speak, eyes, but cannot see.* (Psalm 135:15–16 NIV)

Images of God—Lord's Day 35—Wednesday

Read: Acts 17:16–34
"Distressed by idols"

PAUL WAS DISTRESSED. WALKING through the great metropolis of Athens, the city was full of idols. Statues abounded to every so-called god imaginable. Paul cannot stay silent. He argues first in the synagogue and then in the marketplace, proclaiming the good news of Jesus.

Paul does not mince words on the nature of the Athenian gods. This is front and center in Paul's evangelistic message. He affirms their religious impulses and even their humility to admit there is a god they do not know. However, Paul refuses to pretend that the Greek idols share anything in common with the one true God. They are not the same being with a different name, but the LORD is real and the idols are deaf and mute statues. They did not know the one true God, and Paul makes him known to them. In doing so, he must reveal that their gods are dead and always have been.

Do we feel the same distress that Paul did at the presence of idols? Does the fact that people worship things other than the one true God stir in us a desire to proclaim Jesus risen from the dead? Perhaps we are not troubled enough.

Prayer: *Those who make them [idols] will be like them, and so will all who trust in them. All you Israelites, trust in the LORD—he is their help and shield.* (Psalm 115:8–9 NIV)

Images of God—Lord's Day 35—Thursday

Read: Habakkuk 2:18–20
"Silent Idols"

ONE SUMMER IN COLLEGE while working at the school, a professor let me use his office. Every day I worked uncomfortably in a room filled with small statues of pagan gods. Yet, no matter how long I was there, none of those idols ever talked to me. No matter how much I read about the greatness of the LORD, the idols remained silent.

The prophet Habakkuk points out the futility of trusting in idols. When making an idol, the maker trusts in what it has made—a reversal of how things should be. We should trust in the one who created us, but with an idol, we trust in what we have made. Additionally, "the product is only an idol that cannot speak" (v. 18), "and there is no breath in it at all" (v. 19). It cannot talk or teach. It cannot answer prayer. Not so the LORD. "But the LORD is in his holy temple; let all the earth keep silence before him!" (v. 20)

The worthlessness of idols demonstrates the overwhelming goodness of God. God speaks. God lives. God hears. God is worthy of our trust, because he created and redeemed us. "Let all the earth keep silence before him!"

Prayer: *I will exalt you, LORD, for you lifted me out of the depths and did not let my enemies gloat over me.* (Psalm 30:1 NIV)

Images of God—Lord's Day 35—Friday

Read: 2 Peter 1:16–21
"Living preaching of the Word"

OUR CULTURE PRIZES THE eyes over the ears. Filled with screens, we trust what we see far more than what we hear. The opposite is true in Scripture. Unlike the eye-centered cultures of the world that were filled with idols, God's people were to be people of the ear, people of the word.

As Christians, we have been given not a visual spectacle, but the word of God to build up, strengthen, and confirm our faith. Peter witnessed Jesus' transfiguration and heard the voice from heaven while on the mountain. The apostles spoke the truth, "what we have heard, what we have seen with our eyes, what we have looked at and touched with our hands, concerning the word of life" (1 John 1:1). However, Peter calls us to pay greatest attention to scripture, saying how the Holy Spirit moved people to speak from God. We, the church, have been given the Word. This is enough for us.

The promise of God comes to us not primarily through our eyes, but through our ears. This is why the public reading of Scripture (and preaching and prayer) have always been so central to true Christian worship. We are people who hear again and again the words of life.

Prayer: *The voice of the LORD twists the oaks and strips the forests bare. And in his temple all cry, "Glory!"* (Psalm 29:9 NIV)

Images of God—Lord's Day 35—Saturday

Read: Leviticus 10:1–7
"Unholy Fire"

THE CAT AT THE greenhouse considered me its favorite. With pride, it would bring me the heads of birds it caught. The cat believed this was a loving and caring gesture. I did not agree. The cat was sincere in his gift, but it was not what I wanted.

We do not determine how God should be worshipped. On the very first day of tabernacle worship, Nadab and Abihu seek to worship God their own way. They put fire and incense in their censers and offered it before the LORD. We might think, "Their hearts are in the right place, and they want to worship him how they connect best with God." However, God is holy and cannot be approached on our terms, but only as he has given us. This is for our own safety. God responds to the "unholy fire" with the consuming fire of judgement. Sincerity was important, but it was not enough. God's people were to worship according to God's Word. Like the cat's offering to me, it might have been sincere, but it was not proper worship.

This is a hard passage, but it should lead us not to fear but should lead us to Christ. This is the heart of worshipping according to God's Word. Jesus takes our worship, takes our best and fumbling efforts, and perfects them and places them before the Father. Though we should beware of trying to worship or approach God apart from Christ (even sincerely), when we come before the Father trusting in Jesus, we are worshipping not our way, but God's way.

Prayer: *Guide me in your truth and teach me, for you are God my Savior, and my hope is in you all day long.* (Psalm 25:5 NIV)

The Holy Name of God—Lord's Day 36—Sunday

Q99. What is the aim of the third commandment?
A. That we neither blaspheme nor misuse the name of God
    by cursing, perjury, or unnecessary oaths,
    nor share in such horrible sins
    by being silent bystanders.
    In summary,
    we should use the holy name of God
    only with reverence and awe,
    so that we may properly
    confess God,
    pray to God,
    and glorify God in all our words and works.

Q100. Is blasphemy of God's name by swearing and cursing
    really such a serious sin
    that God is angry also with those
    who do not do all they can
    to help prevent and forbid it?
A. Yes, indeed.
    No sin is greater
    or provokes God's wrath more
    than blaspheming his name.
    That is why God commanded it to be punished with death.

A NAME IS MORE than just a set of sounds. When you give someone power of attorney, you are empowering them to make decisions "in your name." When you sign a contract, you put your name on it, making promises you will do what you said. The name of God is a revelation of who he is and a claim of his authority. That is the reason we pray "in Jesus' name" and that we say that "blessed is he who comes in the name of the LORD."

We misuse the name of the LORD, take it in vain, when we use God's name for our own ends. We take what we want and stamp them with God's name to give them respectability or authority. On a more personal level, we use God's name as a blank check for our decisions and activities. If God always approves of everything I want and strive for in my life, then perhaps I am not dealing with the real God. Perhaps I just stamping what I want with God's name in order to make myself feel good about my decisions. We should be diligent to discern God's will, according to his Word, and then still be cautious about stamping things with God's name. God's name is to be feared, not used for our ends.

Prayer: *Let the praise the name of the LORD, for his name alone is exalted; his splendor is above the earth and the heavens.* (Psalm 148:13 NIV)

The Holy Name of God—Lord's Day 36—Monday

Read: Matthew 5:33–37
"Oaths"

WHY DO PEOPLE SWEAR oaths? We occasionally hear people say, "I swear to God that . . . " But why do we swear? Is our word not good enough? To swear by someone else is to call upon their authority to back what you are saying. God permitted the use of oaths (Numbers 30:2; Deuteronomy 23:21), but called for us to keep them.

Jesus strengthens the Mosaic prohibitions against rash oaths by saying we should not need to give oaths at all. Oaths exist because of a lack of trust in someone's promise. However, if we call upon God as our witness and break our promise, we dishonor the name of God. We should not even swear by our own heads, but should let our word stand on its own. As those who have been called by God and have the Spirit dwelling within us, our promise should be sure enough in itself.

Jesus calls for us to have integrity between what we say and what we will do. Swearing in God's name will not change our character. If we are already trustworthy that should be enough. To call upon God's name to make others trust us is not a sign of faith, but "comes from the evil one" (v. 37).

Prayer: *May integrity and uprightness protect me, because my hope, LORD, is in you.* (Psalm 25:21 NIV)

The Holy Name of God—Lord's Day 36—Tuesday

Read: Leviticus 24:10–21
"Blaspheming the Name"

WHAT DO WE DO with this story? It is in the Bible for a reason. It should impress upon us just how seriousness we should treat God's name.

There is a fight between two people in the Israelite camp. In the midst of the fight, one of the Israelites "blasphemed the Name in a curse" (v. 11). To blaspheme is to speak with contempt or without reverence to God. We are not told what he said. God commands the man be brought out of the camp (symbolizing being cut off from God's people), the congregation lay their hands on his head, and then stone him to death. This killing was a form of judgment, not a murder. The LORD then gives instructions about the penalty for specific actions. Blaspheming God's name and murder are both deserving of death. The death of an animal should be repaid life for life. Injury should have an equal recompense.

The concluding instructions help us to understand this story. How we treat God's name is parallel to how we treat God. To blaspheme God's name is equivalent to killing someone. We should treat it with that level of seriousness. This is why the catechism could say that "No sin is greater or provokes God's wrath more than blaspheming his name" (Q100).

Prayer: *Tremble and do not sin; when you are on your beds, search your hearts and be silent.* (Psalm 4:4 NIV)

The Holy Name of God—Lord's Day 36—Wednesday

Read: Psalm 113
"Praising the Name"

IN SONG AND PRAYER, Christians gather weekly to praise God. It forms the backbone of our life with God. But why do we praise Him?

Psalm 113 begins and ends with praise. Praise is both the beginning and the end of life with God. There is reason to praise. At the center of the psalm is the question, "Who is like the LORD our God?" (v. 5). In short, no one. We praise God for who he is and what he has done. The LORD, who is enthroned on high, stoops down to us. He lifts the poor from the dust and the needy from the ash heap. They are seated with the princes of God's people. He gives barren women children. Pain, suffering, and difficult circumstances are still very real (barrenness and sitting in the ash heap can be seen no other way). However, the psalm declares God's goodness in and through those difficult circumstances. This allows the psalmist to end where he began: "Praise the LORD!"

Why do we praise God's name? There is none like our God. None can sit on his throne above. But our God stoops down to raise us up. Praise the LORD!

Prayer: *Praise the LORD. Praise the LORD, you his servants; praise the name of the LORD.* (Psalm 113:1 NIV)

The Holy Name of God—Lord's Day 36—Thursday

Read: Leviticus 19:11–18
"Do Not Blaspheme the Name"

GOD'S NAME IS WRAPPED up in who he is, in his reputation, his glory, his holiness. Protecting God's name is glorifying it, and, in connection, glorifying God. To honor or dishonor God's name is to honor or dishonor God. Because God reveals his character through his name, he commands us to protect it.

Tucked in the middle of a series of commands that culminate with "love your neighbor as yourself" is the command not to swear falsely by God's name. The reason given is "I am the LORD." When we swear by God's name, we attach his reputation, his identity, and his authority to our promise. When we break it ("swear falsely") our actions demean God's name and reputation.

But we also profane God's name when we break any of the other commandments in Leviticus 19. Christians are people who bear the name of God. When we belong to Jesus Christ, we have been given his name. When we walk out of the doors here into the world, we bear the name of Jesus for all to see. When we say one thing on Sunday morning and live another during the week, we treat the privilege of bearing God's name as if it was nothing.

Prayer: *Save me, LORD, from lying lips and from deceitful tongues.* (Psalm 120:2 NIV)

The Holy Name of God—Lord's Day 36—Friday

Read: Isaiah 45:22–25
"Echoing the Promise"

STAND IN JUST THE right place, speak, and your voice will bounce back to you, a little fainter, but still clear. However, the echo only comes back if you speak something first. The same thing is true when it comes to our relationship with God. We can speak back to him only because he spoke first.

Because God promises, we are to promise ourselves to him. Our promise echoes his. In Isaiah 45, God has sworn (promised) by his own name that he will save. Those who turn to him will be rescued, they will proclaim the deliverance and strength of the LORD. God has promised and put his own name on the line for it. God says, "my mouth has gone forth in righteousness a word that shall not return" (v. 23). God has promised and will keep his word. Part of what God promises is that "To me every knee shall bow, every tongue shall swear" (v. 23). Because God has sworn to save, we will swear our lives to him. Our "pledge of allegiance" is in response to God's unshakable promise.

We honor God's name by pledging our lives to him. However, our promise is an echo and response to his promise to save us.

Prayer: *May your unfailing love come to me, LORD, your salvation, according to your promise.* (Psalm 119:41 NIV)

The Holy Name of God—Lord's Day 36—Saturday

Read: Acts 4:1–22
"No other name"

WHEN YOU ARE DROWNING, it matters who you call for help. As you struggle to keep from going under, you need someone who can save you. Someone unqualified and incapable will only let you drown (and may drown too). You need someone to dive in to where you are and pull you out to safety.

"There is salvation in no one else, for there is no other name under heaven given among mortals by which we must be saved" (v. 12). Peter makes that claim because no other name is strong enough. Not to share would be uncaring and unloving. No other is strong enough to save us, only Jesus. To call out to anyone else, to look to Allah or Vishnu or Buddha or even your stellar resume or reputation is not going to work, because only Jesus is powerful enough to raise you up, only Jesus can reach deep enough to lift us up, only Jesus has a grip strong enough to never let us go.

So why does Peter tell about Christ? There is no other name but Jesus. When we care about someone, we want them to know and trust the only one powerful enough to save them.

Prayer: *Yet he saved them for his name's sake, to make his mighty power known.* (Psalm 106:8 NIV)

Promoting Truth—Lord's Day 37—Sunday

**Q101. But may we swear an oath in God's name
if we do it reverently?**

A. Yes, when the government demands it,
    or when necessity requires it,
    in order to maintain and promote truth and trustworthiness
    for God's glory and our neighbor's good.
    Such oaths are grounded in God's Word
    and were rightly used by the people of God
    in the Old and New Testaments.

Q102. May we also swear by saints or other creatures?

A. No.
    A legitimate oath means calling upon God
    as the only one who knows my heart to witness
    to my truthfulness
    and to punish me if I swear falsely.
    No creature is worthy of such honor.

WHEN EVERY OTHER COMMANDMENT gets only one week, why does the catechism spend two weeks on the third commandment? At the time the catechism was written, the question of oaths was incredibly significant. Oaths and loyalty served to bind society together. The common people swore to their local lord, who swore to his lord, who swore to his lord. Oaths, usually spoken in the name of the LORD, tied peoples and nations together. Rejecting oaths (as some groups did at the Reformation) was seen as a rejection of civilization itself, undermining law and order, and promoting anarchy. Against this, the Reformed argued for the right use of oaths. Not only did many people in Scripture swear oaths, many were commanded to do so. The Reformed focused on the nature of true oaths and the context in which they can be demanded. Oaths promote truth and trustworthiness and should not be used to cover dishonesty. Oaths are meant for God's glory and our neighbors good and should not be used simply for our own gain.

Outside of weddings and court rooms, we are rarely asked to swear oaths or make vows today. Yet these oaths should be taken seriously as a means of promoting truth, glorifying good, and working for the good of our neighbor.

Prayer: *I have taken an oath and confirmed it, that I will follow your righteous laws.*
(Psalm 119:106 NIV)

Promoting Truth—Lord's Day 37—Monday

Read: Deuteronomy 6:4–15
"Swear by his name"

YOUR NAME SAYS WHETHER people can trust you. "You are one of the Vos kids. I know your family, when you say you will pay me, you will." Or, "You belong to *that* family. You have treated me like dirt before. I won't do that again." Your name is connected with your reputation.

When God calls Israel, he tells them to swear in his name. This was a gift. God gives them his name, his reputation, his identity and authority. "The Lord your God you shall fear; him you shall serve, and by his name alone you shall swear" (v. 13). God places his name upon his people that they would remember who they are and carry his name with them. Swearing by God's name would be a consistent reminder to whom they belonged. Every time they made an oath in the LORD's name, they would remember him and his oath to them.

Even though Israel took God's name lightly, they were still marked as his people, as the people who bear his name. We, who bear the name "Christian," do not swear in the name of Jesus, but we are similarly marked. We belong to Jesus and should never forget him.

Prayer: *He determines the number of the stars and calls them each by name.* (Psalm 147:4 NIV)

Promoting Truth—Lord's Day 37—Tuesday

Read: Hebrews 6:13–20
"Swear by himself"

SOME LARGE PURCHASES REQUIRE collateral, an item you give to back your promise. The larger the promise, the more you need to assure others you will keep it. Some loans might require you promise your house if you cannot pay. This is the logic of swearing oaths in someone's name. Who will assure you keep your promise? For small promises, your name is often good enough. But if it is large, who will make sure you follow through?

God made his covenant with Abraham with an oath. People swear by something greater than themselves. However, when God promised to be God to Abraham, to bless him, to give him land and descendants, and ultimately to bring about the blessing of the world through his seed, God swore this immense promise by the greatest thing he could: God's own name. There is nothing greater than God, so God could not swear by anything greater than his name. God put forward the greatest thing he had, his own name, as a pledge he would keep his promise.

When we make promises, we sometimes need more than our word to back them up. When God promises, his name is enough. God keeps all his promises and will continue to keep all his promises to us.

Prayer: *He remembers his covenant forever, the promise he made, for a thousand generations.* (Psalm 105:8 NIV)

Promoting Truth—Lord's Day 37—Wednesday

Read: Genesis 31:43-55
"Jacob and Laban"

WHEN I SIGNED A loan for college, my parents signed as well. They co-signed because my name was not good enough for the bank to be confident I would pay it back. My parents signed guaranteeing if I did not pay it back, they would.

Jacob calls upon God to guarantee that he will keep his covenant with Laban. When Laban catches up to Jacob, they decide to make a covenant that will ensure peace between their two peoples. Both men call upon the LORD to watch between them, and Jacob "swore by the Fear of his father Isaac" (v. 53). Jacob's name is not good enough to make Laban confident that Jacob will do as he says. In using this name of the LORD, Jacob calls upon God as co-signer of his covenant (who guarantees it will be kept), and as the judge who will enforce the terms of the covenant.

Throughout the Bible, God's people swear oaths in his name. We should never be flippant with using God's name, especially as we make promises. However, the example of Scripture shows that "such oaths are grounded in God's Word and were rightly used by the people of God in the Old and New Testaments" (Q 101). When we swear by God's name, we acknowledge that God knows our hearts, and we are asking him to help us keep our word.

Prayer: *Before a word is on my tongue you, LORD, know it completely.* (Psalm 139:4 NIV)

Promoting Truth—Lord's Day 37—Thursday

Read: 1 Kings 1:28-37
"David's Oath"

SLOW OBEDIENCE IS NO obedience. When we are asked to do something, but delay and dawdle, we are not truly showing obedience. When we promise to do something, but procrastinate on carrying it out, this is not a true sign that we take our promises seriously.

David does not dawdle in doing what he promises. David calls Bathsheba and swears to put her son, Solomon, on the throne. David swears by the name of the LORD and keeps his promise that same day. Solomon is brought to Gihon to be anointed as king. David knows who should take his place as king, he swears it, and then does not delay in making it so. In this instance, delay and hesitation would have been costly, for David's other sons were already seeking the throne. If David did not act swiftly, the wrong son would have become king. David's quick action not only honors his oath, but honors the LORD in whose name he swore.

When we know what God wants us to do, we should not delay. Like David, we should keep our word quickly and follow God swiftly. We should be wary of our hearts when we seek to delay doing what we know we need to do.

Prayer: *Teach me your way, LORD, that I may rely on your faithfulness; give me an undivided heart, that I may fear your name.* (Psalm 86:11 NIV)

Promoting Truth—Lord's Day 37—Friday

Read: James 5:7–12
"Not swearing by creatures"

WHEN THE HEIDELBERG CATECHISM was written, many people swore oaths in the names of saints. The Reformers rejected this practice on biblical grounds. Only God's name should be used in an oath. As the catechism remarks, "No creature is worthy of such honor."

In most circumstances, our word—our name—should be enough to ensure that we can be trusted. We should have such integrity that when we say "yes, I will do it" or "no, I will not" people know we will do what we say. Though there is no mention of swearing by saints or other creatures, the command not to swear by "heaven or earth" would include this. James echoes the words of Jesus in the Sermon on the Mount. To swear by heaven or earth (or any creature in heaven or earth) is to "fall under condemnation" (v. 12). If you must swear by something greater than yourself, swear by God who is the Judge standing at the door (v. 9).

While there are times to swear oaths in God's name, we should not swear oaths in any other name. Either we appeal to the God who is judge of all, or we stand on our own name. Anything else is foolishness.

Prayer: *Set a guard over my mouth, LORD; keep watch over the door of my lips.* (Psalm 141:3 NIV)

Promoting Truth—Lord's Day 37—Saturday

Read: Exodus 20:7
"Bearing God's Name Lightly"

EVERY YEAR, OUR CHURCH participates in a citywide food drive. We go out in pairs, wearing official name tags from the churches of the city, to collect food for the food bank. We were told that once we wear the name tags, how we act will reflect upon the churches. When we bore that name on our name tags, our actions shaped how people would see the churches.

Christians are people who bear the name of God. When we belong to Jesus Christ, we have been given his name. When we walk out of the doors of the church into the world, we bear the name of Jesus for all to see. While the translation of Exodus 20:7 as "make wrongful use of the name of the Lord your God" is right, it more accurately says, "bear God's name for nothing." Through our lives, we can treat God's name as if it was nothing, as if it was worthless. The name of Jesus might be on our lips, but our actions could treat his name as if it was nothing. The biblical word for speaking one way and living another is hypocrisy. We bear God's name not only with our lips, but with the whole of our lives.

When we profess Jesus publicly on Sunday, but dishonor him with how we live on Tuesday, we treat the name of God lightly. We break the third commandment. In our lives, how we live will impact how people see Christ and his Church.

Prayer: *Sing the glory of his name; make his praise glorious.* (Psalm 66:2 NIV)

Keeping the Sabbath—Lord's Day 38—Sunday

**Q103. What is God's will for you
in the fourth commandment?**
A. First, that the gospel ministry and education for it be maintained,
and that, especially on the festive day of rest,
I diligently attend the assembly of God's people
to learn what God's Word teaches,
to participate in the sacraments,
to pray to God publicly,
and to bring Christian offerings for the poor.
Second,
that every day of my life
I rest from my evil ways,
let the Lord work in me through his Spirit,
and so begin in this life
the eternal Sabbath.

WHAT DOES IT LOOK like for you to keep the Sabbath? Are there particular things you do every Sunday and things you do not do on Sundays?

The catechism defines obedience to the fourth commandment with two practices: worship and rest. Keeping Sabbath means doing some things and refusing to do others. Sabbath is a day for worship. We hear the Word, participate in the sacraments, pray, and give our offerings. We might read the Word and pray throughout the week, but on the Lord's Day we gather together publicly to sit under the Word. The catechism highlights giving gifts for the poor. Those trapped in poverty have a difficult time entering into God's rest, so we practice Sabbath by giving them rest through our offerings and care. Keeping Sabbath involves entering rest ourselves and allowing others to do the same.

Keeping Sabbath also involves resting from certain activities, particularly work. The Law (and later tradition) spends a lot of effort defining what does and does not count as work. However, we rest not just from work, but from our "evil ways." Keeping Sabbath means ceasing, in particular, ceasing from evil in order to let the LORD work in us through the Spirit.

Prayer: *Truly my soul finds rest in God; my salvation comes from him.*
(Psalm 62:1 NIV)

Keeping the Sabbath—Lord's Day 38—Monday

Read: Hebrews 10:23–25
"Do It Together"

SOME THINGS YOU CANNOT do by yourself: play rock-paper-scissors, talk on the phone, or enjoy a seesaw. Some things are meant to be done together.

Discipleship is not something you are meant to do by yourself. Forgiveness, love, bearing one another's burdens, and encouragement cannot be done on our own. However, the whole Christian life is more difficult when we try to go it alone. Hebrews cautions us about "neglecting to meet together" (i.e. being an active part of the church, v. 24). Apart from the church, it is hard to "hold fast to the confession of our hope without wavering" (v. 23). It is easy to swerve off course or begin to lose hope. Apart from the church, we have to stir up love and good deeds ourselves, instead of being encouraged by the love, support, admonishment, and example of others. Christian discipleship is simply something God does not want us to do alone, but together in the church.

Much of the week, Christians are scattered in our homes, schools, and workplaces. Yet, God has given us the Sabbath, not only for rest, but so that we would gather together as the church. Some things we are not meant to do alone.

Prayer: *I long to dwell in your tent forever and take refuge in the shelter of your wings.* (Psalm 61:4 NIV)

Keeping the Sabbath—Lord's Day 38—Tuesday

Read: Hebrews 4:1–11
"Eternal Sabbath"

WE ALL DESIRE REST, but this desire is never completely met in this life. We waffle back and forth between overwork and laziness, but struggle to find true rest. This is because this desire for rest cannot be fulfilled in this life, but only in the next.

Sabbath rest in Christ points ahead to the eternal rest promised in the life to come. However, we are not there yet. One day, we will rest from all our labors in the presence of our King. "So then, a Sabbath rest still remains for the people of God; for those who enter God's rest also cease from their labors as God did from his" (vv. 9–10). This promise should not make us complacent, but stir us to cling more closely to Christ in faith and to walk in his ways. Our desire for the rest of God in Christ should lead us closer to him.

Our Sabbath practice now points ahead to the day when we will enter into the eternal Sabbath. Right now, we get a taste of that heavenly rest, even if all our Sabbaths will be touched by unfulfilled longing. One day, Lord willing, we will enter into that new Sabbath-rest for the people of God.

Prayer: *Yes, my soul, find rest in God; my hope comes from him.* (Psalm 62:5 NIV)

Keeping the Sabbath—Lord's Day 38—Wednesday

Read: Exodus 20:8–11
"Receiving Rest"

EXHAUSTION HAS BECOME A badge of honor in some circles. "Oh, I am *so* busy right now." "Oh, you think your busy, wait til you hear what *I* had to do this week." As if it is some sort of competition to see who can be the most exhausted and most miserable. That is not a contest I want to win.

God commands us to rest because God himself rested ("sabbathed") after creating the world. We are following God's pattern in his great work of creation. On the seventh day, God was not tired, but had finished his work and delighted in the presence of his people. Sabbath rest is a gift of joy. We Sabbath because God Sabbathed.

Sometimes when Christians debate how to keep the Sabbath we can easily forget the joy of the Sabbath. Sabbath is a gift. God rested on the seventh day, and he invites us into that rest by observing the Sabbath. We enter into God's rest, pattern our lives after him, when we keep the Sabbath. Ceasing from labor is not to make sure you are energized on Monday morning, but so that you can enter into the joy of God's rest.

Prayer: *Trust in him at all times, you people; pour out your hearts to him, for God is our refuge.* (Psalm 62:8 NIV)

Keeping the Sabbath—Lord's Day 38—Thursday

Read: Deuteronomy 5:12–15
"Giving Rest"

GOD GIVES THE TEN Commandments twice. At the beginning of the wilderness journey, at Mount Sinai, Sabbath is commanded because God rested on the seventh day. At the end of the journey, in Deuteronomy 5, the commandments are the same but the reason for keeping the Sabbath is different.

Why are we to keep the Sabbath? "So that your male and female servants may rest as well as you" (v. 14). Sabbath is for receiving rest ourselves, but also so we can give rest to others. In both Exodus and Deuteronomy, the master of the household was supposed to receive rest himself and give it to those in his care. Keeping Sabbath is receiving and giving rest. Jesus gives rest every time he heals on the Sabbath or gets accused of breaking the Sabbath. Jesus is keeping the Sabbath because, by healing and serving, he is giving rest to others. Jesus shows the proper meaning of the Sabbath by not just receiving rest, but giving it.

Who is required to work while we are resting? Sabbath rest is supposed to be both a gift we receive from the hands of God, but also something that is given to others. How can we give rest to those in our community who have no rest?

Prayer: *But God will never forget the needy; the hope of the afflicted will never perish.* (Psalm 9:18 NIV)

Keeping the Sabbath—Lord's Day 38—Friday

Read: Matthew 11:28–30
"True Rest"

TRUE REST IS FOUND in Jesus Christ. In Sabbath, ceasing from work one day a week, God teaches us to where to look for rest. "Come to me, all that you that are weary and are carrying heavy burdens, and I will give you rest" (v. 28). For the world, our worth is our work, but sabbath rest is a visible marker that our worth is in Christ. Jesus is the source of our true rest. This is why Christians have traditionally shifted from celebrating the sabbath on the seventh day of the week to the first day, the day of Jesus' resurrection. In Jesus, there is true Sabbath, true rest.

God has made us to find our rest in him. When we search for rest anywhere else, we will find our hearts restless. As Saint Augustine says, speaking to the LORD at the beginning of his *Confessions*, "to praise you is the desire of man, a little piece of your creation. You stir man to take pleasure in praising you, because you have made us for yourself, and our heart is restless until it rests in you." What this restless world needs, what our restless hearts need, is to find true rest—to find Jesus.

Prayer: *God is our refuge and strength, and ever-present hope in trouble.* (Psalm 46:1 NIV)

Keeping the Sabbath—Lord's Day 38—Saturday

Read: 1 Corinthians 9:8–14
"Tending the Field"

EVERY SPRING FARMERS SOW the fields—corn, wheat, soy beans. Throughout the summer they tend the fields. At harvest, they also reap the benefits of the field. The field they work supports them in their life as farmers.

In 1 Corinthians, Paul makes a similar analogy to the life of a minister of the gospel. Through the minister's work, spiritual seed is planted in the life of the church. By God's grace, that seed grows and matures. Just as the farmer is supported materially by the produce of the field, so the minister should be supported financially by the congregation. Ordained ministers are not the only ones called to plant the seed of the gospel, but they are specifically called out of God's people to plant and tend the field of God. As Paul concludes, "those who proclaim the gospel should get their living by the gospel" (v. 14).

If possible, churches should work to provide for their ministers. In doing so, they not only support a brother or sister in Christ, but promote the teaching of the gospel. By supporting the minister, they encourage more spiritual seed to be planted and the field of God tended well.

Prayer: *But I am like an olive tree flourishing in the house of God; I trust in God's unfailing love for ever and ever.* (Psalm 52:8 NIV)

Q104. What is God's will for you in the fifth commandment?

A. That I honor, love, and be loyal
  to my father and mother
  and all those in authority over me;
  that I submit myself with proper obedience
  to all their good teaching and discipline;
  and also that I be patient with their failings—
  for through them God chooses to rule us.

As the Ten Commandments turn from loving God toward loving our neighbor, the first place we love our neighbor is in the family, in a relationship that none of us chose. The first relationship that God tells us to care for is one we did not choose. It is a relationship that was handed to us before we could speak, could move, could do anything but trust that we would be cared for.

We do not get to choose who we are called to honor. We don't pick our parents. You might wish you had different parents or think you have the best parents in the world, but you don't get to choose them. They are given to us. Before we were ever born, they were there. The child-parent relationship is universal. Whether our home was broken, blended, or whole, we are all children. Whether we are orphaned, adopted, or sick of all our siblings, we are all children. It is one of the few relationships we have that is simply a given in our lives, not something chosen. Before words, before we can do anything but eat, sleep, and poop, we are already embedded in this relationship.

And it is here where our love of neighbor begins. We honor and respect the parents God has given us. It is here in the unchosen, given relationship of a child to a parent that we are called to continue our discipleship as one belonging to Jesus Christ.

Prayer: *Blessed are all who fear the LORD, who walk in obedience to him.* (Psalm 128:1 NIV)

Honor, Love, and Loyalty—Lord's Day 39—Monday

Read: 1 Timothy 5:1–8
"Honoring and Caring for your Elders"

"You are my retirement plan. When we get old we are coming to live with you." As a teenager, this joking line from my parents made me uncomfortable. I was eager to get out of the house, live independently, and did not want to imagine my parents coming to live with me again.

However, caring for your parents and elders in the faith is an integral part of Christian discipleship. The church cares for the widows, but only if their families cannot do it themselves. Paul goes so far as to say, "And whoever does not provide for relatives, and especially for family members, has denied the faith and is worse than an unbeliever" (v. 8). Worse than an unbeliever? This sounds harsh, particularly to those with difficult and messy family situations. Yet, we are called to find ways to care for our families, even when it is difficult. Loving our own household and the household of faith is a sign of our Christian faith. This witness is distinctive as the world comes to see the aging as a burden instead of a gift.

My parents may never move in with me. However, I no longer see it as a joke, but as a part of God's calling to care for those who have gone before me and cared for me.

Prayer: *Whoever dwells in the shelter of the Most High will rest in the shadow of the Almighty.* (Psalm 91:1 NIV)

Honor, Love, and Loyalty—Lord's Day 39—Tuesday

Read: Ephesians 6:1–9
"Obey your parents"

As a teen, I looked for arguments and ways to get out of obeying my parents. Knowing that if the Bible was on my side, my parents could not argue, I found Ephesians 6:4. "Fathers, do not provoke your children to anger." Whenever I got asked to do something I didn't want to do, I could proudly claim I was being "provoked."

However, I had ignored what God's Word was actually saying. Parents do have specific responsibilities toward their children: to raise them in the LORD, not to push them beyond what they can bear, to nurture, discipline, and defend them. Masters do have responsibilities toward their slaves, just as all in authority have responsibility toward those in their charge. However, I had forgotten to read anything before verse 4. "Children, obey your parents in the Lord, for this is right" (v. 1). The flip-side of the call for parental responsibility is the call for submission as children. Except in extreme circumstances, I am to obey my parents "for this is right."

Godly authority is part of the LORD's design for the world. When we honor those rightly placed over us, we honor God who has placed them there. When we reject them, we reveal a hardness of our own hearts.

Prayer: *Open my eyes that I may see wonderful things in your law.* (Psalm 119:18 NIV)

Honor, Love, and Loyalty—Lord's Day 39—Wednesday

Read: Romans 13:1–8
"Submit to Authorities"

As an American living in Canada, I am learning some of the differences between the countries. I often say Americans kicked the king out of the country while Canadians asked for sovereignty. Americans have a deeply-rooted resistance to authorities. We don't like anyone telling us what to do.

Something is wrong when our default position is to reject authority. We should resist unjust authorities, but the call to honor and obey goes beyond just our biological parents. In the church, in school, in society, there are people placed in positions of authority. These authorities have been placed over us by God. Resistance should be the exception, not the rule. "Pay to all what is due them—taxes to whom taxes are due, revenue to whom revenue is due, respect to whom respect is due, honor to whom honor is due" (v. 7). Honoring our father and mother includes honoring all those in authority over you. As the catechism puts it, "That I honor, love, and be loyal to my father and mother and all those in authority over me" (Q104).

Sometimes authority goes bad and must be resisted. However, a heart that always resists authority does not honor God who placed us under the authority of others.

Prayer: *The LORD reigns, let the nations tremble; he sits enthroned between the cherubim, let the earth shake.* (Psalm 99:1 NIV)

Honor, Love, and Loyalty—Lord's Day 39—Thursday

Read: Acts 5:12–33
"Listen to God rather than men"

Authority can go wrong. Sin mixed with power leads to destruction and pain. We are right to challenge abusive authority, whether a tyrant in the church or in the home. We are right to challenge neglectful authority, where selfishness and self-absorption leaves the weak and vulnerable suffering. The fifth commandment does not call for silent suffering under abuse. Challenging these sinful perversions of authority is right and justified.

In Acts 5, the Apostles encountered a twisted authority. They were arrested for preaching and healing in the name of Jesus. The high priest himself commanded, "We gave you strict orders not to teach in this name" (v. 28). Legitimate, God-given authorities told them not to proclaim the name of Jesus. What should they do? Obey them when it contradicted Jesus' commands? No. "We must obey God rather than any human authority" (v. 29). When we must decide between obeying the authorities and obeying God, we must listen to God. The council was enraged, but the Apostles were not shaken. They kept their faith and obedience to God, even under threat, and God was faithful in building his church through their work.

Authorities can go wrong. The honor and loyalty we are called to give those in authority must never be placed above the honor and loyalty we are to give to God.

Prayer: *Listen, daughter, and pay careful attention: Forget your people and your father's house. Let the king be enthralled by your beauty; honor him, for he is your lord.* (Psalm 45:10–11 NIV)

Honor, Love, and Loyalty—Lord's Day 39—Friday

Read: Exodus 20:12
"Give Weight"

THE HEBREW WORD FOR "honor" means to make something heavy. In the Bible, to make something heavy is to give it significance, honor, or authority and to make something light is to treat as if it was nothing.

Who do you value, who do you listen to, whose voice is given the most weight in your life? Think about the voices and people given the most weight in our culture today—self, celebrity, youth, wealthy. For some, there is a resistance to recognizing any authority outside of their self. For others, the people on the screen have more authority than the people who know us and are charged with caring for and nurturing us. We want celebrities, not experts, to comment on the issues of the day. Our culture honors the celebrity, the self, the rich, and the famous.

God calls for us to show honor, not to the famous or the wealthy, but to mother and father. Honor the person who changed your dirty diaper, not your favorite character on TV; honor the person who stood by your bed at night, not the hip Youtuber. To value the person right next to you is a reversal of how our culture values people. Our culture tends to value the bold, bright, and beautiful. Instead, the Lord asks you to honor your father and your mother, the people placed in authority in your life.

Prayer: *God sets the lonely in families, he leads out the prisoners with singing; but the rebellious live in a sun-scorched land.* (Psalm 68:6 NIV)

Honor, Love, and Loyalty—Lord's Day 39—Saturday

Read: Ephesians 5:15–33
"Submission"

"PERFECT SUBMISSION, PERFECT DELIGHT." Some sing this line from "Blessed Assurance" with joy, while others squirm uncomfortably, remembering how "submission" has often lead to bondage instead of freedom. How should Christians view submission?

In the Bible, submission is not a way of domination, but a path to freedom and joy. Submission is how wives are to relate to their husbands (v. 22), how the church relates to Christ (v. 24), and also how all Christians are to relate to each other ("Be subject to one another out of reverence for Christ," v. 21). The Christian life includes laying down of our lives, our wills, and our desires for the sake of our brothers and sisters. Submission—surrendering our will to another—is found in the church, in marriage, and in life with Jesus. Because our life is secure in Jesus, we are free to give our lives for others. When practiced well and with love, there is freedom in submission.

The difference between whether submission leads to freedom or bondage has to do with to whom you submit yourself. Submission becomes twisted into domination when the other person has their interests and not yours at heart. Yet, when the other has your best interest at heart and the wisdom to know it, submission is a path of freedom and joy.

Prayer: *Be exalted, O God, above the heavens; let your glory be over all the earth.* (Psalm 57:11 NIV)

Loving Our Neighbor—Lord's Day 40—Sunday

Q105. What is God's will for you in the sixth commandment?

A. I am not to belittle, hate, insult, or kill my neighbor—
    not by my thoughts, my words, my look or gesture,
    and certainly not by actual deeds—
    and I am not to be party to this in others;
    rather, I am to put away all desire for revenge.
    I am not to harm or recklessly endanger myself either.
    Prevention of murder is also why
    government is armed with the sword.

Q106. Does this commandment refer only to murder?

A. By forbidding murder God teaches us
    that he hates the root of murder:
    envy, hatred, anger, vindictiveness.
    In God's sight all such are disguised forms of murder.

Q107. Is it enough then that we do not murder our neighbor in any such way?

A. No.
    By condemning envy, hatred, and anger
    God wants us
    to love our neighbors as ourselves,
    to be patient, peace-loving, gentle,
    merciful, and friendly toward them,
    to protect them from harm as much as we can,
    and to do good even to our enemies.

From Genesis 1 to Revelation 22, God is committed to the preciousness of every human life. It is in light of this story that the commandment comes to us "You shall not murder."

Yet, hardly a day goes by that we do not see more murder. Another shooting in a school, another murder-suicide, another police officer killed, another few young men killed by police officers. It's so frequent, so normal, so numbing that many of us simply turn off the television and ignore the violence. It's too much, so prevalent, that much of it never even makes it on the news.

We might want to think that the "murderers" are out there, that it is other people who struggle with this commandment. We want to think that even when we feel fear and despair at the violence in our world, that *those* people are out there. It is *them* who violate life, who rebel against God's life-ethic. It's *them*, not *us*.

Jesus won't let us pretend this commandment has nothing to say to us. When God says "You shall not murder" the commandment affects not only what we do with our hands, but reaches all the way to the depths of our hearts. God calls us to remove hatred, malice, and slander from our hearts and to love, protect, and do good to our neighbors and even our enemies.

Prayer: *May these words of my mouth and this meditation of my heart be pleasing in your sight, LORD, my Rock and my Redeemer.* (Psalm 19:14 NIV)

Loving Our Neighbor—Lord's Day 40—Monday

Read: Matthew 5:21–26
"Rooting Out Murder"

AT THE ROOT OF murder is hatred, scorn, and malice for another person. If we keep our hands clean, but those desires still burn in our hearts, Jesus says we have sinned. We might be innocent in the eyes of the law, but not in the eyes of God.

Every human life is precious because we are made in the image of God. Even if I don't point a gun and pull the trigger, when I belittle or insult my neighbor, Jesus says I have violated the sixth commandment. When I hate my neighbor, when I plot or seek revenge, I sin in my heart. I undermine God's value on human life. When I become selective in the recipients of my love and start to wonder who "deserves" my help and compassion, I have murdered my neighbor in my heart.

This leaves none of us innocent. Maybe some of you don't struggle the same way I do. Maybe you never find anger in your heart. Maybe you never wish bad things on that person you dislike or feel glee at their struggles. Maybe you never get angry with your family or speak words you regret. Maybe you never do any of these things, but I doubt it.

Prayer: *But who can discern their own errors? Forgive my hidden faults.* (Psalm 19:12 NIV)

Loving Our Neighbor—Lord's Day 40—Tuesday

Read: Genesis 9:1–7
"Every life"

WHAT IS THE REASON, the driving force, behind God's command for us to refrain from murdering each other? For some of us, the command may seem so obvious as to need no explanation. Of course we don't kill people. That's wrong. Yet, because we trust that God's ways are wise, let us ask "why would God command us not to murder?"

Life is precious because we have all been made in the image of God. Having been brought through the flood, God sets Noah and his children upon the dry ground. God tells them to eat plants and animals, but forbids them to eat anything with blood in it. Specifically, God demands an accounting for the shedding of human blood because each of us has been made in the image of God. "Whoever sheds the blood of a human, by a human shall that person's blood be shed; for him his own image God made humankind" (v. 6). Murder is forbidden because of the intrinsic value of every human life. The phrase "image of God" is rarely used in the Bible, but it comes up at the creation of humanity and here when God calls us to protect human life. Each human life is valuable because every person is made in God's image. There is a consistent, pervasive life-ethic in the Bible that forbids murder because it desecrates one who has been made in God's image.

In other words, God is pro-life. All of life is incredibly precious—from womb to tomb. From two minutes in utero to two years over one hundred—life is precious. We value the life of our neighbor, because God created them and imprinted upon them his image.

Prayer: *Turn, LORD, and deliver me; save me because of your unfailing love.* (Psalm 6:4 NIV)

Loving Our Neighbor—Lord's Day 40—Wednesday

Read: Matthew 22:37-40
"The Positive Commandment"

FAMILIES SHOULD LOVE EACH other. It is not enough for a house to be peaceful and free from conflict if there is no love there. In the same way, we keep God's commandment against murder when our hearts are filled with love for our neighbors and enemies.

At the heart of God's commandments is loving God and neighbor. Not only refraining from murder, we must love those around us. As Martin Luther says, "If you send a person away naked when you could clothe him, you have let him freeze to death. If you have seen anyone suffer hunger and do not feed him, you have let him starve. Likewise, if you see anyone condemned to death or in similar peril and do not save him although you know ways and means to do so, you have killed him" (*Large Catechism*). Refusing to love our neighbor is a form of murder. The command against murder is fulfilled by loving our neighbor.

Christian discipleship is wrapped up in loving God and neighbor. The Ten Commandments are often framed as a series of actions to avoid—"Thou Shalt Nots"—but Jesus reveals that at the heart is a "Thou Shall"—"you shall love God and neighbor."

Prayer: *Show me your ways, LORD, teach me your paths.* (Psalm 25:4 NIV)

Loving Our Neighbor—Lord's Day 40—Thursday

Read: 1 John 2:7-11
"Love or Hate"

WHEN THE LORD BROUGHT Israel out of Egypt, he called them to be set apart. They were to dress differently, eat differently, and act differently than the nations around them. While we no longer always dress or eat like Israel did, Christians are still called to live a distinctive way.

Christians are distinctive in how we love one another. We walk in the light when we love one another. The love we show to our brothers and sisters in Christ is a witness to Christ and a visible sign of our life in Christ. Our love for each other should echo Christ's love for us. We can say all the right words about knowing and loving Jesus ("claim to be in the light"), but if we hate our brothers and sisters, our life shows the lie. The difference between walking in light or darkness is seen in a life of love for others versus a life of hatred.

True faith in Christ leads to a distinctive way of life. The catechism rightly says "by condemning envy, hatred, and anger God wants us to love our neighbors as ourselves" (Q107). To walk in God's ways means loving those around us. To refuse to love them is to refuse to walk with God.

Prayer: *You, LORD, keep my lamp burning; my God turns my darkness into light.* (Psalm 18:28 NIV)

Loving Our Neighbor—Lord's Day 40—Friday

Read: 1 John 3:15–18
"Love in deed"

WHAT IF YOU HAVE more than enough? Sometimes when we have too much, we work to find more places to store it. We buy storage containers, but we do not wrestle with the fact that we have too much to begin with. Other times, we throw our excess away. In Canada, we waste over 2.2 million tons of food each year. When we have been blessed with abundance, what are we supposed to do with it?

The biblical solution to abundance is sharing. Even where many have plenty, there are still many struggling for food and shelter. Abundance is an opportunity for compassion. "How does God's love abide in anyone who has the world's goods and sees a brother or sister in need and yet refuses help?" (v. 17). Christ laid down his life for us and calls us to lay down our lives for others. In light of Christ's immense gift, what is a little stuff? If love is pouring out your life for others, why hold so tightly to what you have?

If you have enough, perhaps you do not need a bigger house, but to give more away. When God meets our needs and gives us abundance, this is an opportunity for compassion for others, to share what we have been given as a witness to the goodness of God.

Prayer: *The LORD is a refuge for the oppressed, a stronghold in times of trouble.* (Psalm 9:9 NIV)

Loving Our Neighbor—Lord's Day 40—Saturday

Read: Ephesians 4:25–32
"Removal"

EVERY TIME MY NOSE starts to run, my family wants to "nip it in the bud." Even before I start to feel lousy, I have been stuffed with tea and honey and Echinacea drops and wrapped in a blanket. In particular, they want to make sure the cold does not develop while I sleep.

Sickness of the heart is far more serious than an oncoming cold. When anger burns in our hearts and we let it grow, it leads to sin. Hatred that festers is incredibly toxic to everyone it touches. We should not let the sun set on our anger, but deal with it so it has no chance to grow and give the devil leverage for worse work in our hearts. Like my family dealing with my runny nose, we are to "Put away from [ourselves] all bitterness and wrath and anger and wrangling and slander, together with all malice" (v. 31). We are to do this at the first signs of sickness in our hearts, not wait until it has developed into more grievous sins.

When anger sets in our hearts, we are to "nip it in the bud." If we cut murderous feelings off at the roots, they will never grow to bear wicked fruit.

Prayer: *Whoever is pregnant with evil conceives trouble and gives birth to disillusionment.* (Psalm 7:14 NIV)

Q108. What does the seventh commandment teach us?
A. That God condemns all unchastity,
    and that therefore we should thoroughly detest it
    and live decent and chaste lives,
    within or outside of the holy state of marriage.

Q109. Does God, in this commandment,
    forbid only such scandalous sins as adultery?
A. We are temples of the Holy Spirit, body and soul,
    and God wants us both to be kept clean and holy.
    That is why God forbids
    all unchaste actions, looks, talk, thoughts, or desires,
    and whatever may incite someone to them.

MARRIAGE IS A REFLECTION of our covenant relationship with God. Human marriage is exclusive because our relationship with God is exclusive. The first commandment to have no other gods but the LORD runs directly parallel with the commandment to have no other lovers than your spouse. This runs contrary to polygamy, open marriages, etc. The command to love the LORD with our whole heart, soul, mind, and strength runs parallel to the command to love our spouse. Christ giving himself up for the church runs parallel to the call for husbands to give themselves up for their wives. Christ and his church, God and his people, are not the same; they are distinct and different from each other, which is one of the reasons for the commands against incest and same-sex relationships. Christ and his church were also made for each other, to be in union with one another, which runs parallel to the commands against things such as bestiality, where the parties are too different. God sets boundaries on who, when, and how when it comes to the marriage bond because human marriage images the covenantal relationship we have with God.

When a fire is in the fireplace, it gives warmth, light, heat, and can be the center of the home, drawing people in. It is good and brings blessing to others. So too with marriage and sexuality. However, when a fire gets out of the hearth, it burns and destroys. So too with marriage and sexuality. May the fire of sexuality burn brightly in the hearth of marriage.

Prayer: *My soul yearns, even faints, for the courts of the LORD; my heart and my flesh cry out for the living God.* (Psalm 84:2 NIV)

Chastity—Lord's Day 41—Monday

Read: Leviticus 18
"Unchastity"

"But I want it!" This child-like reasoning is now common in the world of adults. I want something so I should be allowed to have it, whether it is what we buy or with whom we sleep. As if every desire I have is right, and I have a right to everything I desire.

However, desire can go wrong. "Unchastity" is the word Christians use for sexual desire run amok. Leviticus 18 lists a series of relationships where unchecked desire causes pain and judgment for us. Some desires run contrary to what God has designed for us. These relationships are either too close (daughter-in-law), too similar (same sex), or too different (animals). In the law, the LORD does not comment on the sincerity of the desire, for that is not the point. No matter how deeply or sincerely we want something, we can want the wrong thing.

The people of God are to be different. For the rest of the world, "I want it" is enough of a reason to have it. However, God's people have their desires governed and directed by God's Word, both for our good and for our witness in the world.

Prayer: *Teach me to do your will, for you are my God; may your good Spirit lead me on level ground.* (Psalm 143:10 NIV)

Chastity—Lord's Day 41—Tuesday

Read: Matthew 5:27–30
"Cut It Off"

Before the courts of the world, we are only guilty of a crime if we actually go through with it. But before the court of the Lord, motive is enough. What do we do when attraction transforms into lust, when a glance starts to linger, or when we find our hearts traveling down the same lustful road again and again?

Jesus recommends amputation—cut it off. Jesus speaks with exaggeration and with utmost seriousness. He calls for cutting off your hand or removing your eyes: whatever is keeping you from following God, it needs to be removed. This should not be taken literally, but spiritually. Like a surgeon looking at your wound and saying, "a band-aid won't do. Stitches won't do. It needs to be removed." If watching that show or hanging out with those people leads you to lust, remove it from your life for your own health. If thoughts swirl and you cannot seem to reign them in, bring them to Jesus and ask him for help. Like a surgeon removing a dangerous and infected part of our body, there is mercy in being merciless in dealing with our sin.

Lust is destructive—it damages marriages when it enters the home, it can kill friendships, and can even lead to shame when we find ourselves giving in to desire, to porn, or to self-pleasure again and wondering why we feel so empty inside. Whatever it is that is leading you away from God, it needs to go so that we can be free.

Prayer: *Do not let my heart be drawn to what is evil so that I take part in wicked deeds along with those who are evildoers; do not let me eat their delicacies.* (Psalm 141:4 NIV)

Chastity—Lord's Day 41—Wednesday

Read: 1 Corinthians 7:1–11
"Marriage"

PAUL'S WORDS CHALLENGE BOTH the marriage culture of the church and the sexualized culture of the world. On the one hand, we are told not everyone in the church should be married. Earthly marriage is by no means a requirement for a full Christian life. This should lead Christians to give greater value and appreciation for the unmarried in the church. On the other hand, sexual fulfillment is not central to a full human life either. Paul upholds a chaste singleness and a disciplined marriage. Husbands and wives should have mutual rights to one another's bodies (a shocking claim at the time). It is not only the husband who has the right to desire and expect sex with his wife, but the wife has the right to desire and expect sex with her husband. They are equal partners. Marriage is described as a concession for those lacking self-control. Sex or the desire for sex is not inherently bad, but it is not at the center of what it means to be human. We can exercise self-control, never have sex, and still be a completely fulfilled human (and, perhaps, a more faithful Christian).

In a world both demeaning of marriage and obsessed with sex, 1 Corinthians 7 offers a helpful corrective. Marriage is good, sex is good, but neither are the ultimate good of life. Singleness, as marriage, can be a full and faithful way of living as a disciple of Jesus Christ.

Prayer: *My soul thirsts for God, for the living God. When can I go and meet with God?* (Psalm 42:2 NIV)

Chastity—Lord's Day 41—Thursday

Read: 1 Corinthians 7:12–24
"Remain where you are"

RELATIONSHIPS ARE HARD, INSIDE and outside of marriage. When Christ gets a hold of our life, sometimes our relationships get more complicated and difficult, not less.

Christians are never called to remain *as* they are, but often to remain *where* they are. God calls many to leave behind people and place and go to where he sends. For most, however, God's call to be changed is also a call to remain where they are. "However that may be, let each of you lead the life that the Lord has assigned, to which God called you. This is my rule in all the churches" (v. 17). Conversion does not mean abandoning your vows and your relationships. Even in marriages where one spouse comes to faith and the other does not, this does not mean the marriage ends. If the unbelieving spouse is willing to remain in the marriage, the Christian is called to keep their vows and, perhaps, even witness to their spouse. However, if the unbelieving spouse separates, the Christian should allow it. The Christian should not be the one to break the oath and abandon the family. Though we do not remain as we are, we are, when possible, to remain where we are.

Prayer: *I wait for the LORD, my whole being waits, and in his word I put my hope.* (Psalm 130:5 NIV)

Chastity—Lord's Day 41—Friday

Read: 1 Corinthians 7:25-40
"To marry or not"

Is it wise to get married or not? This decision is not a simple matter between right and wrong. Neither marriage nor singleness is sinful, but they can be wise or foolish to pursue depending on the person and the circumstance. It might be good for one person to get married and not for another.

Paul names three specific factors to consider on whether those betrothed should get married. First, we must consider our self-control and our passions. "If his passions are strong, and so it has to be, let him marry as he wishes; it is no sin" (v. 36). Second, we must consider our anxiety and our attention. Marriage requires time and effort, which may mean sacrificing certain ambitions and desires. Third, Paul urges many not to marry because the time is short. There is much work to do and little time before Christ returns. At times, the urgency of the work the LORD has given to us will lead us not to marry.

Marriage is good, but it is not for everyone. We are called to consider our character, our calling, and the urgency of our work when discerning whether to pursue marriage.

Prayer: *All my longings lie open before you, Lord; my sighing is not hidden from you.* (Psalm 38:9 NIV)

Chastity—Lord's Day 41—Saturday

Read: 1 Thessalonians 4:1-8
"God's will is your sanctification"

What is God's will for my life? We ask this question in the big decisions and the daily tasks of life. How do I know I am pursuing what God calls me to pursue?

We know this: God's will for your life is sanctification. "For this is the will of God, your sanctification" (v. 3). "Sanctification" is the work of God making us holy and conforming our lives to Jesus Christ. As the details of a sanctified life are laid out, it includes controlling our bodies by abstaining from sexual immorality. What we do with our bodies matters. It is a way of either honoring God or disregarding God. It is not an optional or indifferent matter. Set apart for God's service, our bodies are not directed by lustful passions like those who do not know God, but directed by the Spirit of God who calls us into holiness.

What is God's will for my life? While we may still struggle with what job to take or what school to attend, we do not need to wonder what God's will is. God desires us to be sanctified, made holy by the Spirit, which includes what we do sexually. In this way, we "live decent and chaste lives, within or outside of the holy state of marriage" (Q108).

Prayer: *The fear of the LORD is the beginning of wisdom; all who follow his precepts have good understanding. To him belongs eternal praise.* (Psalm 111:10 NIV)

Our Neighbor's Good—Lord's Day 42—Sunday

**Q110. What does God forbid
in the eighth commandment?**
A. God forbids not only outright theft and robbery,
punishable by law.
But in God's sight theft also includes
all scheming and swindling
in order to get our neighbor's goods for ourselves,
whether by force or means that appear legitimate,
such as
inaccurate measurements of weight, size, or volume;
fraudulent merchandizing;
counterfeit money;
excessive interest;
or any other means forbidden by God.
In addition God forbids all greed
and pointless squandering of his gifts.

**Q111. What does God require of you
in this commandment?**
A. That I do whatever I can
for my neighbor's good,
that I treat others
as I would like them to treat me,
and that I work faithfully
so that I may share with those in need.

Like many, I love a good heist movie. Watching the highly-skilled crew in *Oceans 11* hoodwink the casino owner is deeply satisfying. I enjoy seeing how this clever and skilled group will get and out with the goods without getting caught.

However, we have no rights to what belongs to our neighbor, no matter how clever we are. The eighth commandment rules out gas station robberies, the clever schemes of bank heists, and even dealing dishonestly with someone else for your own advantage. It may look (and even be) legal, but if we take what belongs to our neighbor, we sin and break the eighth commandment. If we cheat someone out of what is fair, we steal. If we sell for far more than something is worth, or pay someone far less than they deserve, we steal. Yet, the commandment cuts deeper. When we squander our gifts, hoard our possessions, and refuse to share with our neighbor, we also steal. When we have more than we need, but refuse to share with those that have need, we steal.

The eighth commandment not only tells us to refrain from taking what is not ours, but also to share what is ours with others. To keep the commandment will mean doing "whatever I can for my neighbor's good."

Prayer: *Better the little that the righteous have than the wealth of many wicked.* (Psalm 37:16 NIV)

Our Neighbor's Good—Lord's Day 42—Monday

Read: Deuteronomy 25:13–16
"Deception"

IN THE ANCIENT WORLD, goods were measured using scales. Three one-pound weights are placed on one side of the scale and the other side is loaded up with chunks of cheese until it is balanced out. One way to cheat people was to have "one-pound" weights that weighed less than they should. With these unjust weights, you could sell someone less cheese for the same price, increasing your profit.

Having honest scales was an issue of justice. The prophets frequently condemned the rich for using dishonest scales to defraud the poor. In Deuteronomy 25, God says that those who keep honest scales will dwell long in the land. The implication is that if they cheat their neighbors, God may remove them from the land of Israel (which did eventually happen for a time). To love our neighbors, we must deal with them honestly.

Today, we might not worry about light or heavy weights, but our neighbors are still cheated and defrauded through telemarketer scams, pay-day loans, and deceptive fine print in contracts. As Christians, we keep the eighth commandment by not only dealing honestly with others ourselves, but by working so such wicked practices are ended.

Prayer: *My whole being will exclaim, "Who is like you, LORD? You rescue the poor from those too strong for them, the poor and needy from those who rob them."* (Psalm 35:10 NIV)

Our Neighbor's Good—Lord's Day 42—Tuesday

Read: Exodus 22:1–4
"Repayment"

WHEN I STEAL SOMETHING, what am I truly taking? If my daughter takes a toy from her sister, more than a toy is taken. She cries, she feels loss, her relationship with her sister takes a small hit. Giving the toy back stops the tears, but does not undo all the damage.

Theft requires repayment. In the Bible, it is not enough simply to return what was taken. If the property is used or destroyed, you must pay back five times what was stolen. If the property itself can be returned, you must still pay double. Theft breaks trust and relationship. Restoration requires more than just giving back what was taken, we must work to restore the lost honor and trust of the one from whom we stole. When we steal, we must repay all that was lost, not just return what was stolen.

The Bible is concerned with the fabric of relationships that make up our life. The command against stealing is about more than protecting private property rights. When we return more than we have stolen, we acknowledge the extent of the damage that is done by theft. In this way, we show the value we place on the relationships in our lives and in our community.

Prayer: *Do not trust in extortion or put vain hope in stolen goods; though your riches increase, do not set your heart on them.* (Psalm 62:10 NIV)

Our Neighbor's Good—Lord's Day 42—Wednesday

Read: James 2:1–13
"Favoritism"

VISITING FOR THE FIRST time, Evan went to shake the pastor's hand to thank him for the message. Evan's disheveled clothes meant he wasn't worthy of his time. "He saw right through me," he recalled as the pastor quickly moved on to talk with more well-dressed visitors.

Greed can manifest itself through favoritism. The wealthy or well-educated often get more attention and respect in our congregations. When a visitor drives up in a expensive car, everyone stops to talk with him and invite him back. When a woman arrives in her best clothes, which are quite worn and ragged, everyone looks uncomfortable. This favoritism is sin. "Has not God chosen the poor in the world to be rich in faith and to be heirs of the kingdom that he has promised to those who love him?" (v. 5). To favor the rich is the way of the world, but God's way is different.

Favoritism is not necessarily greed for money, but for honor, power, or respect. We like to be surrounded by the famous, the powerful, and the influential. However, God calls us to "show no partiality as you hold the faith" (v. 1 ESV).

Prayer: *Trust in him at all times, you people; pour out your hearts to him, for God is our refuge. Surely the lowborn are but a breath, the highborn are but a lie. If weighed on a balance, they are nothing; together they are only a breath.* (Psalm 62:8–9 NIV)

Our Neighbor's Good—Lord's Day 42—Thursday

Read: Matthew 25:14–30
"Wasting Gifts"

SOMETIMES THE WORST RESPONSE is to do nothing. We understand this when someone stands idly by watching someone suffer or die. But what about when we have gifts or resources and refuse to use them for others?

We are called to use our gifts for the glory of God. In the parable of the talents, only the servant who did nothing is rebuked. The first servant receives five talents (about a hundred years worth of wages), goes out, and makes five more. He is praised and rewarded. The second servant receives two talents (about forty years worth of wages) and makes two more. He, too, is praised and rewarded. The last servant distrusts his master and buries the talent. He did not lose the money, but because he did not use it, he is rebuked and cast out. His failure to act was his downfall. By refusing to use what he has been given, the servant stole from his master. He stole the profit the master should have been able to expect.

When we refuse to use our gifts for God's glory, we steal from God and our neighbor. Hoarding our talent, money, or time denies our neighbor in their need and dishonors God.

Prayer: *Do not be overawed when others grow rich, when the splendor of their houses increases; for they will take nothing with them when they die, their splendor will not descend with them.* (Psalm 49:16–17 NIV)

Our Neighbor's Good—Lord's Day 42—Friday

Read: Ephesians 4:25–32
"No longer steal"

AT THE HEART OF greed is the fear that there is never enough. So I need more. I either take more, hoard more, or feel unable to give because I fear not having enough. Underneath the fear that we do not have enough is the deeper fear that we are, ourselves, not enough. We can live with greedy anxiety when we do not believe our worth in Jesus.

The antidote to fearful anxiety is security in Jesus Christ. We need something that stuff and money, no matter how much, can never offer. Nothing you do can make God love you less, and nothing you do can make God love you more. Only Jesus Christ, who was born for you, lived for you, died for you, rose for you, and is seated at God's right hand for you, can make your life secure. When we belong to Jesus, our hope, our future, our life, our identity is secure. When this is true, we don't need to take; we don't need to grab and hoard and hold on.

Instead, we can see all that we have as an opportunity to love our neighbors. "Thieves must give up stealing; rather let them labor and work honestly with their own hands, so as to have something to share with the needy" (v. 28). In Christ, our hearts are set free to work so that we might share with others.

Prayer: *They will have no fear of bad news; their hearts are steadfast, trusting in the LORD.* (Psalm 112:7 NIV)

Our Neighbor's Good—Lord's Day 42—Saturday

Read: Isaiah 58:1–10
"Loose the bonds of injustice"

EVERY FLIGHT HAS THE same safety training. In an emergency, oxygen masks will appear. Secure your own mask before helping others. Sadly, the church has become good at fixing our own oxygen mask and watching while others struggle to put theirs on.

Isaiah revealed Israel was good at keeping all the religious ceremonies, but at the same time, they were oppressing others through their work. They worshipped God in the sanctuary, but treated their employees like dirt in the workplace. They fasted, praised, and prayed, but they spent their days fighting, scheming, and breaking the backs of the weak. God calls for a different way. The fast he desires is one where the poor are set free, the straps that keep the oppressed in bondage are loosened. He tells Israel, "if you offer your food to the hungry and satisfy the needs of the afflicted, then your light shall rise in the darkness and your gloom be like the noonday" (v. 10). By caring for the poor and weak, Israel will be a light among the nations.

The eighth commandment calls for us to care for the poor and the weak. It is not enough simply to put our oxygen mask on and leave others to struggle. Our Sunday worship should be joined with Monday through Saturday compassion.

Prayer: *Even in darkness light dawns for the upright, for those who are gracious and compassionate and righteous.* (Psalm 112:4 NIV)

Love the Truth—Lord's Day 43—Sunday

Q112. What is the aim of the ninth commandment?

A. That I

never give false testimony against anyone,

twist no one's words,

not gossip or slander,

nor join in condemning anyone

rashly or without a hearing.

Rather, in court and everywhere else,

I should avoid lying and deceit of every kind;

these are the very devices the devil uses,

and they would call down on my God's intense wrath.

I should love the truth,

speak it candidly,

and openly acknowledge it.

And I should do what I can

to guard and advance my neighbor's good name.

WHAT DOES CHRISTIAN DISCIPLESHIP look like in light of the ninth commandment? I think the Catechism gets it right when it says that "I should love the truth, speak it candidly, and openly acknowledge it."

In our world today, we are tempted to separate honesty and compassion. Candor holds them together. We often fear that we must either speak the truth or save the relationship. However, speaking candidly is gently, patiently speaking the truth for the good of your neighbor. Candor involves speaking truth face-to-face, not behind another's back. Candor is avoiding flattery or silence out of a misguided desire to protect another with half-truths. Candor avoids using the truth as a bludgeon. Candor encourages and corrects. Candor also avoids believing and speaking the worst about someone else before all the facts are in. Speaking truthfully, candidly, holds together honesty and love.

The church, of all places, should be where the truth is told. We tell the truth about ourselves: we are beautiful and broken, made in God's image and rebels against God. We tell the truth about God—Father, Son, and Holy Spirit—his holiness, his goodness, his love and his grace poured out in Jesus Christ, the coming judgment, and the call to repentance and faith. In short, the church needs candor.

Prayer: *For the word of the LORD is right and true; he is faithful in all he does. The LORD loves righteousness and justice; the earth is full of his unfailing love.* (Psalm 33:4–5 NIV)

Love the Truth—Lord's Day 43—Monday

Read: Acts 5:1–11
"Loving the Truth"

THE STORY OF ANANIAS and Sapphira is a difficult one for many of us to hear. It comes on the heels of incredible works of God in growing the church. Yet, despite all the good that is happening and all the good that Ananias and Sapphira may have done in the church, there are certain behaviors God desires to be rooted out of the church for its own good.

Ananias and Sapphira were judged for their lying more than their greed. This couple generously sold some property to give the proceeds to the church for its ministry. They claimed to give the whole amount to the church, but secretly held some back for themselves. They wanted to look generous while secretly hoarding some for themselves. Yet, when Peter confronts them, it is for lying and testing the Holy Spirit. They have been called before the apostle and given false testimony. It was for this, even more than their greed, that they were judged.

Ananias and Sapphira serve as a caution to the church today. Lying is the sin God most swiftly rooted out of the early church. A lying tongue and a lying spirit are toxic to the church, no matter how much money someone gives.

Prayer: *Save me, LORD, from lying lips and from deceitful tongues.* (Psalm 120:2 NIV)

Love the Truth—Lord's Day 43—Tuesday

Read: Psalm 15
"Speaks the Truth in his Heart"

LANGUAGE IS ONE OF the most precious gifts that God has given humanity. Right now, if you are reading this out loud, your mind is working with muscles in your vocal chords, lips, cheeks, tongue, and jaw all to produce words. These words carry meaning, communicate desire, information, and wonder. The ability to speak is an incredible gift of God.

God cares deeply about the words that we speak. In Psalm 15, only the blameless can approach God in the tabernacle for worship. However, four of the eight ways to be blameless are related to our speech. The one who can sojourn in God's tent speaks the truth from his heart (v. 2), does not slander with his tongue (v. 3), does not take up reproach against a friend (v. 3), and swears to his own hurt and does not change (v. 4). At the head of these descriptions is speaking the truth. God delights when we speak the truth and keep our word.

Language is a gift from God. It is a gift that can be used to slander or to speak the truth and praise God. May we use this gift well and come into the Lord's house for worship.

Prayer: *Lord, who may dwell in your sacred tent? Who may live on your holy mountain? The one whose walk is blameless, who does what is righteous, who speaks the truth from their heart.* (Psalm 15:1–2 NIV)

Love the Truth—Lord's Day 43—Wednesday

Read: Proverbs 19:5–9
"False Witness"

WHAT DOES A FALSE witness do? A false witness causes the innocent to be condemned and the guilty to go free. "A false witness will not go unpunished, and a liar will not escape" (v. 5). Proverbs 19 repeats this same admonition twice for emphasis. To pervert justice through a lying tongue should not be excused. In between are several proverbs about gift-givers and the poor. Those who are generous and give gifts find people flocking to them, while the poor find even their closest family hate them. Why put these proverbs between statements about false witnesses? The wealthy and generous often benefit from false witnesses. People assume the best of them, excuse their crimes, or believe the good outweighs the bad. The poor receive the worst from false witnesses. People assume the worst and magnify their crimes. False witnesses often malign the poor and benefit the wealthy and generous.

Whenever we are called to testify about our neighbor, in the courtroom or conversation, we must speak the truth. We do not consider their wealth, past reputation, or future good works, but only the truth of what happened. In this, we are true witnesses by not showing partiality, but upholding justice and truth.

Prayer: *I hate and detest falsehood but I love your law.* (Psalm 119:163 NIV)

Love the Truth—Lord's Day 43—Thursday

Read: 1 Corinthians 13
"Love rejoices in the Truth"

IS IT MORE LOVING to keep the peace or tell him the truth? I can tell him the truth, but he may no longer want to be friends with me. If I love her, I cannot tell her how harmful her actions were. At times, we feel we must either tell the truth or save the relationship.

This is a false choice. Love "rejoices in the truth" (v. 6). Christian love finds joy in the Truth (Jesus Christ) and in all the things that are true. Love is not begrudging or tolerating the truth, but rejoicing in it. Love is not simply accepting the truth and loving anyway, but finding joy in speaking and knowing the truth. Truth can encourage and correct us. Truth can lead us closer to Christ and deeper into who God calls us to be. Sometimes the truth about ourselves or others will hurt for a time, but ultimately love will rejoice in it.

Love and Truth strengthen one another. When we love someone, we will want to tell them the truth for their good. And we will want them to do the same with us. When truth is spoken in love, then in love we can rejoice in the truth as it leads us to the Truth.

Prayer: *The LORD is compassionate and gracious, slow to anger, abounding in love.* (Psalm 103:8 NIV)

Love the Truth—Lord's Day 43—Friday

Read: 1 Peter 3:8–12
"Zeal for the truth"

IF YOU COULD BUILD a perfect church, what would it look like? Not the design of the building, but the shape of the people. What traits or habits would be best for forming a family that loves and serves God?

Thankfully, we do not need to guess what God desires for his church. God tells us what virtues and habits should make up his people. Our minds should be united. We should be filled with sympathy, brotherly love, and have a humble mind. Our hands are to turn from doing evil to do good. We do not repay evil for evil, but bless those who curse us. The character of the church is also seen in how we talk. When people revile us, we do not revile them back. We keep our tongue from evil and our lips from deceit. In the church, our minds, hearts, lips, and hands should be shaped *by* God and *for* God.

When God's Word instructs us, "You shall not give false testimony against your neighbor," this instruction touches our actions in the courtroom, in the sanctuary, the classroom, the kitchen, and the workplace. The Christian church is marked by how we use our lips.

Prayer: *Guide me in your truth and teach me, for you are God my Savior, and my hope is in you all day long.* (Psalm 25:5 NIV)

Love the Truth—Lord's Day 43—Saturday

Read: 2 John
"Testifying and walking in the truth"

"I JUST WANT MY children to be happy." When parents say this, I wonder, "Is that all?" What if they were happy kicking puppies? What if they were happy never growing up and maturing? What if what they think will make them happy will never truly satisfy them?

John wants more than happiness for his children in the faith. "I was overjoyed to find some of your children walking in the truth, just as we have been commanded by the Father" (v. 4). Throughout John's letter, truth is of vital importance. John loves the recipients of the letter "in the truth" (v. 1). He is joined in that love by all who know the truth because the truth abides in them. Grace, mercy, and peace come from God in truth and love. But the great joy that John experiences is that the people are walking in the truth. They not only speak the truth, but live their lives according to it.

What do you desire most for your children, your friends, your family, and your neighbors? I hope that they are happy, but far more than that, I hope that they are walking in the truth according to the Word of God.

Prayer: *Your statutes are my heritage forever; they are the joy of my heart.* (Psalm 119:111 NIV)

Q113. What is the aim of the tenth commandment?
A. That not even the slightest desire or thought contrary
   to any one of God's commandments should ever arise in our hearts.
   Rather, with all our hearts we should always hate sin
   and take pleasure in whatever is right.

Q114. But can those converted to God obey these commandments perfectly?
A. No.
   In this life even the holiest have only a small beginning of this obedience.
   Nevertheless, with all seriousness of purpose, they do begin to live
   according to all, not only some, of God's commandments.

Q115. Since no one in this life can obey the Ten Commandments perfectly,
   why does God want them preached so pointedly?
A. First, so that the longer we live the more we may come to know our sinfulness
   and the more eagerly look to Christ for forgiveness of sins and righteousness.
   Second, so that we may never stop striving, and never stop praying to God
   for the grace of the Holy Spirit, to be renewed more and more after God's image,
   until after this life we reach our goal: perfection.

THE TEACHER HANDS BACK your test with an 82 written on it. You studied hard and feel good. Moments later, a classmate reveals they barely studied and got an 87. What happens in your heart? You might feel angry or bitter toward the person with the 87. You might feel discouraged about yourself. For a moment, you were content with the fruit of your hard work, but comparison sucks it all away.

Coveting is wanting what our neighbor has. "You shall not covet your neighbor's house"—not just their home, but their whole life. "You shall not covet your neighbor's wife." We have a tendency to covet other people's families at times. *Her* marriage must be wonderful. *His* kids are always well-behaved. Even in ancient times, this was a reality. "His male or female servant, his ox or donkey." We can covet success at work. Those extra dollars that would make life easier. That recognition she gets, but you never do. Coveting can touch all areas of our life. In case we thought anything was left out, God includes "or anything else that belongs to your neighbor."

The opposite of coveting is contentment, trusting in the goodness of God. In this life, you will have troubles. Yet if my life is about Jesus, serving him by serving my neighbor, and sharing the name of Christ, then why do I care if my neighbor has a better lawn, a better job, or a more put-together family? Because I am secure in Jesus, I can fully commit to who God has given me and where he has placed me.

Prayer: *Keep me safe, my God, for in you I take refuge. I say to the LORD, "You are my Lord; apart from you I have no good thing." (Psalm 16:1–2 NIV)*

Small Beginnings of Obedience—Lord's Day 44—Monday

Read: 2 Samuel 11
"A multitude of sins"

As a kid, I liked to set up dominoes in different patterns and let the first one topple. Every time the first would knock over the second, the second the third, the third the fourth, until eventually every one of them was knocked down.

When it comes to sin, coveting is often the first domino to fall. King David looks out and sees Bathsheba bathing. He wants her. Though she is Uriah's wife, David desires her, so he takes what he desires. Coveting leads to adultery. Bathsheba gets pregnant. To cover his crime, David attempts to get Uriah to sleep with Bathsheba. Coveting leads to lying and deception. Failing, David places Uriah at the front line of battle so he will be killed. Coveting leads to murder. Only after the prophet Nathan confronts David are his eyes opened. The first domino of coveting falls, and all sorts of sins start crashing down around David.

Coveting cuts right to the heart, to our desire for things contrary to God's will for us. From these mismatched desires, all sorts of other sins flow. The sin of coveting may start alone, but it never ends alone. It always leads to other sins.

Prayer: *For the sake of your name, LORD, forgive my iniquity, though it is great.* (Psalm 25:11 NIV)

Small Beginnings of Obedience—Lord's Day 44—Tuesday

Read: Psalm 139:17–24
"No Wicked Way In Us"

"Search me and know my heart." A beautiful and dangerous thing to ask. Do we really want God, who knows us completely, to test our hearts, to reveal any wickedness there, and to lead us in the way everlasting? Things we let fester in the darkness would come out into the light. Things we hold dear might be left behind. God will cut, prune, and heal as he wants, not as we would like.

Psalm 139 invites us to come to God completely transparent. We place our lives before the LORD to do the work only he can do—kill and make alive, prune and make grow, forgive and heal. This confession will not be comfortable, but it is good. There is wisdom for Christians to gather to confess their sins every week in worship. We need the God who knows us to come and change us. We need him to search and test us, to convict us of all the ways our hearts have gone wrong so that in his healing light he might lead us in the way everlasting. We come to God in confession to have our hearts revealed and to have them reshaped into the way of God.

Prayer: *Search me, God, and know my heart; test me and know my anxious thoughts. See if there is any offensive way in me, and lead me in the way everlasting.* (Psalm 139:23–24 NIV)

Small Beginnings of Obedience—
Lord's Day 44—Wednesday

Read: Philippians 3:12–16
"Striving for Righteousness"

"ARE WE THERE YET?" Though the question gets exhausting, I admire my children's eagerness to get to the destination. Though the journey is long, they have only one focus: to arrive. We should pursue Christ and his calling upon us with the same single-minded focus.

None of us has arrived at perfect holiness. As the Catechism states, "In this life even the holiest have only a small beginning of this obedience" (Q114). We have not arrived, but we still strive for righteousness. In Philippians 3, Paul uses the image of a runner racing toward the finish line. He strains with all his effort to move toward it, shedding everything else that might get in the way. The runner must have a single-minded focus on the finish line if he is going to win. Paul runs this race, pushes forward to claim Christ, because Christ has already claimed him. Because Christ has already made Paul his, Paul can run wholeheartedly for Jesus.

Are we there yet? No, none of us have arrived when it comes to following Jesus. Yet, Christ has taken hold of us. Because he has made us his own, we should daily strive to move forward in running after Jesus.

Prayer: *With your help I can advance against a troop; with my God I can scale a wall.* (Psalm 18:29 NIV)

Small Beginnings of Obedience—Lord's Day 44—Thursday

Read: Psalm 1
"Meditating on God's Word"

THE WORD "MEDITATE" OFTEN brings to mind silent, detached concentration or focus. We imagine Buddhist monks, detached from the world and meditating for enlightenment. The Biblical image of meditation—*Hagah*—couldn't be more different.

Hagah is the sound a lion makes when it eats its food, a deep throated growl of pleasure. This is biblical meditation. "But their delight is in the law of the Lord, and on his law they *Hagah* day and night" (v. 2). We savor God's Word, salivate over it, hunger for it. Like an animal with its bone, we chew on God's Word, roll it around in our mouth, set it aside for a bit and come back to it. Twice, God demanded this literally from his servants. God has Ezekiel write God's Word on a scroll and then commands him to eat it and fill his stomach with it. The Apostle John on Patmos was told to take the scroll from the hands of the angel and eat it.

While God is not calling for us to eat the pages in our Bibles, the image is still there. *Hagah*—to meditate on God's Word day and night with an active delight. To meditate on it, ingest it, and allow God to change us through it.

Prayer: *but whose delight is in the law of the LORD, and who meditates on his law day and night.* (Psalm 1:2 NIV)

Small Beginnings of Obedience—Lord's Day 44—Friday

Read: Psalm 32
"Why Teach the Ten Commandments?"

WHAT HAPPENS WHEN WE fail yet again? If we fail so consistently to keep the Ten Commandments, why should we keep teaching them?

Teaching the Ten Commandments regularly reminds us where to go to find forgiveness for our sins. One of the purposes of the Ten Commandments is to help us see our need for Jesus Christ. Psalm 32 is a prayer of joy after coming to confession. After recognizing his sin, David runs to the Lord. In coming to God and baring his sin in repentance, David found forgiveness. This forgiveness leads to a psalm of joy and gladness. It leads to a prayer of praise to the goodness, grace, and mercy of God. David's example reminds us where to run when we have fallen into sin. When we hear again the Ten Commandments and sense how poorly we have kept them, we can run to Jesus, in whom our transgression is forgiven and our sins are covered.

None of us keeps the Ten Commandments perfectly. Yet, we need them taught to us regularly. Not only so we know how God calls us to live, but so we can see our sin and run swiftly to Christ, our only refuge and hope.

Prayer: *Blessed is the one whose transgressions are forgiven, whose sins are covered.*
(Psalm 32:1 NIV)

Small Beginnings of Obedience—Lord's Day 44—Saturday

Read: Romans 7:14–25
"We have just a beginning in this life"

I WAS SITTING ON the end of my son's bed. He had been sent to bed early for hitting his sister. He looked sad and admitted to me, "Sometimes I like to do bad things." I replied, "Me too, buddy. I feel those same desires too sometimes."

Paul admits to a war raging in his heart. He knows what he should do. Yet, at times, he lacks the ability to carry it out. He finds himself doing the evil he does not want to do and not doing the good he wants to do. The sin that dwells within him refuses to go quietly. It flails within Paul, wreaking havoc in his life. No wonder he says, "Wretched man that I am! Who will rescue me from this body of death?" (v. 24).

There is hope for all of us with war raging in our hearts. After lamenting his situation, Paul gives us the one true hope we have: "Thanks be to God through Jesus Christ our Lord!" (v. 25). We are not saved through the purity of our lives or our desires. We are saved by the purity of Christ, who redeems us from this body of death into eternal life with him.

Prayer: *Answer me, LORD, out of the goodness of your love; in your great mercy turn to me.*
(Psalm 69:16 NIV)

Q116. Why do Christians need to pray?

A. Because prayer is the most important part
of the thankfulness God requires of us.
And also because God gives his grace and Holy Spirit
only to those who pray continually and groan inwardly,
asking God for these gifts
and thanking God for them.

**Q117. What is the kind of prayer
that pleases God and that he listens to?**

A. First, we must pray from the heart
to no other than the one true God,
revealed to us in his Word,
asking for everything God has commanded us to ask for.
Second, we must fully recognize our need and misery,
so that we humble ourselves in God's majestic presence.
Third, we must rest on this unshakable foundation:
even though we do not deserve it,
God will surely listen to our prayer
because of Christ our Lord.
That is what God promised us in his Word.

Q118. What did God command us to pray for?

A. Everything we need, spiritually and physically,
as embraced in the prayer
Christ our Lord himself taught us.

Q119. What is this prayer?

A. Our Father in heaven,
hallowed be your name.
Your kingdom come.
Your will be done,
on earth as it is in heaven.
Give us this day our daily bread.
And forgive us our debts,
as we also have forgiven our debtors.
And do not bring us to the time of trial,
but rescue us from the evil one.
For the kingdom
and the power
and the glory are yours forever.
Amen.

DINNER IS READY. SPAGHETTI has been strained. Garlic bread is out of the oven. Plates are set and glasses full. As the delicious smells fill our nostrils, we stop, bow our heads, and pray. Why?

Christians are people who pray, but why? In the midst of every increasing busyness, unfolded laundry, and unfinished to-do lists, Christians take time to stop and speak with God. The Heidelberg Catechism devotes the whole last section to the practice of prayer and, specifically, the Lord's Prayer. By placing prayer toward the end of the catechism, we are not saying it is less important or just an appendix to the rest of the Christian life. Instead, prayer is part of our gratitude. As the catechism writes, "prayer is the most important part of the thankfulness God requires of us" (Q116). Prayer flows from a heart that has tasted and seen the goodness of God.

Dinner is on the table. We stop and bow our heads. We pray with thanks. Prayer is more than simply thanking God, but certainly not less than that. We are to pray for "Everything we need, spiritually and physically" (Q118). We cry out in distress, ask in our need, and lament in our sorrow. However, the catechism puts prayer in its proper place—principally as an act of gratitude and thankfulness to God.

Prayer: *Give thanks to the LORD, for he is good. His love endures forever.* (Psalm 136:1 NIV)

Learning to Pray—Lord's Day 45—Monday

Read: Matthew 6:5–8
"We must pray from the heart"

IMAGINE MOM AND DAD are dressed up and ready to go out to dinner. They pull up to a nice restaurant and sit down. However, instead of talking together, Dad spends the whole night telling the waiter how amazing his wife is. Shouldn't he be telling this to his wife instead?

In prayer, we speak to God. Whoever else is listening, God is our conversation partner in prayer. When prayer becomes about being seen by everyone else, it is like coming before God and, instead of talking to him, spending the whole time telling everyone else about how much you love and trust God. Jesus calls this "praying like the hypocrites." In the time of Jesus, hypocrites were masked actors in the theatre. They present one face to the world, but keep their true face hidden. Hypocrites are those who want others to know they are praying more than they want to pray themselves. They present one face to the world—"I am someone who prays"—but their real face is hidden. Prayer itself is secondary to being known as someone who prays.

Jesus tells us to remember who you are talking to when you pray. Pray like no one is watching even if someone is. Keep your focus on your Heavenly Father. When you are by yourself, when you lock the door and are alone in your room, God is with you. Your Father sees your heart.

Prayer: *From the ends of the earth I call to you, I call as my heart grows faith; lead me to the rock that is higher than I.* (Psalm 61:2 NIV)

Learning to Pray—Lord's Day 45—Tuesday

Read: Psalm 116
"Prayer is the most important part of the thankfulness which God requires of us"

A MAN'S PARENTS HELPED him buy a house. It was an incredibly generous gesture and he was so thankful. But the gift was so big he did not know how to begin saying, "Thank you." How do you say thank you for extravagant gifts?

God has given us extravagant gifts. During times of distress, anguish, and imminent death, we cried out to the Lord and were saved. When we were low, God saved us. When we were weary, God gave us rest. With all the Lord has done for us, how shall we respond? "What shall I return to the Lord for all his bounty to me? I will lift up the cup of salvation and call on the name of the Lord" (vv. 12–13). We respond to God's grace and mercy by calling upon his name in prayer. Prayer is both our ready response in times of distress and danger and the perfect response when God has poured out his blessing. God hears our prayers in need and delights in our prayers of thanks after he delivers us.

How do we say thank you to God for his extravagant gifts in our lives? We pray. Prayer is, as the catechism says, "the most important part of the thankfulness which God requires of us" (Q116).

Prayer: *I love the LORD, for he heard my voice; he heard my cry for mercy.* (Psalm 116:1 NIV)

Learning to Pray—Lord's Day 45—Wednesday

Read: Acts 17:16–31
"To the one true God, revealed to us in his Word"

IN ATHENS, PAUL WAS distressed by all the idols he saw. There was even "an altar to unknown god." People prayed, even to a God they did not know. Many also pray today to a God they do not know. They may pray to other so-called gods, to the universe, or simply send up "good vibes." Yet all these attempts at prayer are aimed at a God they do not know.

When Christians pray, we pray to the God we know. He has told us about himself. He has shown us his character. He has done great things for us in the past and promises to do much more in the future. God has revealed himself in the Scriptures, has come to us and for us as Jesus Christ, and lives within us in the person of the Holy Spirit. We know God because he has made himself known to us. When Paul stands up in the Areopagus to address the people of Athens, he remarks about their altar "to an unknown God," and says, "What therefore you worship as unknown, this I proclaim to you" (v. 23).

Christians pray confidently because we know the God who hears our prayers. He alone can be trusted with our prayers, our needs, and our thanks.

Prayer: *But I pray to you, LORD, in the time of your favor; in your great love, O God, answer me with your sure salvation.* (Psalm 69:13 NIV)

Learning to Pray—Lord's Day 45—Thursday

Read: John 14:8–17
"God will surely listen to our prayer because of Christ our Lord"

"IN JESUS' NAME. AMEN." We often end our prayers with these simple words. Why? What is the reason for offering our prayers "in Jesus' name"?

Jesus tells us to ask for what we need from the Father, but to ask it in his name. "I will do whatever you ask in my name, so that the Father may be glorified in the Son. If in my name you ask me for anything, I will do it" (vv. 13–14). Using Jesus' name is not a magic formula for all our prayers to be answered exactly as we want them. Instead, Jesus gives us confidence our prayers will be heard. His name gives us the strength to offer our prayers to the Father. We do not pray in our own name because we cannot stand before God on our own. We stand before God in Jesus' name, in his strength.

"In Jesus' name" is not a superstitious appendix to our prayers, but reveals the ground we stand on as we pray. Because we belong to Christ, because he gives us his name, we can pray in his name and know God will listen to our prayers.

Prayer: *You who answer prayer, to you all people will come.* (Psalm 65:2 NIV)

Learning to Pray—Lord's Day 45—Friday

Read: 1 Peter 5:6–11
"we humble ourselves in God's majestic presence"

BY THE SPIRIT, PETER urges us to "humble [ourselves] therefore under the mighty hand of God. (v. 6). Augustine once said there were three ways to walk before God, "That first way, however, is humility, the second way is humility, and the third way is humility" *(Letter 118)*. Humility before God is not thinking too low or too high of oneself, but recognizing ourselves in proper relationship to God. The posture is essential to prayer and cultivated in prayer. We are not God. This is good news. We must be humble to pray and learn humility by praying.

We humble ourselves before God in order to struggle against sin and evil. Peter tells us to keep alert, resist, and be steadfast against the devil (vv. 8–9). God calls us to resist everything in us and in the world that fights against the reign of Christ. We resist even to the point of suffering (vv. 9–10). Resisting evil is also essential to prayer and cultivated by prayer. Humbly trusting God, we stand firm against evil. Eyes alert to wickedness in us and in the world, we pray for God's kingdom to come on earth as it is in heaven.

Prayer: *My heart is not proud, LORD, my eyes are not haughty; I do not concern myself with great matters or things too wonderful for me.*
(Psalm 131:1 NIV)

Learning to Pray—Lord's Day 45—Saturday

Read: Matthew 7:7–11
"All things we need for body and soul"

SOME PEOPLE ARE SKILLED at picking out just the right gift. They know how to find something personal, practical, and fun all at the same time. Others of us fumble with our hearts in the right place but the wrong gift in our hands.

God never gives us the wrong gift. We would all do our best to give what is best to our children. Jesus says "Is there anyone among you who, if your child asks for bread, will give a stone? Or if the child asks for a fish, will give a snake?" (vv. 9–10). Even those who struggle to find the right gifts would not fail to give their children food when they ask for it. We may fail, but God will not. Our heavenly Father is far greater, far more loving, and far more generous than any of our earthly parents will ever be. What he gives us is always good.

Jesus talks about gifts to urge us to pray. We are to "ask, seek, and knock"—to come regularly to the Father in prayer for all that we need for our body and soul. We can pray knowing that God's gifts to us are good, far better than anything our parents will give us.

Prayer: *The LORD is my shepherd, I lack nothing. He makes me lie down in green pastures, he leads me beside quiet waters.* (Psalm 23:1–2 NIV)

God Our Father—Lord's Day 46—Sunday

**Q120. Why did Christ command us
to call God "our Father"?**

A. To awaken in us
at the very beginning of our prayer
what should be basic to our prayer—
a childlike reverence and trust
that through Christ God has become our Father,
and that just as our parents do not refuse us
the things of this life,
even less will God our Father refuse to give us
what we ask in faith.

**Q121. Why the words
"in heaven"?**

A. These words teach us
not to think of God's heavenly majesty
as something earthly,
and to expect everything
needed for body and soul
from God's almighty power.

AT THE BEGINNING OF the Lord's Prayer, we come near to the heart of the gospel. Jesus teaches us to pray "Our Father in heaven." We are welcomed to God's presence as children in his family. Though we are not naturally children of God, we are brought into God's family through Jesus Christ. He looks upon us with the Father's love. Christians are children of God.

God has only one Son, Jesus Christ. The rest of us are not naturally children of God. We are creatures. We are created in God's image and likeness, but we are not children of God. We are created with dignity and purpose and beauty, but we are not God. We cannot approach the throne of God. Not only is there a natural gap between God and everything that is not God, including us, we have created an additional problem. Sin creates another layer of separation between us and God. Our hearts are turned away from God and our lives have reflected that.

The good news is that "through Christ God has become our Father." The Son came into the world so that we might be called sons and daughters of God. He went down into the flesh, down into the manger, down in humility all the days of his life, down to the cross, down to the tomb, so that we might be raised up from the grave, up from the dust, up from our sins, to be seated at the table of the king, children in the Father's house.

Prayer: *As a father has compassion on his children, so the LORD has compassion on those who fear him.* (Psalm 103:13 NIV)

God Our Father—Lord's Day 46—Monday

Read: Matthew 6:9–13
"Our Father"

MY CHILDREN USED TO love reading a book called, "Just Me and My Dad," about a boy camping with his father. However, all three children wanted to be on my lap at the same time. It was hard to say "just me and my dad" to my son, with his two sisters sitting there too. It is really "us and our dad" since they are all siblings.

Jesus teaches us to pray "our Father" because our relationship with God joins us together with a whole family of siblings, the church. The Lord is *our* Father." We cannot go it alone. There might be times we want to. The church is a messy place. It might feel more spiritual to have a relationship with Jesus apart from these people. God's wisdom puts us together into a family called the church, warts and all. We pray "our Father" because even as Jesus saves sinners personally, he joins them together into a family. We are in this together.

Our Father in heaven. We pray this prayer together. Especially when we feel alone, we pray "Our Father in heaven" with the church. Christians pray together, even when we pray by ourselves. The opening of the Lord's Prayer reminds us we are bound together as a family.

Prayer: *How good and pleasant it is when God's people live together in unity.* (Psalm 133:1 NIV)

God Our Father—Lord's Day 46—Tuesday

Read: Luke 15:11–32
"The Prodigal Father"

I SAT PAINED WITH the parents as the news of their runaway daughter settled in. They were frustrated and hurt, but they loved her immensely. They waited months, watching and praying for any sign of her. When she finally came home, I received the happiest text in the world, "She's home!"

Jesus tells us a parable of a father of two lost sons. One—the older, dutiful son—remains at home, but remains lost. The other—the younger, reckless son—runs away with his portion of the estate. The heart of the parable is the Father's love for these two boys. When the younger son wakes up to his miserable life and heads back, the Father sees him from a distance and runs to him. In a culture where adult men never run, this was a scandalous act of love. Hiking up his robes, his feet padding the earth, this stately, older man runs for his son, even though others might think it undignified. The Father embraces him and brings him home, celebrating that the lost one has been found. When the older brother hears, he is bitter and remains outside of the party. Again, the Father goes out to his son to invite him in. Both sons have a Father who loves them enough to run out to them and bring them home.

The Father in the Lord's Prayer is the same Father in this parable. He loves us enough to run out to us and embrace us, bringing us home.

Prayer: *Restore us, LORD God Almighty; make your face shine on us, that we may be saved.* (Psalm 80:19 NIV)

God Our Father—Lord's Day 46—Wednesday

Read: John 1:1–18

"Through Christ God has become our Father"

WHEN OUR DOCTOR PLACED our newborn son on my wife's chest, he insisted I cut the umbilical cord. While I was initially uncomfortable, the doctor reminded me that this was part of the natural way children are born. My wife carried our son in her womb and bore him into the world. It is the way children have been brought into families for generations. It was completely natural.

However, becoming children of God is anything but natural. This birth is "not of blood or of the will of the flesh or of the will of man, but of God" (v. 13). We become children of God by receiving Jesus, by believing in his name. We are adopted through Jesus Christ. This adoption is a gift of God, we receive through faith. Not because of anything we have done or will do, does God redeem us. Not because of where we come from or what we can offer, does God adopt us as his children. It is the gift of God for all who receive him and believe in his name.

Becoming children of God may not be natural, but it is real. We call God "Father" because through receiving Jesus Christ we have received the gift of adoption into the family of God. We who believe in the name of Jesus are truly the children of God.

Prayer: *He put a new song in my mouth, a hymn of praise to our God. Many will see and fear the LORD and put their trust in him.* (Psalm 40:3 NIV)

God Our Father—Lord's Day 46—Thursday

Read: Isaiah 64

"Our Father In Heaven"

FEW THINGS CUT THE heart like being unable to help your children. When we moved to another country, my children struggled finding new friends, getting used to our new church, and even feeling settled in our new home. No matter how much I loved them, I couldn't make that struggle go away.

In our deepest struggles, we need an all-powerful Father. Seeing the pain and desperate need of God's people, Isaiah prays, "O that you would tear open the heavens and come down" (v. 1). God causes the mountains to shake and the nations to tremble. His coming judges the world (and Israel) for their sin.

Yet, there is hope for mercy. "Yet, O Lord, you are our Father; we are the clay, and you are our potter; we are all the work of your hand" (v. 8). God is both the one who shakes the mountains and the one who molds and fashions us in his hand. He is holy and loving, judging and merciful, Almighty God and our Father.

Unlike earthly fathers, God does not lack strength to help his children. God is the one who sits enthroned in power in heaven and the Father who molds us in his hands. The Father is powerful and loving enough to care for us.

Prayer: *Your kingdom is an everlasting kingdom, and your dominion endures through all generations. The LORD is trustworthy in all he promises and faithful in all he does.* (Psalm 145:13 NIV)

God Our Father—Lord's Day 46—Friday

Read: Psalm 113
"Heavenly power"

WHAT DOES IT LOOK like to be strong? In the world, the strong push down the weak to make themselves stronger. Bullies belittle to strengthen their position. Nations undermine enemies and rivals to gain advantage and power. Is this what true strength looks like?

God shows his strength, not by pushing down the weak, but by lifting up the lowly. God is seated upon the throne of heaven. He has all power and authority, having created the world and everything in it. He is the King of kings on the throne. He will one day vanquish all those who stand against his kingdom. However, in his great power, God shows us what power looks like. "He raises the poor from the dust, and lifts the needy from the ash heap, to make them sit with princes, with the princes of his people" (vv. 7–8). God shows power by lifting up the lowly and giving them seats with the powerful.

When we were brought lowest in our sin, God himself stooped down to raise us up to give us a seat at his table. As one old hymn says, "When I was sinking down beneath God's righteous frown, Christ laid aside His crown for my soul." That is true strength.

Prayer: *From the rising of the sun to the place where it sets, the name of the LORD is to be praised.* (Psalm 113:3 NIV)

God Our Father—Lord's Day 46—Saturday

Read: Isaiah 59:1–8
"The Lord's Long Arm"

AFTER POURING OUT HIS life story, Edward looked me in the eye across the table. "Can someone be too far gone to be saved?" The unspoken, more personal question hung between us, "After all I have done, could God still save me?"

God's arms are long enough to save even those we might think beyond his reach. While in exile, Israel may have wondered if God could still save them. "Your iniquities have been barriers between you and your God" (v. 2). Had they fallen so far that God could no longer reach them? Isaiah proclaims that "Behold, the Lord's hand is not shortened, that it cannot save" (v. 1 KJV). No matter how far they had fallen away, they were not beyond the reach of God. God alone is strong enough to save. He alone can reach deep enough to reach us in our sin. He alone is strong enough to lift us up and bring us to himself.

No one is too far that they are beyond God's reach. This should give us patience to wait for God to work in the hearts of those we love, persistence in sharing the gospel with them, and hope that they can never be too far. God's arm is long enough to save.

Prayer: *Your arm is endowed with power; your hand is strong, your right hand exalted.* (Psalm 89:13 NIV)

Hallowed Be Your Name—Lord's Day 47—Sunday

Q122. What does the first petition mean?

A. "Hallowed be your name" means:

Help us to truly know you,
to honor, glorify, and praise you
for all your works
and for all that shines forth from them:
your almighty power, wisdom, kindness,
justice, mercy, and truth.
And it means,
Help us to direct all our living—
what we think, say, and do—
so that your name will never be blasphemed because of us
but always honored and praised.

PRAYING "HALLOWED BE YOUR name" is a way of saying we want the world to know the greatness, power, and goodness of God. We want the world to know our Holy God. May his name be lifted up, may it be exalted, may it be known. May the Lord be known for who he is.

This task is too big for us. We cannot make God's name holy, so we ask God to do it. And he has. We saw God's glory when he broke the power of Pharaoh and brought us out of Egypt on dry ground. We knew God's holy name when he planted us in the promised land. We saw God's holiness when he cast us out of the land for our sin, but also when he brought us back. God's name was hallowed most of all when God himself came as the man Jesus Christ and died on a cross and rose from the grave, breaking death itself and rescuing us from sin. God has made his name holy, because we cannot.

Yet, we are called to live so God's name is honored and not disgraced through us. God has made his name holy, so we can set about living so the world would see his holy name in us.

Prayer: *I will exalt you, my God the King; I will praise your name for ever and ever.*
(Psalm 145:1 NIV)

Hallowed Be Your Name—Lord's Day 47—Monday

Read: Exodus 3
"The Name of God"

AS A YOUNG CHILD, I decided to call another child "William," even though that was not his real name. I honestly do not remember why I would do such a thing (or even what his real name was), but I had decided his name should be "William," so that is what I called him. He was confused and not at all pleased with me. Our friendship did not survive. Instead of learning his name, I chose to give him a name.

We do not choose God's name. He has given it to us. Moses did not go looking for God and find God at the end of his search. God came to Moses, and then God revealed his name to Moses. Adam named all the animals. He had authority over the animals and knew them well enough to choose a fitting name. Neither of these things apply to our relationship with God. When Moses encounters the LORD at the burning bush, he must receive the name as a gift, as an act of revelation from God. God's name—YHWH—tells us he is always faithful to who he is.

God told us who he is, what he is like, by giving us his name. This is the name we pray to be hallowed. Because he has given us his name, we can know him. The gift of his name gives us the possibility of relationship with God.

Prayer: *Every day I will praise you and extol your name for ever and ever.* (Psalm 145:2 NIV)

Hallowed Be Your Name—Lord's Day 47—Tuesday

Read: Isaiah 6:1–8
"The Holy Name of God"

CHRISTIANS CAN SOMETIMES BE too quick to speak of being "friends of God." It is true and faithful to what we have in Christ. However, when we forget what it is like to stand before a holy God, we can forget how great is the gift of friendship with God.

Isaiah sees God seated on his throne, high and lifted up. God is so perfect, holy, and powerful even the angels cover their faces. Isaiah is stunned. He cries, "Woe is me! I am lost, for I am a man of unclean lips, and I live among a people of unclean lips; yet my eyes have seen the King, the Lord of hosts!" (v. 5). Isaiah is gripped with awe and terror. God is holy and he is a sinner. How could he come before God's throne?

At that moment, an angel brings a coal that purifies Isaiah's mouth. God himself cleansed Isaiah. "Now that this has touched your lips, your guilt has departed and your sin is blotted out" (v. 7). Now he can stand, respond, and be sent.

Christians are rightly called "friends of God." Yet the more we consider God's holiness, the more precious it becomes to be called his friends.

Prayer: *I will praise God's name in song and glorify him with thanksgiving.* (Psalm 69:30 NIV)

Hallowed Be Your Name—Lord's Day 47—Wednesday

Read: Psalm 115
"Living God or Dead Idols"

THE DIFFERENCE BETWEEN GOD and idols is the difference between life and death. The idols of the ancient world were statues in the images of gods made of gold, silver, wood, or stone. However well made they were, these statues were not alive. The artist might give them a mouth, but the idols could not talk. They were dead and useless, nothing but a figurine. "Those who make them are like them; so are all who trust in them" (v. 8). If we place our trust in idols, we will become as dead as they are. But if we place our trust in the living God, we will have life.

Idols are objects of worship. While the Bible repeatedly calls them dead and worthless, they have power in our lives. Idols claim our devotion, our time, our loyalty, and turn us away from the Creator. Today idols do not always look like golden statues, but whatever captures our heart—money, success, security, or acceptance and the objects that promise them. As William Perkins once said, "Look what a person loves most and cares most for and delights most in: that is his God." Will we worship the living God or dead idols?

Prayer: *Not to us, Lord, not to us but to your name be the glory, because of your love and faithfulness.* (Psalm 115:1 NIV)

Hallowed Be Your Name—Lord's Day 47—Thursday

Read: Matthew 5:13–16
"always honored and praised"

A YOUNG MAN WAS the first person in his family to go to college. When he was offered drugs, he refused. When the dealer insisted, saying that no one would ever know, the student responded, "That's not the point. My mother cleaned houses and washed floors to send me to this college. I am here because of her. I am here for her. I wouldn't do anything that might demean her sacrifice for me." This young man lived in light of the sacrifice his mother had made for him. He wanted to honor her name.

Christ has placed his church to be visible, so the light of Christ within her would radiate outward for the world to see. A hidden light, a light no one can see, is not doing what it was made for. Our light—our life and good works—are to be light that shines so others will see and give glory to the Father.

Christians live to glorify the name of God. Because Jesus Christ died and rose again for us, Christians shouldn't steal, cheat in their marriages, murder, gossip or slander. Like that young man, we shouldn't do anything that would demean his sacrifice for us.

Prayer: *Ascribe to the Lord the glory due his name; worship the Lord in the splendor of his holiness.* (Psalm 29:2 NIV)

Hallowed Be Your Name—Lord's Day 47—Friday

Read: Jeremiah 31:31–34
"To truly know you"

GOD'S PEOPLE HAD TURNED their backs on the LORD. Instead of wanting to know God, to know his Word, or to walk in his ways, they chased after the power and "gods" of other peoples. This hardened their hearts to the point they barely knew God anymore.

The LORD promised Jeremiah one day things would be different. God will establish a new covenant—a new form to our relationship with him which could not break. Unlike the time of Moses, where God wrote his law on stone tablets, this new covenant will be written on the human heart. This relationship will be secure. God will be our God and we will be his people, he will forgive our sins, and we will no longer need to be taught to know the LORD. "For they shall all know me, from the least of them to the greatest" (v. 34).

That new covenant has come in Jesus. When Jesus sat with his disciples at the last supper, he took a cup of wine and said, "This cup is the new covenant in my blood." Jesus proclaimed that the new covenant was beginning in him. We know God truly when we trust in Jesus.

Prayer: *I will declare that your love stands firm forever, that you have established your faithfulness in heaven itself.* (Psalm 89:2 NIV)

Hallowed Be Your Name—Lord's Day 47—Saturday

Read: 1 Peter 2:1–10
"All that shines forth from them"

ONE OF THE REASONS we gather to sing and pray and read God's Word on Sundays is to praise God for what he has done for us. Part of "hallowing God's name" is praising him for all his good works.

Christians are called to praise God for his saving work in Jesus Christ. We have an identity and calling as the people of God: "you are a chosen race, a royal priesthood, a holy nation, God's own people" (v. 9). Peter's words echo and summarize the calling of Israel in the Old Testament, now for all who believe in Jesus Christ. Our calling also has a purpose: "that you may proclaim the mighty acts of him who called you out of darkness into his marvelous light" (v. 9). We have been called out of the world in order to proclaim in the church and then to the world what God has done in Jesus Christ to save. Part of our purpose is praise.

We praise God both for what he has done for us, but also for who that shows him to be. As the catechism puts it, we praise God for "all your works and for all that shines forth from them: your almighty power, wisdom, kindness, justice, mercy, and truth" (Q122).

Prayer: *Praise be to his glorious name forever; may the whole earth be filled with his glory. Amen and Amen.* (Psalm 72:19 NIV)

Your Kingdom Come—Lord's Day 48—Sunday

Q123. What does the second petition mean?

A. "Your kingdom come" means:

> Rule us by your Word and Spirit in such a way
> that more and more we submit to you.
> Preserve your church and make it grow.
> Destroy the devil's work;
> destroy every force which revolts against you
> and every conspiracy against your holy Word.
> Do this until your kingdom fully comes,
> when you will be
> all in all.

EVERYONE SERVES SOMETHING. THE question we must face is not *whether* we will serve, but *who*. In the midst of all the voices clamoring for our hearts, Jesus teaches us to pray, "your kingdom come." Christians pray for God's Kingdom, for every square inch of creation to know God alone is king.

In this kingdom of Jesus, there is a good shepherd, not a tyrant, on the throne. Jesus says, "I am the good shepherd. The good shepherd lays down his life for the sheep" (John 10:11). This king does not consume the lives of his subjects, but pours out his own life for them. This king, Jesus, brings life by giving his life, brings joy by enduring sorrow, and brings peace by the blood of his cross. In the kingdom of God, the hungry are fed, the naked are clothed, the thirsty are sated, and the poor are lifted up from the dust. A different kind of kingdom and a different kind of king.

Everyone serves something. To pray "your kingdom come" is to renounce every other kingdom and every other king—everything else we might put at the center of our lives—and place our hope in the one true self-giving King, Jesus Christ.

Prayer: *Your kingdom is an everlasting kingdom, and your dominion endures through all generations. The Lord is trustworthy in all he promises and faithful in all he does.* (Psalm 145:13 NIV)

Your Kingdom Come—Lord's Day 48—Monday

Read: Psalm 47

"A Kingdom Has A King"

GROWING UP IN THE United States, I grew up hearing the stories of the Boston Tea Party and the American Revolution. Kingship was connected with oppressive tyranny. The last time we had a king, we kicked him out. We—the people—would be king. Imagine, then, opening the Bible and seeing God everywhere described as King. Jesus spoke frequently of the Kingdom of God and even instructed us to pray for that kingdom to come on earth as it is in heaven.

However, we should rejoice that the LORD is King. "Clap your hands, all you peoples; shout to God with loud songs of joy. For the Lord, the Most High, is awesome, a great king over all the earth" (vv. 1–2). Human kings might be good and faithful to God, but they might be wicked and oppressive. The rulers of the nations might fear the LORD or seek to destroy his people. Through it all, the LORD is king.

In a world of wicked kings, the LORD is the perfect king. In a world of powerful rulers who fight against God's people, the LORD is stronger. Even in a world where we want to be king, the LORD is the true king. This is a reason to rejoice, clap our hands, and sing songs of praise.

Prayer: *For the Lord Most High is awesome, the great King over all the earth.* (Psalm 47:2 NIV)

Your Kingdom Come—Lord's Day 48—Tuesday

Read: Revelation 22

"The fullness of your kingdom comes"

IN OUR HOUSE, DESSERT always waits until after dinner. Thinking of dessert changes how we eat the rest of their meal. Beets become exciting because it gets us closer to ice cream.

The Bible saves the best for last. The book of Revelation tells us what it will be like when Jesus Christ returns. There will be the resurrection of the body, judgment, and a setting right of all that is wrong. Tears will be wiped away, death will be completely vanquished, and heaven will come down to earth.

Yet, the best part of the kingdom of God is that the King is there. The best part of heaven is not all the things you will do, but that Jesus is there. "But the throne of God and of the Lamb will be in it, and his servants will worship him; they will see his face, and his name will be on their foreheads" (vv. 3–4). The joy of the saints is that they will see Jesus' face.

"See, I am coming soon" (v. 22) Jesus tells John on Patmos. This hope and expectation has guided and strengthened Christians for two thousand years. Thinking of the end changes how we live as we wait.

Prayer: *Look to the Lord and his strength; seek his face always.* (Psalm 105:4 NIV)

Your Kingdom Come—Lord's Day 48—Wednesday

Read: Matthew 12:22–30
"Destroy the work of the devil"

CHRISTIANITY INVOLVES SPIRITUAL STRUGGLE. Everywhere Jesus goes, he encounters both faith and firm resistance. Everywhere the apostles go preaching the gospel, some believe while others are enraged. Behind resistant humans is a greater enemy—the devil.

Once, after casting out a demon that had kept a man blind and mute, Jesus was questioned about the source of his power to set people free from demons. Jesus replied that to take what belongs to someone strong, you must first tie them up, otherwise they will work to stop you. Jesus tells us the devil is strong and has taken many people captive. Jesus also proclaims that he is stronger, strong enough to incapacitate the devil and take those whom the devil wants to keep from God.

"Your kingdom come" is a prayer of defiance. We pray confessing the kingdom of Jesus is stronger than the kingdom of Satan. Jesus Christ is King and every power that resists him will ultimately be defeated. The strong man has been bound. As Martin Luther wrote in the hymn "A Mighty Fortress Is Our God," "The prince of darkness grim, we tremble not for him, his rage we can endure, for lo his doom is sure, one little word shall fell him."

Prayer: *Contend, Lord, with those who contend with me; fight against those who fight against me. Take up shield and armor; arise and come to my aid.* (Psalm 35:1–2 NIV)

Your Kingdom Come—Lord's Day 48—Thursday

Read: Matthew 16:13–23
"Preserve and increase your Church"

MY CHILDREN LOVE BUILDING tall towers with wooden blocks. They enjoy the challenge of building it as high as they can before it topples. However, each of them wants to be the one to build the tallest tower. In our human nature, we often desire to take control and do the work ourselves to accomplish great feats. However, Jesus tell us that he will be the one to build his church.

Jesus Christ will build his church. It is not our task to build it. When Jesus reached Caesarea Philippi with his disciples, he has a conversation with them about his identity. Who is he? After the disciples list what everyone else has said, Jesus asked more directly. "But who do you say that I am?" Peter boldly replied, "You are the Messiah, the Son of the living God" (vv. 15–16). In the midst of affirming Peter's answer, Jesus promises to build his church. Jesus is the foundation, and he is the master builder. Only Christ can build the church, and he promised to do it. Nothing, not even the gates of hell, will stand against it.

Jesus' promise should make us bold. Since the pressure to build the church does not lie on our shoulders, we are now free to live fully for Christ. We can be bold in telling others about Jesus and courageous in how we live as his disciples.

Prayer: *There is a river whose streams make glad the city of God, the holy place where the Most High dwells. God is within her, she will not fall; God will help her at break of day.* (Psalm 46:4–5 NIV)

Your Kingdom Come—Lord's Day 48—Friday

Read: Psalm 119:105–112
"Rule us by your Word and Spirit"

WHENEVER I GO OUT into the woods at night, I always bring a flashlight so I can see where I am going. If I forget, I can sometimes make my way for a little while, but eventually I trip over a tree root, lose my balance, or run into something. I need light to see where I am going.

Like a lamp in the darkness, God's Word shows us the difference between good and false paths, so that we do not stumble and fall into sin (v. 105). Like a light on a path, God's Word holds forth Jesus Christ, the light of the world. When we walk in the light of God's Word—trusting in Jesus and living in gratitude—we will experience life even in the midst of suffering (v. 107). In the Bible, we hear God's promises, learn to pray, and hear the voice of the God who saves us. When we let God's Word guide us, it brings joy to our heart (v. 111).

We do not have to stumble around in the dark to know God. He has given us his Word, the Bible. Praying "your kingdom come" is to ask that our lives would be lived more and more in the light of God's Word.

Prayer: *Your word is a lamp for my feet, a light on my path.*
(Psalm 119:105 NIV)

Your Kingdom Come—Lord's Day 48—Saturday

Read: Matthew 13:24–33
"The kingdom of heaven is like . . ."

WHAT DOES GOD'S KINGDOM actually look like? Jesus often explained the kingdom of God through a type of story called a parable. Matthew 13 contains a few of the dozens of Jesus' parables about the kingdom of God.

The kingdom is compared to a field of wheat where weeds were sown by the enemy. The man refused to let the workers pull the weeds, so the wheat was not accidentally damaged. The kingdom of God will be mixed until the final day of harvest. We cannot know everyone who is part of the kingdom until the last day.

The kingdom is a small mustard seed that later grows large enough for birds to perch in it. The kingdom starts small, but will grow to bless others.

The kingdom is a lump of dough and a small bit of yeast (leaven) worked through the whole batch. The little yeast impacts and transforms the whole batch of dough. The kingdom begins small, but transforms everything around it.

The kingdom we pray for is like a field, a mustard seed, and a lump of dough. It is a mixed community until the last day. It starts small, but grows. It blesses others and changes the world around it. This kingdom is worth praying for.

Prayer: *The Lord is righteous in all his ways and faithful in all he does.*
(Psalm 145:17 NIV)

Your Will Be Done—Lord's Day 49—Sunday

Q124. What does the third petition mean?

A. "Your will be done, on earth as it is in heaven" means:

> Help us and all people
> to reject our own wills
> and to obey your will without any back talk.
> Your will alone is good.
> Help us one and all to carry out the work we are called to,
> as willingly and faithfully as the angels in heaven.

"Your will be done on earth as it is in heaven" is no small prayer. We pray for God to set all things right, make all things new, and to see God's will worked out on earth. It is a prayer for God to act and change things, even us.

We might be fine praying for God's will to be done when we see *others* walking against the will of God. But what about us? If we consider ourselves among the just, we can be content praying for God's justice to be done on the earth, hoping that God would finally hold accountable all the bullies and tyrants, all the slanders and predators, all the wicked of the world who defy the will of God and trample upon the weak. What about the ways *we* walk against God's will? Can we pray "your will be done" then?

Praying for God's will to be done does not include an exception clause. It means us. It means placing God's will ahead of ours, even when it may cause suffering in our lives, and trusting his will, even if we think we have a better way of doing it ourselves. It will not always be easy, our Lord Jesus can attest to this. "Your will be done on earth as it is in heaven" is a prayer with astounding hope for the future, that God will finally set all things right, even us.

Prayer: *I have sought your face with all my heart; be gracious to me according to your promise.* (Psalm 119:58 NIV)

Your Will Be Done—Lord's Day 49—Monday

Read: Matthew 6:9–13
"On earth as it is in heaven"

WHEN WE OPEN A door, we turn it on its hinges. The hinge sits at the intersection between the wall and the door and allows it to turn. Without the hinge, the door cannot open.

"On earth as it is in heaven" is the hinge of the Lord's Prayer. It connects all that we learned to pray before—God's name, kingdom, and will—with all that will come after—give us, forgive us, rescue us. In heaven, the Lord's name is hallowed, the Lord is acknowledged as king, and the Lord's will is done. Not so on earth. On earth, the unborn are stripped of their voices and their lives, children must learn to defend themselves from predators, and bullies take what they want.

When we pray "On earth as it is in heaven," we are asking God to make the earth just a little more like heaven. It is a prayer of people weary of all that is broken and aching for all to be set right. It is a prayer of those longing to see the lost found, the weak made strong, and the dead raised to life. It is a prayer for those longing for the salvation of the Lord to come rushing into this world.

Prayer: *He upholds the cause of the oppressed and gives food to the hungry. The LORD sets prisoners free.* (Psalm 146:7 NIV)

Your Will Be Done—Lord's Day 49—Tuesday

Read: Revelation 4
"Tune our hearts"

ONCE MY WIFE AND I were playing guitar and piano together. We sounded terrible. I assumed it was me, so I stopped and tuned my guitar. We started again, but no improvement. I tuned the guitar again. After the third time, my wife turned and said, "It is not the guitar that is out of tune, but the piano."

Because the piano is so much louder as an instrument, I assumed something was wrong with me, with my guitar, and how I was playing. Even though my guitar was right, it sounded wrong because of how loud the piano was.

Revelation 4 gives us a vision of heavenly worship in tune with the will of God. The more in tune we become with the Lord through prayer, the more out of tune we may feel in a world that denies him and seeks after other gods. We may be tempted to think something is wrong with us, like I did with the guitar. The sheer volume of the music the world is playing can threaten to drown out the tune of the gospel and make the church wonder if somehow we are the ones out of tune. Revelation 4 reminds us which tune truly matters.

Prayer: *Sustain me, my God, according to your promise, and I will live; do not let my hopes be dashed.* (Psalm 119:116 NIV)

Your Will Be Done—Lord's Day 49—Wednesday

Read: Matthew 16:24–28
"To reject our own wills"

THE MANTRA OF OUR culture is to "be true to yourself." No one knows what is best for us better than we do. No one knows how to be "me" better than I do. But is this true? Do we really know what is best for us? Are our desires always the best for us?

Jesus has no such confidence that we know what is best for us. The call to follow Jesus is to lay down ourselves—our desires, our plans, even our sense of identity—and take up a cross. We are to find our hope, our identity, our truest self in Jesus Christ. This is a form of death, but it is also the only way to life. "For those who want to save their life will lose it, and those who lose their life for my sake will find it" (v. 25). We find true life when we lay aside our life to find life in Christ.

Anything else will lead only to death. We can gain everything in this world, but apart from Christ, it is vanity. We are not to be "true to ourselves" as *we* see ourselves, but to be "true to who you are in Christ."

Prayer: *You discern my going out and my lying down; you are familiar with all my ways.* (Psalm 139:3 NIV)

Your Will Be Done—Lord's Day 49—Thursday

Read: Titus 2
"Renounce ungodliness"

IF ONLY DISHES WOULD wash themselves. Dirty dishes pile in the sink and we wish, just this once, they would do it themselves. However, dirty dishes cannot clean themselves. They cannot put themselves away in the cupboard. It must be done for them.

We cannot cleanse ourselves either. We need God to do it for us. In the Word and at the Table, Jesus' work of grace cleanses us and loosens the grip of ungodliness on our lives (v. 14). But grace is also the way God trains us to walk in the path of righteousness. "For the grace of God has appeared, bringing salvation to all, training us to renounce impiety and worldly passions, and in the present age to live lives that are self-controlled, upright, and godly" (vv. 11–12). We do not learn to be godly by trying really hard. When God cleanses us, the dirt and grime of evil begins to lose its power, and we can begin to live for God.

Whenever we struggle with sin, we need to be trained again by grace. God's grace alone will set us free and enable us to live for God in this world.

Prayer: *Do not bring your servant into judgment, for no one living is righteous before you.* (Psalm 143:2 NIV)

Your Will Be Done—Lord's Day 49—Friday

Read: Romans 12:1–8
"to carry out the work we are called to"

MOVING HOMES IS HARD. My father-in-law, in particular, loves to be home and be close to family. Yet, he moved across an ocean to Canada because he believed God called him to be a dairy farmer. He was seeking to live out God's calling upon his life.

In Romans 12, both our work and our worship is part of our calling. We worship, renew our minds, and live humbly. We also use our gifts. All Christians are called. Each of us is to present our whole lives before God for his service, as thanks for the grace we have received in Jesus Christ (v. 1). Service, teaching, generosity, leadership, and mercy are all different ways we live out our Christian calling. We do this within the four walls of the church and in our homes, our workplaces, and in our schools. Daily life is where we live out the calling to be "living sacrifices."

We live out God's calling on weekdays as well as in worship. As Martin Luther said, "A dairymaid can milk cows to the glory of God." Live to the glory of God in your worship each Sunday, but also live to the glory of God wherever God places you Monday morning.

Prayer: *Teach me to do you will, for you are my God; may your good Spirit lead me on level ground.* (Psalm 143:10 NIV)

Your Will Be Done—Lord's Day 49—Saturday

Read: Psalm 103:20–22
"As the angels in heaven"

THE HEIDELBERG CATECHISM SAYS that we should carry out God's will "as willingly and faithfully as the angels in heaven" (Q124). Why compare us to angels? How are we to imitate angels?

In the Bible, angels are messengers from God. The word "angel" in both the Old and New Testament literally means "messenger." These heavenly beings bring God's message from heaven to earth. In Psalm 103, the angels are commended for their obedience to the word of God. While there are fallen, disobedient angels (like Lucifer), what sets the angels apart in the psalm is their willingness to "obey the voice of the LORD." These angels are "doers of the word, and not merely hearers" (James 1:22). When God said to do something, they do it. When God sends them, they go. They are "willing and faithful" in obeying the will of God.

While the Bible nowhere tells us to try to become angels, their ready obedience to God should inspire us. When we pray "your will be done," we should be as eager as the angels to see God's will done—and to do it ourselves. Our prayer should be joined by a heartfelt desire to do God's will in every moment of our lives.

Prayer: *Praise the LORD, all his works everywhere in his dominion. Praise the LORD, my soul.* (Psalm 103:22 NIV)

Our Daily Bread—Lord's Day 50—Sunday

Q125. What does the fourth petition mean?

A. "Give us this day our daily bread" means:

> Do take care of all our physical needs
> so that we come to know
> that you are the only source of everything good,
> and that neither our work and worry
> nor your gifts
> can do us any good without your blessing.
> And so help us to give up our trust in creatures
> and trust in you alone.

WE WERE MADE TO hunger and to be filled. I've had the privilege of being in the room when each of our three children were born. Within a few minutes of being born, doctors recommend skin-to-skin contact between mom and baby and try to get the child to latch onto her breast and eat. From the moment we are born, we know how to be hungry. The first thing we show a newborn child is where to go for that hunger to be satisfied.

We were made this way—made to hunger and to be filled. We need daily bread. The physical way our bodies were made by God points to something deeper. We hunger for purpose, for meaning, for love, for friendship, for wholeness. But in and behind all these hungers, we hunger for God. It is as Saint Augustine once said, "O Lord, you have made us for yourself and our hearts are restless until they rest in thee" (*Confessions*). We were made to hunger and for that deep hunger to be satisfied by the Lord.

What are you hungry for and where do you go to satisfy your hunger? Our Lord Jesus taught us to pray, "Give us this day our daily bread." In praying this, we come to the LORD as hungry people—physically, spiritually, emotionally, relationally—and look for God to satisfy us. "Give us this day our daily bread" is a prayer that, through whatever means he chooses, God would give us enough for today. It is a prayer that we would not forget where our bread comes from, where our needs are truly met.

Prayer: *For he satisfies the thirsty and fills the hungry with good things.*
(Psalm 107:9 NIV)

Our Daily Bread—Lord's Day 50—Monday

Read: Exodus 16
"Daily Bread—Manna"

EVERY DAY FOR FORTY years, the people got up, went out of their tents, and found bread-like manna to eat. For forty years, God provided enough, including double on the day before the Sabbath. God gave them daily bread.

Daily bread was God's way of teaching us where to go to satisfy our hungers. We need the peace, grace, and satisfaction only God can provide. However, we have learned to look for satisfaction in all the wrong places. There is no app that will quiet the deep questions in our hearts, there is no amount of money in the bank that will make us truly secure, and there is no amount of success in our life or the lives of our children that can truly give us worth. Everywhere we look but God only ends in slavery, pain, and suffering.

The Lord rained down bread from heaven—daily bread—that we would know to go to him for all the true hungers of our hearts. For forty years, the Lord taught us where to go for our physical hunger, to train our hearts to know where to go for all the deeper hungers of life.

Prayer: *You, God, are my God, earnestly I seek you; I thirst for you, my whole being longs for you, in a dry and parched land where there is no water.* (Psalm 63:1 NIV)

Our Daily Bread—Lord's Day 50—Tuesday

Read: John 6:1–14
"Feeding the Crowds"

IN SOME CHURCH TRADITIONS, the bread and cup for the Lord's Supper are brought forward with the offering. It is not usually much, just a loaf or two and a chalice. The church places them on the table, offering these small gifts of bread and a cup, trusting that they will be enough.

In the hands of Jesus, even a little becomes enough. When Jesus asks the disciples to feed the crowd, there is not enough money and certainly not enough food. All they could scrounge up was one young boy's lunch. Five loaves and two fish. In the eyes of the disciples, it will not be enough. Yet, Jesus takes the bread, gives thanks, and gives them away. In doing so, Jesus multiplies and fills. Five thousand people are fed "as much as they wanted" until they "were satisfied" (vv. 11–12). In the hands of Jesus, these few loaves are enough. The more Jesus gives, the more there seems to be. Jesus multiplies not just enough, but so much that there are leftovers.

When placed in the hands of Jesus, even five loaves and two fish become enough. Jesus gives extravagantly, transforming a small lunch into a feast.

Prayer: *I cling to you; your right hand upholds me.* (Psalm 63:8 NIV)

Our Daily Bread—Lord's Day 50—Wednesday

Read: Psalm 23
"Green Pastures"

HAVING THE LORD AS our shepherd is a promise that God will always give us what we need, though not everything we want. We live in trust, not in comfort. "I shall not want" does not mean we will get everything we want. It does not mean living in affluence. It means getting enough for today—daily bread.

The "green pastures" of Psalm 23 look nothing like the thick fields of grass in North America. In Israel, the shepherd's green pastures are full of dust, sand, and rocks. Yet at the shady base of those rocks are small tufts of grass, maybe an inch or two long. These are the green pastures of Israel. The sheep are given a mouthful at a time. Day by day and step by step, the shepherd teaches the sheep to trust his voice. The sheep follow the shepherd from one tuft of grass to the next, trusting that, where the shepherd leads, there will be more for the next mouthful.

The LORD, our shepherd, provides for us. He always leads us where we will get just what we need. He does this day by day, step by step as we listen to him and trust his voice.

Prayer: *The LORD is my shepherd, I lack nothing. He makes me lie down in green pastures, he leads me beside quiet waters.* (Psalm 23:1–2 NIV)

Our Daily Bread—Lord's Day 50—Thursday

Read: James 1:16–18
"The only fountain of all good"

A FRIEND OF MINE was once overcome by a swift and brutal bout of pneumonia. He lay for days doing his best to take one breath after another. Later, his response to his illness was one of gratitude, saying, "God did not owe me one more breath. Each breath was a gift."

All our life is dependent upon God. James warns us not to be deceived, but to know that "Every generous act of giving, with every perfect gift, is from above, coming down from the Father of lights" (v. 17). As the catechism says, the Lord is "the only source of all good" (Q125). Everything we have and everything we need is a gift from God—the extraordinary gifts of salvation, adoption into the family of God, and the presence of the Holy Spirit and the very ordinary gifts of food, shelter, warmth, and family. It even includes one breath after another. All are good gifts from God.

We can live as if all our blessings come from our hard work or from human ingenuity. Yet, Christians are called to regularly pray for "our daily bread." It is a reminder that everything in our life comes from the hand of our loving Father.

Prayer: *All creatures look to you to give them their food at the proper time. When you give it to them, they gather it up; when you open your hand, they are satisfied with good things.* (Psalm 104:27–28 NIV)

Our Daily Bread—Lord's Day 50—Friday

Read: Psalm 146
"Withdraw our trust from all creatures"

WE GET HURT WHEN we trust the wrong person. A common team building exercises is the "trust fall." One person stands with their back facing another and falls backwards, trusting the person behind them to catch them. In our life, we are given daily opportunities to trust others, but we must know whose arms we're falling into in order to have the courage to take the fall and be held up.

Psalm 146 calls us to put our trust in our Creator and not in his creations. The LORD is worthy of our trust in a way that no human leader ever will be. The heart of the contrast between God and human leaders lies in two statements: God keeps faith forever (v. 6) and the LORD will reign forever (v. 10). Human leaders fail and fade. Even the best human leaders cannot save us. Even the greatest and most powerful leaders in human history eventually die and return to the earth. Even the best laid plans of the best minds will eventually turn to dust. Not so with God. God alone can save us and God alone has a kingdom that will never end.

Who can you trust? When we trust the wrong people, we end up getting hurt. But when we trust in the LORD, who keeps faith forever, we can rest in good hands.

Prayer: *Do not put your trust in princes, in human beings, who cannot save.* (Psalm 146:3 NIV)

Our Daily Bread—Lord's Day 50—Saturday

Read: Jeremiah 17:5–8
"place it only in you"

WHEN EACH OF OUR children was born, we planted a tree for them. We could not control how cold it would get that winter, nor how much rain would come in the spring. We could only plant them and trust. Like the trees, we could only bring our children into the world and do our best to root them in a strong foundation.

Our life depends on where we plant our trust. According to Jeremiah, the person who trusts in human beings will be like the shrub in the desert, dry and anxious. They may survive, but never thrive. They live in the "parched places of the wilderness" (v. 6) Those who trust in the LORD, however, are like a tree planted by streams. When there is no rain and the heat beats down on them, they are not afraid. They remain fruitful and green in drought. Both plants experience dry, difficult seasons, but one thrives while the other withers.

Planting our trust in the LORD does not guarantee life will always be easy. However, it will change how we live during the dry seasons. We will thrive or wither. Those who place their trust in humans "shall not see when relief comes" (v. 6), but those who trust in the LORD "in the year of drought [will not be] anxious" (v. 8).

Prayer: *That person is like a tree planted by streams of water, which yields its fruit in season and whose leaf does not wither—whatever they do prospers.* (Psalm 1:3 NIV)

Q126. What does the fifth petition mean?

A. "Forgive us our debts,
    as we also have forgiven our debtors" means:
    Because of Christ's blood,
    do not hold against us, poor sinners that we are,
    any of the sins we do
    or the evil that constantly clings to us.
    Forgive us just as we are fully determined,
    as evidence of your grace in us,
    to forgive our neighbors.

FORGIVENESS IS COMPLICATED BECAUSE many of us feel stuck. We feel stuck wondering if there are sins in our past or in our present that cannot be forgiven. We feel stuck wondering if we can ever let go of the pain and sins of others. The business of forgiveness seems all straight-forward until we need to do it ourselves. It all seems great until we make huge mistakes and really hurt someone. Forgiveness all seems like a nice idea until someone wounds us deeply. Forgiveness? Really? For me? For them?

Yes. We who are in Christ have been forgiven everything. Forgiveness means you don't bear the weight of your sins and mistakes anymore. God does not hold our sins against us because of Jesus Christ. Forgiveness means your relationship is healed, made right again. There is no sin in your past or present too deep to be reached by the forgiveness of Jesus Christ. Since we have been forgiven our lives should be marked by forgiveness of others.

We forgive because we have been forgiven. To refuse to forgive is to cut off the very branch you are standing on. To forgive others is a powerful witness in the world to the reality of God's forgiveness of us. In Jesus' name, we call upon God not to hold our sins against us. In Jesus' name, we are then called to forgive others. God's grace in us unsticks us—freeing us from our sins and freeing us to let go of the sins of others.

Prayer: *As far as the easy is from the west, so far has he removed our transgressions from us.* (Psalm 103:12 NIV)

Forgiven & Forgiving—Lord's Day 51—Monday

Read: Psalm 51:1–7
"I know my transgressions"

THE PROCESS OF HONESTLY examining the motives of our hearts, the works of our hands, and the words that come from our lips can be devastating. We rarely like what we see. When we compare our lives with God's Word, we continually fall short.

David knew this about himself too. Though a "man after God's own heart," when David was confronted with his sin with Bathsheba, he was crushed. David certainly sinned against Bathsheba and Uriah, but ultimately, he sinned against God (v. 4). David's sin was not an isolated incident, but part of his nature from the womb (v. 5). Most severely, his sin is not something he can fix himself. He needs God to wash him, purge him, cleanse him, have mercy on him, and blot out his transgressions. David cannot forgive himself, he must be forgiven by God.

Like David, our sins are great and something we cannot fix. Yet, David models for us the proper response. When we see our sin, we must lift up our eyes to the LORD and cry for mercy. We respond to sin best when turn from it and turn toward the LORD in prayer.

Prayer: *Restore to me the joy of your salvation and grant me a willing spirit, to sustain me.* (Psalm 51:12 NIV)

Forgiven & Forgiving—Lord's Day 51—Tuesday

Read: Romans 7:21–25
"Wretched sinner"

RECENTLY, I ASK MY three year old why she pushed her sister. She simply said, "Sometimes, I want to do bad things." Adults become practiced at pretending we are good, even when we are not. If only we were all so honest.

Even Christians struggle because we want to do bad things. Having been forgiven and adopted into God's family, the battle with sin does not stop. In Romans 7, Paul describes the internal struggle all Christians face between the new person, who desires to please God, and the old self that desires to please ourselves. Until we see Jesus Christ face to face, these desires will wage war within us. We have only one hope in this battle: Jesus Christ. "Wretched man that I am! Who will rescue me from this body of death? Thanks be to God through Jesus Christ our Lord!" (vv. 24–25). We have a continual struggle, but we also have a powerful and faithful Savior. Jesus Christ will ultimately deliver us.

We should be honest as children about the desires we find within our hearts. Sometimes we want to do bad things. We should also be equally honest about our hope in the struggle: Jesus Christ.

Prayer: *Unless the LORD had given me help, I would soon have dwelt in the silence of death.* (Psalm 94:17 NIV)

Forgiven & Forgiving—Lord's Day 51—Wednesday

Read: Matthew 18:15–22
"As we forgive our debtors"

EVEN IN THE CHURCH, we will sin against each other. We will have debts and we will have debtors. Jesus assumes this when he teaches us to pray, "Forgive us our debts as we also have forgiven our debtors." What do we do with the debts of sins owed to us and what can be done about our debt of sin? Peter asks, "Lord, if another member of the church sins against me, how often should I forgive? As many as seven times?" (v. 21)

Peter is trying to be generous here. Seven is plenty. There has to be a limit to forgiveness, right? Even if I am generous in my forgiveness, there must be a point at which I no longer have to forgive.

Jesus pushes farther than Peter imagined. Forgive seventy-seven times or even seventy times seven. The message becomes clear: Forgive and forgive and forgive until you begin to lose count.

While Peter may think he is generous is being willing to forgive seven times, Jesus multiplies that forgiveness. Seventy-seven times, seventy times seven. This call to a wide mercy and abundant forgiveness is rooted in what God has done for us in Jesus Christ.

Prayer: *He does not treat us as our sins deserve or repay us according to our iniquities.* (Psalm 103:10 NIV)

Forgiven & Forgiving—Lord's Day 51—Thursday

Read: Matthew 18:21–35
"Forgive as we forgive"

EACH OF US BEGINS as a debtor. Before we are told to forgive others, we are called to pray for our own forgiveness. We are those in need of forgiveness before we are forgivers.

In this parable, we are reminded of the simple truth that we ourselves are debtors before God and we cannot get out from under it. A debt we cannot pay and yet "out of pity for him, the lord of that slave released him and forgave him the debt" (v. 27). That forgiveness should change everything. We are forgiven, so we forgive.

The good news is that our debt has all been forgiven through the blood of Jesus Christ on the cross. Through Jesus, our slate has been wiped clean. We have been released and our debt, which we could never pay, has been forgiven.

Now we are called to forgive others the smaller, but not insignificant, debts they owe to us. Christians live by forgiveness. We live *because of* forgiveness: God's forgiveness of our sins. We have life because God has forgiven us. We also live *through* forgiveness: we forgive because we have been forgiven. As we are taught to pray, "Forgive us our debts as we also have forgiven our debtors."

Prayer: *Then I acknowledged my sin to you and did not cover up my iniquity. I said, "I will confess my transgressions to the Lord." And you forgave the guilt of my sin.* (Psalm 32:5 NIV)

Forgiven & Forgiving—Lord's Day 51—Friday

Read: 1 John 2:1–6
"Do not impute to us . . . any of our transgressions"

WHAT DO WE DO when we sin? What do we need? With three words John shows how Jesus gives us all we need in response to our sin.

First, Jesus is our "advocate before the Father." Think of a lawyer in a courtroom. Jesus speaks on our behalf to the Father. He advocates for guilty sinners. Second, Jesus is "the righteous." Jesus lived a perfect life, not only by never sinning, but also by always obeying God's word. Jesus is righteous. Only those who are righteous can stand before God, but we are not. Through faith in Christ, we are "counted as righteous" before the Father. Jesus, the righteous one, gives us his righteousness. Lastly, Jesus is the "propitiation for our sins," which means that he takes on the punishment we deserve so that God's wrath is satisfied. We deserve judgment for our sins, but Christ takes that judgment for us.

What do we do when we sin? What do we need? We need Jesus. We need Jesus to plead our case, to give us his righteousness, and to make us right with God. We need Jesus every day. This is why "Forgive us our debts" is not a one-time-only prayer, but the daily prayer of the Christian.

Prayer: *Let the redeemed of the LORD tell their story—those who redeemed from the hands of the foe.* (Psalm 107:2 NIV)

Forgiven & Forgiving—Lord's Day 51—Saturday

Read: Colossians 3:12–17
"Forgive Others"

CHRISTIANS LIVE BY FORGIVENESS. The poet George Herbert said: "He that cannot forgive others breaks the bridge over which he must pass himself, for every man hath need to be forgiven."

We forgive because we have been forgiven. Refusing to forgive is cutting off the very branch you are standing on. Each of us can stand before God only because Christ has forgiven us. In Colossians 3, Paul calls us to put on Christian virtues like a cloak. In Christ, we put on kindness and patience. We wear humility and compassion. In the midst of these virtues, Paul calls us to forgive others, because we have been forgiven. Christ-likeness looks like forgiving as we have been forgiven. It looks like living what we pray for in the Lord's Prayer.

In a world consumed with revenge politics, nursing grudges, and where everyone is focused on getting what they deserve, we pray "forgive us our debts as we also have forgiven our debtors." Perhaps our forgiveness will be a sign to the world of just how good the good news is.

Prayer: *Blessed is the one whose transgressions are forgiven, whose sins are covered.* (Psalm 32:1 NIV)

Rescue from Trials—Lord's Day 52—Sunday

Q127. What does the sixth petition mean?

A. "And do not bring us to the time of trial, but rescue us from the evil one" means:
> By ourselves we are too weak to hold our own even for a moment.
> And our sworn enemies—the devil, the world, and our own flesh—
> never stop attacking us. And so, Lord, uphold us and make us strong
> with the strength of your Holy Spirit, so that we may not go down to defeat
> in this spiritual struggle, but may firmly resist our enemies
> until we finally win the complete victory.

Q128. What does your conclusion to this prayer mean?

A. "For the kingdom and the power and the glory are yours forever" means:
> We have made all these petitions of you because, as our all-powerful king,
> you are both willing and able to give us all that is good; and because your holy name,
> and not we ourselves, should receive all the praise, forever.

Q129. What does that little word "Amen" express?

A. "Amen" means:
> This shall truly and surely be! It is even more sure that God listens to my prayer
> than that I really desire what I pray for.

TRIALS AND EVIL. THIS is how the Lord's Prayer ends—struggling with trials and evil. It is not the cheery ending we might have hoped for in the pattern prayer for the Christian life.

Life may become more challenging, not less, if you take up the mantle of faith in Christ. Alongside the joy that comes from being in Christ, there is also immense struggle. Your favorite sinful habit is not going to give up without a fight. Your old social group may not take your following Jesus as a welcome development. This world that Christ came to redeem is filled with forces that will resist the saving work of Christ.

This is why we are taught to pray "Do not bring us to the time of trial," but that we would be rescued and delivered. We pray that we would not be vulnerable to those powers that rage against God's kingdom.

The Lord's Prayer ends in trials, but that is not exactly true. Of course, that is where Jesus ends in Matthew, but that is not where the prayer ends. Some of the earliest Christians with great wisdom added, "For yours is the kingdom and the power and the glory, forever and ever. Amen."

As much as we need to know that there are trials in this life as a follower of Jesus, we need even more to know that trials and evil are not the end of the story. The Lord's Prayer ends not with trials, but with praise. So too the Christian life.

Prayer: *Hear me, my God, as I voice my complaint; protect my life from the threat of the enemy.* (Psalm 64:1 NIV)

Rescue from Trials—Lord's Day 52—Monday

Read: Psalm 103:14-19
"We are so weak"

THE LORD'S PRAYER ENDS with an invitation to remember our weakness. Praying with Jesus means admitting we cannot stand on our own in this life. We are in continual, desperate need of God.

Psalm 103 reminds us to two connected truths: we are weak, but God is strong. We are "dust," "like grass," "like the flowers of the field," and withering under the wind. Our lives are fragile, short, and temporary. Even the healthiest of us will eventually die. Even the most noble of us will eventually fade from human memory. However strong we are, we are dust.

Yet, while we are weak, God is strong and faithful. We have a beginning and an end, but the steadfast love of the LORD does not. It is "from everlasting to everlasting" (v. 17). Our hope lies in the LORD's strength, not in the power of human strength. His love for us lasts long after we have returned to dust. His strength continues when even the fiercest trials come.

On our own, "we are too weak to hold our own even for a moment" (Q127). Thankfully, our hope is ultimately in the strength of the God who hears our prayers.

Prayer: *But from everlasting to everlasting the LORD's love is with those who fear him, and his righteousness with their children's children.*
(Psalm 113:17 NIV)

Rescue from Trials—Lord's Day 52—Tuesday

Read: Ephesians 6:10-20
"In this spiritual war"

WHEN CHRISTIANITY BECAME LEGAL in the Roman Empire, it was a time of both joy and struggle for the church. It was joyous because Christians could worship freely. However, it was also a struggle because comfort and ease caused many Christians to lose sight of the spiritual battle taking place.

The Christian life is a battle. Christians are called to put on spiritual armor to make a stand in the fight "against the rulers, against the authorities, against the cosmic powers of this present darkness, against the spiritual forces of evil in the heavenly places" (v. 12). Paul describes the complete set of armor used by soldiers at the time: belt, breastplate, shoes, shield, helmet, and sword. Instead of wearing physical armor, Christians are to be fully armored with truth, righteousness, readiness, faith, salvation, and the word of God. We are to use spiritual weapons in our spiritual battle. Belonging to Christ enlists us into a fearful struggle.

When Christianity finally became legal, some Christians fled into the desert to recover a sense of the spiritual battle of the Christian life. God may not be calling you to the desert, but we all must learn to stand in the spiritual battle.

Prayer: *Praise be to the LORD my Rock, who trains my hands for war, my fingers for battle.*
(Psalm 144:1 NIV)

Rescue from Trials—Lord's Day 52—Wednesday

Read: Psalm 2
"The Laughter of God"

EVERY CHILD GETS UPSET sometimes. They don't get a toy they want, their sibling is reading their favorite book, or they want dessert but don't want to eat dinner. Their emotions spill over and they flop on the floor or hop up and down. In those moments, many parents must resist the urge to laugh.

God laughs at the kingdoms of this world. When the nations rage against his kingdom and against his Messiah (Anointed), God laughs. When rulers plot and plan against God's will, the Lord laughs. We look out at the world and grow anxious. Yet, God is not fearful. In fact, their resistance is laughable, like the toddler's tantrum. God has put his anointed, Jesus, on the throne—King of kings and Lord of lords. His kingdom, power, and glory will go on forever.

When Christian's pray, "For yours is the kingdom and the power and the glory forever," we are joining God's laughter at the way things are because we know that is not how things will always be. We pray this way because the end of the story is secure, no matter how the nations rage, because the LORD is seated on the throne of heaven.

Prayer: *The One enthroned in heaven laughs; the LORD scoffs at them.* (Psalm 2:4 NIV)

Rescue from Trials—Lord's Day 52—Thursday

Read: 1 Corinthians 10:1–13
"Keep us from falling"

GROWING UP, MY PARENTS often sat me down to talk about other's bad behavior. It could be my brother, my school friends, or even someone on the news. I had not done anything wrong, but they wanted me to see the consequences, instead of experiencing them myself. They warned me using the example of others.

Speaking to the Corinthian church, Paul warns us with the example of Israel in the wilderness. "These things happened to them to serve as an example, and they were written down to instruct us, on whom the ends of the ages have come" (v. 11). They desired evil, were idolaters, were sexually immoral, put Christ to the test, and they fell. We are given this warning so that the same does not happen to us. Yet, this passage ends with a promise: "God is faithful, and he will not let you be tested beyond your strength, but with the testing he will also provide the way out so that you may be able to endure it (v. 13)."

When we pray for God to "deliver us from evil," we are asking for him to provide that way of escape. We are asking him to help us endure, so that we do not fall.

Prayer: *But as for me, my feet had almost slipped; I had nearly lost my foothold.* (Psalm 73:2 NIV)

Rescue from Trials—Lord's Day 52—Friday

Read: John 15:1–11
"Apart from me you can do nothing"

P. T. FORSYTH ONCE said, "the worst sin is prayerlessness." It is the "sin behind sin." In prayer, we seek God and find our life in him. To neglect prayer is to neglect God and look for life elsewhere.

Branches only live if they are connected to the vine. In John 15, Jesus speaks of a grape vine to describe the deep, living connection between us and Jesus. A branch cut off from the vine is cut off from the source of its life. It will die. A branch connected to the vine, "abiding" in the vine, continues to draw life from it. Similarly, Christians cannot live cut off from Christ. He is the source of our life. We must be intimately connected to him to live, drawing our life and hope from him. Apart from Christ, we are like a branch cut off from the vine—dead and useless. The first call of the Christian life is to abide, to stay, to remain in Jesus.

Prayer is an essential part of abiding in Jesus. When we neglect to pray, we neglect to abide in Jesus Christ, the life-giving vine. Yet, in prayer, we find our life in Jesus Christ.

Prayer: *You who answer prayer, to you all people will come.* (Psalm 65:2 NIV)

Rescue from Trials—Lord's Day 52—Saturday

Read: Isaiah 65:17–24
"Certainly hears my prayer"

AMEN IS A LITTLE word that carries so much weight. Ending our prayers with "Amen" expresses confidence that God will hear our prayer. As the catechism says, "It is even more sure that God listens to my prayer than that I really desire what I pray for" (Q129).

The Christian confidence that God listens to our prayers comes because God has promised to hear. When the LORD promises a new heaven and a new earth filled with joy and gladness, he also promises to hear us. "Before they call I will answer, while they are yet speaking I will hear" (v. 24). Before a word enters our mouth, God is already answering our prayers. Before we ever get to "amen," God has already heard exactly what we need. As Jesus promises, "your Father knows what you need before you ask him" (Matthew 6:8). Even when we are not sure what to say or don't know what we need, the Lord hears.

So we end our prayers with "Amen" because we trust God's promises. We trust God to keep his word: to hear us when we pray and give us what we need, even when we do not know what to ask.

Prayer: *You answer us with awesome and righteous deeds, God our Savior, the hope of all the ends of the earth and of the farthest seas.* (Psalm 65:5 NIV)

Bibliography

Augustine. *Confessions*. Translated by Henry Chadwick. Oxford: Oxford University Press, 2008.

―――. *Letters 100–155*. II/2 of *The Works of Saint Augustine*, translated by Roland Teske, SJ. Hyde Park: New City, 1990.

Bray, Gerald L., ed. *Galatians, Ephesians*. Reformation Commentary on Scripture, New Testament 10. Downers Grove: IVP Academic, 2011.

Forsyth, P. T. *The Soul of Prayer*. Vancouver: Regent College, 2002.

Herbert, George. *The Autobiography of Edward, Lord Herbert of Cherbury*. Edited by Sidney Lee. London: Routledge, 1906.

Kierkegaard, Søren. *Works of Love*. Translated by Howard and Edna Hong. New York: Harper & Row, 1962.

Luther, Martin. *The Large Catechism of Martin Luther*. Translated by Robert H. Fischer. Minneapolis: Fortress, 1959.

―――. *The Ninety-Five Theses and Other Writings*. Edited and translated by William Russell. New York: Penguin, 2017.

Manton, Thomas. *Puritan Sermons 1659–1689*. 6 vols. Wheaton: Roberts, 1981.

Made in United States
North Haven, CT
08 March 2023